The Uprooted

Southeast Asia

POLITICS, MEANING, AND MEMORY

David Chandler and Rita Smith Kipp

SERIES EDITORS

The Uprooted

Race, Children, and Imperialism

in French Indochina, 1890–1980

CHRISTINA ELIZABETH FIRPO

UNIVERSITY OF HAWAI'I PRESS   *Honolulu*

Printed in the United States of America

22 21 20 19 18 17   6 5 4 3 2 1

Library of Congress Cataloging-in-Publication Data

Firpo, Christina Elizabeth, author.
    The uprooted : race, children, and imperialism in French Indochina, 1890–1980 / Christina
Elizabeth Firpo.
        pages cm.
    Includes bibliographical references and index.
    ISBN 978-0-8248-4757-9 cloth : alk. paper
    1. Eurasians—Indochina—History.   2. France—Colonies—Race relations—History—19th
century.   3. France—Colonies—Race relations—History—20th century.   4. Indochina—
Relations—France—History.   5. France—Relations—Indochina—History.   I. Title.
    DS546.5.F8F57 2016

    305.80095909'04—dc23

                                                                                      2015028391

ISBN 978-0-8248-7515-2 (pbk.)

For my parents, John and Katherine Firpo

CONTENTS

ACKNOWLEDGMENTS

As this book took more than a decade to research and write, I owe great debt to countless individuals and institutions. The research for *The Uprooted* was made possible by the generosity of the following fellowships: University of California Pacific Rim Research Grant, Fulbright-Hays Dissertation Research Grant, American Philosophical Society Franklin Research Grant, Center for Khmer Studies Senior Research Grant, French Historical Studies Fellowship, American Historical Association Bernadette Schmitt Grant, National Endowment for the Humanities Summer Research Stipend, Cal Poly University Robert Detweiler Research Grant, and a writing fellowship from the International Institute for Asian Studies in the Netherlands.

At University of Hawai'i Press, I would like to extend a warm thank-you to Pamela Kelley, Debbie Tang, Rita Smith Kipp, David Chandler, who enthusiastically encouraged me to pursue this project when I was still a graduate student, and Peter Zinoman, who reviewed this book.

The Uprooted grew out of research that I started at UCLA. I am grateful for the guidance of Geoff Robinson and Thu Huong Nguyen-Vo, as well as George Dutton, Kate Norberg, and Ned Alpers. I was lucky to be part of a thriving intellectual community of friends including Cari Coe, Emily Musil-Church, Jinny Oh, Juliana Wajaya, and Awet Weidemichael.

After UCLA, I found a home at Cal Poly University in beautiful San Luis Obispo, California, where I have wonderful students and colleagues. In particular, I thank CLA dean Douglas Epperson, CLA librarian Brett Bodemer, the History Department, the Women's and Gender Studies Department, and those colleagues whom I am proud to call my closest friends: Regulus Allen, Kim Barton, Julie and Jay Bettergarcia, Maggie Bodemer, Denise Isom, Devin and Don Kuhn-Choi, Jane Lehr, Andrew Morris, Kate Murphy, José Navarro, Dawn Neil, Elivra Pulitano, and Jay Singh.

In my countless research trips to Vietnam, Hoa Sen University in Ho Chi Minh City and the University of Social Sciences and Humanities in Hanoi graciously hosted me with open arms. I am specifically grateful to Bùi Trân Phượng, Đặng Thị Vân Chi, Hoàng Anh Tuấn, Nguyễn Thu Hương, Thái Thị Ngọc Dư, and Trần Thị Phương Hoa.

From the bottom of my heart, I thank Laby Camara, Phạm Ngọc Lân, Emile Tissot, Rolland Raymond, and other former wards of the *métis* protection societies who wished to remain anonymous for trusting me with their personal stories. I can only hope this book does justice to those *métis,* their mothers, and the extended families whose lives were touched by the *métis* removal policy.

Shawn McHale and Ron Spector have been the biggest influences on my intellectual development. I am forever grateful to them for igniting my passion for Vietnamese studies as a young undergraduate student and generously continuing to provide advice and mentorship. To this day they remain my good friends. I also owe a great debt to my French teacher, Madame Esther Gordon. Elisa Camiscioli, David Del Testa, Eric Jennings, Charles Keith, David Marr, Shawn McHale, Ed Miller, and Erica Peters graciously commented on drafts of my chapters. I can only hope that the final product pleases them. Over the years, colleagues whom I met in the field and in various archives have provided invaluable feedback, friendship, and fun. In addition to the colleagues and friends already mentioned, I would like to sincerely thank David Biggs, Jennifer Boittin, Pascal Bordeaux, Pierre Brocheux, Haydon Cherry, Brad Davis, Olga Droor, Katie Dyt, Claire Edington, Katie Edwards, Gilles de Gantes, Chris and Agathe Goscha, Marie Paule Ha, Erik Harms, Tom Hoogervost, Margaret Jacobs, Micheline Lessard, Van Nguyen-Marshall, Lien-Hang Nguyen, Martina Nguyen, Philippe Pappin, Patricia Pelley, Philippe Peycam, Emmanuelle Saada, Hue Tam Ho Tai, Keith Taylor, Philip Taylor, Michele Thompson, Richard Tran, Owen White, and my colleagues in the Vietnam Studies Group.

The following individuals do not necessarily fit neatly into any of the categories previously mentioned but I am very grateful for their intellectual support and friendship: Neetu Bali, Tiffany Chung, George Cotkin, Hoàng Lan Hương, Alyson Holob, Christina Kaviani, Meme Lobecker, Fabien Lotz, Hong Anh Ly, Nguyễn Thị Hồng Hạnh, Nguyễn Thị Hoa, Marta Peluso, Suzie Smith, and the staff at Joe Mamma's Coffee in Avila Beach, who let me spend countless hours writing this book while watching the waves roll in.

I am grateful to my big Italian family for their love and support throughout this project, even if it meant bringing my work on family vacations. I thank my ông xã Mike Chen for being a supportive and loving partner in crime. The Sangiacomo family, the Cozzi family, Gabriella Lofaro, Salvatore Lofaro, Laura Lofaro-Freeman, Jim Freeman, and June and Ross Stoddard cheered me on from afar. I am deeply indebted to Erica Firpo; Darius,

Emilia, and Xanthe Arya; and Patrice, Joseph, Audrey, and Jack Guitreau. Sadly, Joe Guitreau passed away while I was finishing this book, but I promise to celebrate by cracking open a bottle of wine for him. Finally, words cannot express my gratitude to my parents, Kathy and Johnny Firpo. From the beginning, they made my education a priority while teaching me, by example, how to truly enjoy life. None of this would have been possible without their support and unconditional love.

ABBREVIATIONS

CAC	Centre des Archives Contemporaines at Fontainebleau
CAOM	Centre des Archives d'Outre Mer
CNA	Cambodian National Archives
FNA	French National Archives
FOEFI	Fédération des Oeuvres de l'Enfance Française d'Indochine
GF	Gouvernment du Fait
GGI	Governor General of Indochina
JBF	Jules Brévié Foundation
MHN	Maire Ville de Hanoi
PTTVNCH	Phủ thủ tướng Việt Nam Cộng Hòa
RF	Résident de France
RSA	Resident Superior of Annam
RSC	Resident Superior of Cambodia
RST	Resident Superior of Tonkin
SET	Service d'Enseignement du Tonkin
SHAT	Service Historique d'Armée de Terre
SLOTFAM	Service de Liason avec les Originaires des Territoiers Française d'Outre Mer
VNNA	Vietnam National Archives

Introduction

As she sat crying, young Eurasian Juliette Varenne did not know how or why she had ended up separated from her Vietnamese mother and confined to the Saint Joseph Asylum, an orphanage and leper colony run by French nuns in Tonkin. That day in 1939 or 1940—she is unsure of the year—she did not feel like playing with other wards but preferred to weep silently by herself. When the nuns asked why she was crying, she told them she missed her cat. Day after day, she stationed herself beside the orphanage gate, head hurting and throat tight, scanning the outside world for traces of her mother and brothers. She promised herself that they would soon appear from beyond the horizon, at which point the ordeal would be over and it would be time to return home. Suddenly, "as if by magic," she would later recall, her older brother appeared outside the gate that isolated the asylum-orphanage from the surrounding Vietnamese village. Through the fence, young Juliette and her brother clasped hands, taking advantage of a moment when the orphanage's one-legged guard was distracted. With his other hand, Juliette's brother slipped her a few grains of rice and a couple of coins. Espying the glint of the coins, the guard barked, "You better pay for a visit. If not, it's over!" Hands still interlinked, the two children did not budge, enraging the guard. He hobbled over, separated the siblings, and shooed Juliette's brother away. When Juliette realized that her brother would probably never return, "it was as if another door had shut" on her, and she was left "empty of hope, in front of the big sad gate." As an adult, Juliette would regret that she never got a chance to tell her brother that French officials had changed her name.[1]

Juliette Varenne was just one of many *métis* (mixed-race) children who were removed from the Vietnamese, Cambodian, and Lao milieus during the French colonial and postcolonial periods (1890–1980).[2] This study investigates the origins and development of French initiatives to "protect" fatherless *métis* children in Indochina and, later, South Vietnam. In the course of my research, I was shocked to find that what initially appeared to be a few isolated stories of colonial officials coercing indigenous mothers to relinquish custody of their *métis* children turned out to be much more—and I was even more astounded to find that this practice lasted twenty-six years beyond the end of French colonial rule, through the Vietnam War.

In this book, I contend that between 1890 and 1980, French colonial authorities and civilian-led protection societies systematically uprooted fatherless *métis* children from the Vietnamese, Cambodian, and Lao cultural environments and placed them in institutions designed to cultivate their loyalties to France. The term "uprooted" (*déraciné* in French and *bật gốc* or *mất gốc* in Vietnamese) appeared multiple times in the Vietnamese and French-language discourse on fatherless *métis* children. One former protection society ward even titled his unpublished memoire *Le Déraciné* (The Uprooted). The term is used to describe the process by which authorities removed fatherless *métis* children from the indigenous cultural environment by offering shelter to orphans and impoverished children; or by convincing, coercing, or forcing mothers to relinquish custody of their children. The children were then raised in French-run institutions that were designed to restrict indigenous cultural influences. In the process of researching this book, I created a database that tracks more than four thousand *métis* protection society wards over multiple decades, from early childhood to late adulthood, and even follows some to France.[3] I estimate that in total, more than ten thousand *métis* children likely passed through these institutions from the early days of colonization through the end of the Vietnam War.[4]

Indochina's *métis* protection system developed out of late nineteenth-century French colonists' concerns about a growing population of *métis* children born to indigenous mothers and French fathers. In many cases, the father left the mother soon after or even before the child was born—whether as a result of divorce, death, the end of a romance, or a return to France, or because he had raped her. While children born of legal marriages automatically inherited their father's French citizenship, those born out of wedlock were considered indigenous under French law unless their fathers had legally recognized them. These unrecognized, fatherless *métis* children were subject to the native legal code and denied the privileges of French citizens; almost all of them lived in poverty with their mothers in the indigenous cultural milieu and had come to identify as Vietnamese, Cambodian, or Lao.

In the 1890s, civilian-led organizations dedicated to the "protection" of fatherless *métis* children cropped up throughout Indochina, as well as in other areas of the empire.[5] Founded by a handful of eager French citizens and colonial officials acting in a civilian capacity, *métis* protection societies initially developed independently of one another. Yet given the regular collaboration that occurred among protection societies and colonial officials, protection societies' rhetoric and actions were strikingly similar. By 1938, the colonial state had taken complete control of the protection societies, underwritten the costs, and integrated the policies towards fatherless *métis* children into the broader plans for Indochina. After World War II, *métis* protection societies moved to civilian control. Under the direction of Indochina's prominent *métis* leaders, the *métis* program continued through the end of the Vietnam War—long after France had ended its claim to Indochina.

Throughout the colonial period, protection societies lobbied the colonial government to treat unrecognized *métis* children as French and afford them the same opportunities as recognized French children. Members saw themselves as following in the antiracist tradition of liberal French republicanism. Protection societies aimed to "save" *métis* children from what they claimed were the dangerous influences of their indigenous mothers and indigenous culture. Drawing on an 1889 metropolitan French law that regulated the moral abandonment of children—titled the "divestiture of paternal powers"— colonial officials and protection societies claimed that growing up in the absence of a French father or French cultural influences and living in the Vietnamese, Cambodian, or Lao milieu was tantamount to abandonment.[6] French officials and protection societies conducted exhaustive searches of the countryside for fatherless *métis* children who were being raised by their mothers. While officials invested most of their resources in searching for children in Vietnam—the focus of this book—they also conducted searches in the Cambodian and Lao countrysides.[7] Colonial authorities took custody of the fatherless *métis* children and removed them from the indigenous milieu—at times against the wishes of their mothers. Authorities then placed the children in institutions run by protection societies, much like the orphanage where Juliette Varenne was raised. There, *métis* wards were raised and educated in a French cultural environment with the aim of transforming them into "little Frenchmen."[8]

The story of the uprooting of these children is absent from the Vietnamese, Cambodian, Lao, and French historical memory. What little talk there is of the subject paints a picture of a benevolent state saving children from the irresponsible parents who had callously abandoned them. Indeed, during the time that the removals occurred, the French and indigenous public knew little about what was happening. Because both colonial French and indigenous society scorned unmarried indigenous women who had sex with Frenchmen, and regarded mixed-race children as outsiders, few people cared about these mothers or their children. With the exception of a series of reportage articles and a few other articles announcing protection society initiatives or gossiping about crimes committed by *métis* adults, Vietnamese newspapers rarely covered stories about fatherless *métis* children.[9] And while French government files pertaining to fatherless *métis* children have been sitting in archives in Vietnam, Cambodia, and France for more than a century, few scholars have acknowledged that the colonial state and protection societies not only uprooted *métis* children from the indigenous cultural environment but, in many cases, forcibly separated them from their own mothers. This story, therefore, has remained largely untold for more than a century.

Over the last few decades, a handful of adult *métis* have told their stories through published and unpublished memoirs.[10] Literary scholars such as Françoise Vergès, Karl Britto, Srilata Ravi, Nathalie Huynh Chau Nguyen, Jack Yeager, Isabelle Thuy Pelaud, and Nguyen Xuan Tue have drawn from these memoirs to explore the experiences of *métis* who grew up in Indochina.[11] Karl Britto, for example, shows that the hybrid and intercultural position occupied by *métis* resulted in "rigid and potentially traumatic conditions."[12] However, we know very little about the historical context within which those *métis* who wrote these memoirs were raised. The most important history of *métis* in Indochina is Emmanuelle Saada's groundbreaking work on the sociocultural history of French colonial legal codes pertaining to race and nonrecognized *métis* throughout the French empire, with a specific focus on Indochina.[13] Gilles de Gantes, Ann Laura Stoler, Pierre Guillaume, David Pomfret, Gregor Muller, Yves Denéchère, Penny Edwards, and Haydon Cherry have also devoted articles, book chapters, and dissertation chapters to *métis* in their larger works on *métis* belonging, colonial sexuality, the history of childhood, the foundations of the early colonial state, and poverty in colonial Saigon.[14]

Among these historical and literary studies, Stoler, Saada, Pomfret, Edwards, Muller, Denéchère, and Vergès have all found incidents of *métis* child removals. Drawing from this important scholarship and from the thousands of cases that I found in the course of my research in the Vietnamese, Cambodian, and French archives, I contend that protection societies and colonial authorities systematically removed fatherless *métis* children from the indigenous milieu. In my investigation of the systematic removal of *métis* children, I explore the reasons why protection societies and the colonial government devoted so much money, time, bureaucratic infrastructure, and other resources to such a small and apparently innocuous population of children. I also trace the development of the *métis* protection system and the many shifts that occurred in the attitudes towards *métis* through the colonial and post-colonial periods. I found that *métis* removals were motivated not only by co-lonial benevolence but also by colonial self-interest. Fearing that fatherless *métis* children might come to resent the French government for denying them the rights of French men and women, officials saw the *métis* removals and the protection system as a means of minimizing the threat of rebellion. More broadly, colonial authorities saw *métis* removals as a way to preserve white prestige and bourgeois class status and, most importantly, of repro-ducing the French race, nation, and, eventually, empire. *Métis* children—including not just Eurasians but also eventually Afro-Asians and Indian-Asians, all of whom could be given a French education and inculcated with French culture and middle-class sensibilities—came to be seen by protection society officials as a key to French imperial permanence.

The removal of children from their parents, and more generally the na-tive milieu, for social, political, economic, and demographic purposes reflects a trend in nineteenth- and twentieth-century imperial statecraft. Through-out much of the French empire, protection societies worked with colonial ad-ministrators to place *métis* children in orphanages. As Emmanuelle Saada has shown, Indochina functioned as a laboratory for the French state to test poli-cies towards mixed-race children before implementing them in other colonies around the empire.[15] In French West Africa, authorities created protection societies to prevent fatherless Eurafrican *métis* children from growing up to rebel against the colonial state. The Eurafrican population, they believed, could potentially offer useful services to the colonial government as an inter-mediary race of petit bourgeois who were acclimated to the West African climate.[16] From 1963 to 1982, in the process of decolonizing the empire and integrating select colonies into the French nation-state, authorities in Ré-union transferred impoverished children from the island to the *métropole,* often against the will of the children and their families.[17]

What transpired in Indochina between 1890 and 1980 also bears a strik-ing resemblance to infamous cases of colonial child removal programs in other empires, including that of the removal of Eurasians in colonial India (the Andaman scheme) and the forced migration of *métis* children from Ruanda-Urundi to Belgium (mid-twentieth century); the forcible removal of aborig-inal children in Australia, also known as Australia's Stolen Generation (1860s–1970s); the forcible removal of First Nation children in Canada, also known as the Indian Residential School System (1860s–1960s); the forcible removal of Native American children for placement in Indian boarding schools (late nineteenth to mid-twentieth century).[18] As in Indochina, child protection societies in the United States, Australia, Canada, and Ruanda-Urundi targeted young children, maligned indigenous mothers, claimed that indigenous culture had deleterious influences on children, removed children, and institutionalized them in boarding schools. In the boarding schools, wards were prohibited from speaking their native languages, practicing native culture and religion, and seeing their families. In their rhetoric, protection societies used what Françoise Vergès describes as the "colonial family romance" to present the state as the protective parent that would replace the wards' own indigenous families.[19]

Yet the motivations underlying *métis* child removals in Indochina differed from those in other removal cases. In India, officials removed Anglo-Indian Eurasians from their parents to prevent the growth of an impoverished, domiciled white population.[20] In the United States, Australia, and Canada, protection societies were part of a larger plan to maintain colonial rule and divest indigenous people of their land by eradicating the indigenous populations. In Indochina, by contrast, the colonial government never intended to eliminate the indigenous population. Because Europeans never constituted more than 0.2 percent of the colony's population,[21] the aim of the *métis* removal program was to aid in reproducing the French nation by raising *métis* wards to identify with French culture and the French nation.

The French state's desire to reproduce the nation was closely linked to security fears. After the Franco-Prussian War of 1870, France associated population growth with military strength and, by extension, national strength. Any challenges to the colonial order—including indigenous nationalism, anticolonial activity, changes in gender roles, or the rise of a disgruntled fatherless *métis* population—fed French colonial anxieties about maintaining colonial security. French colonists believed that both the *métis* threat and the French depopulation problem could be solved by transforming fatherless *métis* children into French men and women.

In colonial society, French identity was defined through a complex calculation of race, culture, class, and citizenship. Although officially illegal,[22] the most important factor in this equation was racial phenotypes, including skin color, hair color, and eye color. Indeed, wealthy, French-educated, and naturalized Vietnamese, Cambodian, and Lao—even those who had been French citizens since birth—were rarely accepted in French colonial social circles as French, but were instead considered "naturalized French." The colonial state deemed fatherless *métis* children politically important precisely because they tended to be easily identifiable as the descendants of colonizers and, with an education and job placement, could be transformed into French men and women in a way that naturalized Vietnamese, Cambodian, and Lao people could not.

Central to Indochina's *métis* removal program was the belief that the racial and cultural identity of mixed-race people remained fluid until puberty. If the state or protection societies stepped in to replace the missing French paternal influence and to educate the wards in French language, culture, and middle-class sensibilities, then fatherless *métis* children could be inculcated with a French identity and taught to be loyal to France and the colonial government.

As colonial security needs evolved in Indochina, the racial categorizations of fatherless *métis* children likewise changed. Moreover, because racial formations depended in part on the personal views of the beholder, *métis* children found themselves caught in the cross fire of competing ideologies and strategies. At any given time, the French public held a variety of opinions about the racial categorization of fatherless *métis* children, and these opinions usually fell on the fault lines of class. As a result, neither "white" nor "French" were stable social categories. After the perceived population decimation resulting from World War I, colonial administrators and protection society members looked to mixed-race children to bolster the colony's white French population and hence colonial strength. Yet the trend towards regarding fatherless Eurasian *métis* as white directly contradicted racial formations in the *métropole,* where, as work by Elisa Camiscioli shows, Frenchness was equated with whiteness, and whiteness in turn meant having two white parents.[23] Although initially the French colonial government used only Eurasian *métis* children who were passably white in their plan to reproduce the white French race, this changed with the Vietnamese revolution (1946–1954) and ensuing decolonization. Desperate for the loyalties of Afro-Asian and Indian-Asian *métis* children, French authorities began to use Afro-Asian and Indian-Asian children to reproduce the "imperial" race and the French nation.

French colonial and protection society officials understood that if fatherless *métis* children could be used to reproduce the French race, then it logically followed that many Vietnamese, Cambodian, and Lao women were giving birth to future French men and women and hence the French nation. Indigenous mothers, therefore, became central to French anxieties. This fear of indigenous mothers introduced a gendered dimension to the "*métis* question," as the French called it.[24] Emmanuelle Saada has shown that the connection between paternity and citizenship rendered the *métis* question a "male affair."[25] The anxiety of French officials vis-à-vis indigenous maternity and the centrality of child removals reveals the *métis* question to have been a female affair in other ways. In addition to deploring the fact that indigenous mothers were giving birth to and socializing their *métis* children into indigenous culture and raising them to identify as racially Vietnamese, Cambodian, or Lao, officials portrayed these mothers as morally corrupt and lacking maternal instincts. From 1890 to 1975, the French state and protection societies demonized the indigenous mothers of *métis* children and the pernicious influence they were believed to have on their children. So consistent were the efforts of these officials that their rhetoric about indigenous mothers scarcely changed over the course of an entire century—from the start of colonialism to the end of the Vietnam War.

Troubled by the perceived contradiction of indigenous mothers giving birth to and raising children who would be the future of the French nation and imperial race, the French state and protection societies asserted a proprietary claim and racial ownership over these children—particularly those who were easily identifiable as *métis* through the popular understandings of racial phenotypes of the time. According to this view, indigenous mothers who gave birth to this valuable French national resource had no claim to or rights over their own children. Whereas single mothers were frowned upon regardless of the race of their children, it was only the mothers of *métis* children whom authorities encouraged—and even pressured—to relinquish custody of their children.

Indigenous mothers were maligned not only by French colonial officials but also by the Vietnamese press and public. Vietnamese women who married Westerners were called *me tây* (wives of westerners or mothers of Western children).[26] In one of the most famous Vietnamese writings on the subject of the colonial era, journalist Vũ Trọng Phụng reported on the phenomenon he called "the industry of marrying Westerners," in which Vietnamese women congregated around French military bases to ensure subsistence through successive "sugar daddy" style relationships with French soldiers. Such relationships frequently produced *métis* children, whom the mothers considered potentially profitable insofar as they could be recognized as French citizens, opening up a world of opportunity that mothers hoped to access through their children.[27]

Yet not all of the women who had sex with foreigners resembled the hardened, money-minded women portrayed by Vũ Trọng Phụng and countless colonial administrators. In many cases, mothers of mixed-race children had been in love with their French husbands or domestic partners and vowed to maintain long-term relationships with them. Other women had been raped—a well-known if rarely discussed reality of the colonial period. As evident in letters from mothers to the colonial government and other government documents, an overwhelming number of mothers who consented to placing their children in protection society institutions acted out of selfless maternal instinct and economic desperation, hoping that the colonial government would give their children the food and education that the mothers themselves were struggling to provide.

While the letters that mothers sent to the colonial government about their fatherless *métis* children bespoke a shrewd sense of how to navigate a bureaucracy—what could be interpreted as "politics of pity"[28]—these letters also served as genuine means of survival for economically and politically marginalized mothers and their children. Indigenous women, after all, were particularly vulnerable to the colonial system of financial exploitation, and for some women, the protection society system was a form of help. While it is possible that, as French administrators claimed, some women relinquished custody of their children out of a reluctance to commit to motherhood, the archival record suggests that such women were in the minority. For these mothers, the protection society system genuinely offered aid to mothers and children—but only within certain limits. Prospective wards had to be prepubescent and have racial phenotypes that indicated that they were children of French men or colonial soldiers, and mothers had to agree to waive some of their rights. Archives in Vietnam, Cambodia, and France include letters from mothers imploring the French government to return their children.

It is evident through the archival record that maternal consent—or nonconsent—to relinquish custody of children was cultural and subject to change. Some mothers who consented to be separated from their children later withdrew their consent and wrote to colonial officials, imploring them to return their children. These mothers were likely used to early twentieth-century Vietnamese cultural practices in which temporary adoption or institutional care was commonplace practice. For parents suffering financial hardship or ill health, adoption and child-care services served as short-term solutions to ensure children's survival; once the parents' financial situation improved, according to Vietnamese custom, they had the option to regain custody of their children. In the case of fatherless *métis* children, however, protection societies rarely granted the mothers' requests to have their children returned to them. Alternatively, some mothers whose children were forcibly removed from them later appeared to approve of their children's education and upbringing in the protection societies. For example, the mother of

Antoine Slovic, who at first, in 1955, refused to let the French take her child, appeared to have reversed her opinion by 1959, when she sent out proud announcements of her son's marriage and scholastic progress under protection society care in France.[29]

It is worth noting that the correspondence located in the archives represents only a certain portion of the letters written by the mothers of fatherless *métis* children placed in institutions. Those letters were written by mothers who were savvy enough to appeal to high-level colonial officials; letters sent to lower-level administrators were likely lost over time, and the historical archives could not preserve the record of those mothers who made verbal appeals or those who did not possess the bureaucratic acumen necessary to contact the right officials.

Given that protection societies were decentralized, independent units for most of their existence and that records from these societies are hence incomplete, it is impossible to quantify how many children were uprooted from their mothers and the native milieu. Colonial-era estimates varied widely, and colonial officials frequently acknowledged their inability to estimate the size of the fatherless *métis* population.[30] Further complicating the issue, fatherless *métis* children were difficult to track, as they often lived on the margins of native society and were recorded in legal records as "*indigène*," the legal classification for natives. This classification meant there was no legal distinction between nonrecognized *métis* children and Vietnamese, Lao, or Cambodian children; hence, they are mostly invisible in statistical records.[31] Unlike the policies pertaining to multiracial people in the Jim Crow American South, there was no rule in Indochina about how many grandparents made someone white, French, *métis,* or Asian.[32] In fact, "*métis*" appears to have been a nebulous category whose definition changed according to the speaker. Some considered Afro-Asian and Indian-Asian children to be French *métis;* others considered them indigenous or did not acknowledge their existence at all.

Because fatherless *métis* children lived on the margins of colonial and postcolonial society, it is difficult to obtain information about them, their mothers, and their experiences as indigenous subjects before authorities removed them. Colonial officials looking to erase fatherless *métis* children's Vietnamese, Cambodian, and Lao pasts and cultural influences deliberately obscured information about the children's lives before they entered the protection society programs or along the way. Colonial officials also successfully withheld from the colonial records voices they considered undesirable or unreliable—namely those of Vietnamese, Cambodian, and Lao mothers. Spaces for the mothers' names were often left blank, or the words "unknown" or "*indigène*" were penciled in for their name. Officials referred to *métis* children as "orphans" or "without family," even though most of them did have families before they were removed. It is not uncommon to find contradictions among the archival files. For the same child, one document might list the mother's name, but another document might list the mother as "unknown." In one particularly egregious case, the 1942 notes by protection society worker Madame Aumont detail the forcible removal of Robert Henri from his mother, Nguyễn Thị Khai, who made multiple attempts to regain custody of her child. Yet the 1946 notes of same Madame Aumont claim that the same mother had been "completely uninterested in her children."[33]

Protection societies also separated siblings to prevent them from finding one another, developing familial ties, or being found by their mother. This policy left some children to lament that they were "treated like dogs, separated [from the litter] according to someone else's whim."[34] When children sought out their siblings, some officials flatly denied their existence.[35] In the 1970s, adult Eurasian men and women who had been members of the last generation of protection society wards and were by then living in France contacted former protection society officials requesting information on their families. However, even the most well-meaning protection society officials could rarely provide that information, given that their colonial predecessors had deliberately obfuscated the channels to the past.

Renaming the fatherless *métis* children was an important part of the transformation process that destroyed the links to the past, as names linked children to their maternal family, culture, and ancestral heritage.[36] Officially, children whose fathers had legally recognized them were permitted to maintain their paternal surnames, nonrecognized children were not. To circumvent laws that deemed nonrecognized children indigenous subjects and denied them their paternal name, colonial authorities assigned them common male first names—such as Bernard, Nicolas, Louis, and Henri—as their last names. This practice effectively bestowed a French identity on these unrecognized children while preserving the anonymity of their fathers. This practice was more common for boys than it was for girls, although it is not clear why. In cases in which the fathers themselves had a last name that could function as a first name, protection societies reversed the two names, as was the case of Henri François, son of François Henri.[37] Although first names that function as last names are not unusual in French culture, some children, such as Henri André, would grow up to resent the French state for not giving them "real" last names and thus implicating them as bastard children.[38] While many nonrecognized *métis* children did use their father's names informally, colonial record keepers added "so-called" to these names to signal their skepticism of the mothers' paternity claims, a practice that was also frequent among *métis* protection societies in French West Africa. [39] Examples included the young Demba "so-called Picard"[40] or "Phạm Thê Anh, so-called Alain-Michel."[41]

The renaming process was a flagrantly political act that severed the bureaucratic ties between children and parents, and divested fatherless *métis* children of their indigenous identity. In most cases, officials did not include indigenous names. When they did, the indigenous names were often couched in doubt. For example, protection society officials recorded the name of a young, nonrecognized girl as "Christielle, so-called Trần Thị Lai."[42] As Owen White shows in the case of *métis* children in the French West African and Equatorial African colonies, the renaming process not only created identities but also denied identities—in this case, indigenous identities.[43] Through changing children's names, authorities erased an important archival as well as symbolic link to their indigenous identities. Only a handful of documents even mention the *métis* children's Vietnamese, Cambodian, or Lao names—usually dismissively. As noted by Juliette Varenne, whose story opened this book, the name changes made it difficult for families to track their *métis* loved ones. Such was the case for Robert Henri, the child whose mother had fought to keep him yet was listed as uninterested in him, who saw his name changed to Robert Charles Henri, to Charles Henri, and then to Charles Robert, rendering it impossible for his older brother to find him.[44]

In some cases, the renaming resulted in a serious problem for fatherless *métis* children, only to be discovered years later, when the child reached a certain bureaucratic milestone. In one case, protection societies assigned two boys the same name, birthday, and birthplace. The protection societies only realized their mistake when it came time for the boys to register for military service.[45] In another case, Fatima Shirif was accused of fraud by another woman whom protection society officials had also named Fatima Shirif; authorities had accidentally issued her the same birthday and same parents. Officials cleared up the situation by changing the name of one of the Fatimas to Fatine Serif, moving her birthday a month later, and changing her parents' names.[46]

Despite the efforts of protection societies to obscure the fatherless *métis* children's indigenous pasts, careful attention to detail reveals these histories in archives, printed sources, or the memories of still-living former protection society wards. Details of their pre-removal lives were mentioned by police in their surveillance of indigenous families and correspondence between officials and mothers, some mothers edging their way back into the picture with letters demanding full custody of their children or imploring officials to at least let them visit. In the decades that followed, many former protection society wards held on tightly to their memories of mothers, siblings, and grandparents. Some reified memories of their families and native culture by writing memoirs or by participating in Internet chat groups or Facebook pages with other former wards. These progeny of the protection societies had not left their indigenous lives in the past. Many continued to consider themselves first and foremost as Vietnamese, Cambodian, or Lao, with some going so far as to leave lucrative jobs to return to the indigenous milieu.[47]

French authorities' extensive efforts to obscure the pasts of fatherless *métis* children reveal just how important these histories are to an understanding of how *métis* children were systematically uprooted from their indigenous families and cultural milieus. Because authorities involved in the uprooting of fatherless *métis* children obfuscated the majority of wards' pasts, researching this subject calls for an alternative methodology. Although this story of child removals focuses on government policies and is therefore told mostly through government documents, it is built on stories that come from intimate spaces: the personal lives of fatherless *métis* children and those of their family members. This study works at the grassroots level, examining the realities of, and responses to, French policies as they played out in day-to-day life.

In the course of my research, I created a database to trace the lives of more than four thousand fatherless *métis* who passed through the protection society program. As I read through hundreds of thousands of documents pertaining to the removal of fatherless *métis* children, I collected just as many complicated anecdotes pieced together from documents spanning multiple decades and filed in archives in Hanoi, Dalat, Ho Chi Minh City, Phnom Penh, Paris, Château de Vincennes, Fontainebleau, and Aix-en-Provence. With these anecdotes about individual children—some consisting of only a sentence or two, others consisting of dozens of pages detailing a child's removal and life in protection society institutions—the database humanizes social history and creates a narrative of interwoven personal stories in a way that is not usually possible, especially for a population as marginalized as children. By entering into the database and piecing together the snippets of information conveyed in each mention of protection society wards across hundreds of thousands of diverse documents, it has been possible to reconstruct the lives of some of these children and to reveal the larger scope of the removal and transformation experience. By making an argument heavily rooted in empirical data, this history conveys the magnitude of French anxiety about the cultural influences of the Vietnamese, Lao, and Cambodian mothers of "half-French" children and, more generally, about the presumed need to reproduce the French nation and preserve the colonial racial order. In a broader sense, this story explores the effects, both insidious and blatant, of colonialism on colonized societies and, in particular, on mothers and children.

The database I created to track the lives of these *métis* children sheds light on the vivid contrast between the official rhetoric about fatherless *métis* children articulated by colonial administrators and the personal stories of the removals as narrated by the mothers and children themselves. When using children's names and their experience as the central organizing factor for this database, a picture of the *métis* protection system emerges that is different from the benevolent discourse promoted in protection society propaganda. Indeed, the personal reminiscences of former wards, written correspondences of their mothers, and even protection society members' own notes often belie the protection societies' claims that they were "rescuing" the fatherless *métis* children. The archival records, not intended for public consumption and often labeled "confidential" or "secret," reveal a significant disconnect between, on the one hand, the colonial government's public narrative about "saving" children from mothers who were supposedly morally corrupt and, on the other hand, the emotionally and culturally violent reality of separating mothers—many of whom were competent and caring—from their children.

The pages that follow place the history of fatherless *métis* children within the context of colonial Indochina's history. Because the French typically made policy in reaction to events in Tonkin, Annam, and Cochinchina—the Vietnamese areas of Indochina—this story focuses mostly on Vietnam. Policies towards fatherless *métis* children changed significantly from the start of colonialism to the end of the Vietnam War. This book is organized chronologically to track the changes in attitudes towards fatherless *métis* children that informed these policy changes—and, conversely, the ways in which policies towards fatherless *métis* changed public attitudes about these children.

Chapter 1 explores the formation of *métis* protection societies within the context of a developing colonial state, and the challenges the state faced from a rebellious indigenous population. The protection system was designed to forestall the development of a disaffected, rebellious class of *métis* by training fatherless *métis* boys in agriculture. Chapter 2 investigates how the massive number of casualties in World War I changed the colony's approach to the *métis* population. French officials capitalized on the rhetoric of pronatalism to make the case that fatherless *métis* were French "by blood" and convince the colonial French population to accept them as French. To facilitate *métis* contributions to French population regeneration, protection societies developed a program for *métis* agricultural settlements in strategic areas of Annam and a program to send wards to the *métropole* to aid in repopulating war-torn areas while learning French culture and professional skills.

Chapter 3 looks at the social and economic changes that occurred during the Great Depression and eventually led the colonial state to take over the *métis* protection system. To alleviate the widespread poverty of this era, the colonial state built child-care institutions throughout Indochina, thereby normalizing institutionalized child care and leading many more mothers to entrust their *métis* children to the protection societies. Meanwhile, Les Français d'Indochine, a group of wealthy and powerful adult *métis* from Cochinchina, lobbied the state to devote more resources to fatherless *métis* children. On the advice of the metropolitan government, the governor general created the Jules Brévié Foundation—a centralized, state-directed *métis* protection program—and a military school for older wards.

Chapter 4 shows how the Japanese occupation of Indochina during World War II led protection societies to obsess over fatherless *métis* children's white racial phenotypes. The Brévié Foundation developed a plan to use wards as the colony's new fixed-French population to settle strategic areas of Annam and the proposed new colonial capital of Dalat, with the long-term goal of transforming them into a permanent French elite population that would counterbalance the colony's Vietnamese, Cambodian, and Lao elites.

After Hồ Chí Minh declared Vietnamese independence and the colony became engulfed in the French-Indochina War, the colonial government placed the *métis* protection system under civilian control, creating the Fédération des Oeuvres de l'Enfance Française d'Indochine (FOEFI). Chapter 5 discusses how FOEFI used the symbolism of abandoned *métis* children to make the case for France to maintain its colony in Indochina while expanding *métis* child removals to include children of African and Indian troops. During the French Indochina War, *métis* protection was no longer about preserving whiteness; it was about preserving the former colony's connection to the empire through its Eurasian, Afro-Asian, and Indian-Asian *métis* children.

Even after the 1954 Geneva Accords dismantled the French empire in Asia, French military officials and civilians continued to remove fatherless *métis* children from Indochina's countryside. As we will see in chapter 6, fatherless *métis* children were held up both as a critique of those French politicians who had abandoned the colony and as a symbolic reminder of French imperial greatness—even as the empire crumbled. Although France no longer had legal jurisdiction over its former colony, FOEFI used defunct colonial-era laws to justify continuing the removal process and sent wards to France—often without maternal consent.

Note on names: In order to respect the privacy of those families affected by the *métis* protection system, and to respect the privacy laws governing French archives, I have used pseudonyms for individuals mentioned in this book. The only real names I have included are those of former wards who have, as adults, published their stories in the form of memoirs, documentaries, or newspaper articles, or appeared on television, thereby indicating their willingness to make their personal stories public. I tried to choose pseudonyms that preserve the character of their names as they appear in the historical documents. For example, I use Vietnamese, French, Corsican, or Senegalese names to follow the spirit of an individual's original name. When authorities assigned wards first names to function as last names, I did the same for pseudonyms. For cases in which mothers gave their children names that were French translations of the mother's Vietnamese name, I have also chosen pseudonyms that reflect this naming process.

Note on diacritic marks: The colonial archives often use incorrect diacritic marks or leave them out all together. Instead of guessing the correct diacritic marks, I maintained the original spelling.

1 Founding of the *Métis* Protection Societies, 1870–1908

In the early years of the twentieth century, French soldiers stationed along the Chinese border in Lạng Sơn alerted colonial officials to a young *métis* boy who had been abandoned by his European father. The authorities declared him legally abandoned and took custody of him, although it is not clear that his mother willingly relinquished her parental rights. In 1905, French authorities placed the boy, whom they had renamed Georges Michel, in the custody of the Society for Métis Children in Hanoi. The society's mission was to "protect" *métis* children from bad influences in indigenous culture and prevent them from joining anticolonial activities by removing them from the indigenous milieu. Their fear was that *métis* children—whose fathers never recognized them, thus denying them access to French citizenship and its privileges—would come to resent the French colonial government. At the society's orphanage, young Georges learned French language and culture and eventually matriculated into a French school in Hải Phòng.[1] A French education, it was thought, would foster loyalties to the colonial government, thereby allaying any threats he might pose as a *métis* living among Vietnamese.

As part of a larger initiative to neutralize the potential threats posed by children like Georges Michel, in 1908 the governor general of Indochina established the Collège Agricole de Hưng Hóa in Tonkin, for fatherless Eurasian boys. Georges was among the agricultural school's enrolled students. The colonial state intended the school to be a surrogate for the French paternal influence missing from the lives of adolescent Eurasian boys; as such, it would presumably prevent them from developing hostile feelings towards the French government. After the wards graduated, the state planned to place them in strategic areas of the colony for the purposes of enhancing the colony's agricultural production. Indeed, the agricultural school of Hưng Hóa was the first of a series of colonial projects launched throughout the span of French rule in Indochina to redeem *métis* through agricultural labor and transform them into loyal middle-class Frenchmen.

The agricultural school project failed. In January 1910, Georges Michel—by then a teenager—acted as ringleader of a student riot protesting mistreatment, harsh labor conditions, and an inadequate and tainted food supply. The children broke out of the school but were soon captured and imprisoned by colonial police. It was only a matter of weeks before authorities shut down the Collège Agricole, returned the students to protection societies, and sent Georges Michel to China, presumably so that he would pose no further risk to colonial order. Soon he disappeared from the purview of colonial police.

This chapter traces the development of *métis* "protection" programs, like the one that raised Georges Michel, in relation to the formation of the colonial state. The *métis* protection system developed out of a sense of urgency on the part of concerned French civilians to stem the supposed debauched influences of indigenous societies, specifically Vietnamese, Cambodian, and Lao mothers, and to prevent the development of a disaffected and impoverished class of *métis* who would potentially grow to resent the colonial state for not imparting them the legal privileges afforded to Europeans. As with much of the colony's bureaucratic infrastructure, the *métis* protection system developed in response to the challenges facing the colonial state and was formed within the context of major metropolitan debates about child welfare and the role of the church in public life. Administrators would draw from the *anciennes colonies* of the French empire, as well as that of the Netherlands Indies, for models of success and failure in dealing with mixed-race children who had been abandoned by their European fathers. By the end of the first decade of the new century, a system developed in which civilian-led protection societies worked with local police to remove fatherless *métis* children from the indigenous milieu, raise them in French-run institutions that were largely isolated from the world around them, and train them in the skills necessary for entering the colonial workforce in professions becoming of French men and women.

ESTABLISHING COLONIAL RULE

Franco–Southeast Asian births date back to at least the seventeenth century, when French missionaries, traders, and government advisers had been involved in Indochina. Many of them—including priests—were rumored to have fathered children with local women. Yet because the French presence was limited, the region's *métis* population would remain sparse through the mid-nineteenth century. In 1847, the French navy first attacked Vietnam, ostensibly to defend the French missionaries who were being persecuted. By 1862, the French military had taken Gia Định, Mỹ Tho, and Biên Hòa in southern Vietnam. In 1863, Cambodia became a French protectorate.

The invasions resulted in an influx of French colonial soldiers and traders. By 1872, 858 Europeans had settled in Cochinchina, as well as 6,289 French men who were temporary stationed as military personnel, colonial officials, or merchant marines.[2] In the early years of colonial rule, interracial concubinage was largely accepted among French colonists. As Gregor Muller shows, officials in Cambodia regarded concubinage as well as prostitution necessary evils that helped prevent homosexual activity and mass rapes of local women by French soldiers. Moreover, these relationships proved to be an asset to French colonists. With their knowledge of local culture and languages, indigenous women helped the French men settle into Indochina and conduct business. In these early years, fathers were inclined to recognize the paternity of their *métis* children—a trend that would change by the turn of the century.[3]

The battle for Tonkin in the 1880s introduced new military units to Indochina. With the conclusion of the Sino-French War (1883–1885), Tonkin and Annam became French protectorates in 1887, completing the takeover of Vietnam. By February 1888, the number of European troops had grown to 12,308 in Tonkin, 2,348 in Annam, 2,090 in Cochinchina, and 614 in Cambodia, as well as roughly 40,000 troops from North Africa stationed throughout the area.[4] Although many of the French and North African soldiers would die in battle or from disease, the large number of single soldiers resulted in *métis* births. This seems even more understandable given that the population of European male settlers—military troops and temporary colonial officials excluded—exponentially outnumbered that of European women. For each European woman in Hải Phòng, there were 4.15 European men; in Hanoi, that number was 4.8.[5] Although there were never more than a handful of mixed-race marriages, many European soldiers, colonial officials, and permanent residents had sexual or romantic relationships with local women.

In the 1880s, French attitudes about mixed-race relationships grew less tolerant. Metropolitan academic debates about racial degeneration made *métissage* an issue of concern throughout the empire. French colonial officials came to believe that cohabiting relationships between European males and indigenous women contributed to the degeneration of the white race as well as the degeneration of European class status. Authorities initially clamped down on interracial marriages, issuing warnings to colonial functionaries in 1887 and again in 1901.[6]

As Marie-Paule Ha shows, the solution proposed was to import white French women from the *métropole* to the colony. Authorities believed the plan would benefit both the *métropole* and the colony. Female emigration would serve as an outlet for some of the social tensions that authorities identified in the *métropole,* including the growing number of single women who had become both *déclassé* and disenfranchised. The belief was that would-be "spinsters" in the *métropole* who could not afford a dowry were only too happy to come to Indochina, where they would be valuable commodities rather than social rejects. Meanwhile, the rewards for the colony would be manifold. As authorities were concerned that the colony's French male population was composed of social rejects and "bad Frenchmen," they believed that white women from the *métropole* could "civilize" French male settlers by encouraging French men in the colony to live according to European bourgeois norms rather than adopt native customs, thereby ensuring a divide between colonizer and colonized. The marriages produced from these unions would form the foundation for a permanent French population, which was essential for long-term colonization in Indochina. The union would also guarantee the production of a "pure" French race in the colony and slow the allegedly corrosive effects of *métissage* on the white race.[7]

In 1897, the Société Française d'Émigration des Femmes was created to facilitate emigration and, in 1900, the Oeuvre Coloniale des Femmes Françaises was founded to assist women once they arrived in the colonies. In Indochina, the colonial government designated office jobs for French wives and daughters of French men to ensure their livelihood and prevent them from resorting to prostitution.[8] Colonial officials' efforts to encourage women to emigrate from the *métropole* were successful. The population of white women in Hanoi, for example, increased tenfold between 1885 and 1900—from 20-some to 219.[9]

By 1897, France had established a colonial government that ruled Indochina, which comprised the Vietnamese colony of Cochinchina, the protectorates of Tonkin and Annam, and the protectorate kingdoms of Cambodia and Laos. The influx of government administrators and soldiers from the *métropole* and other areas of the empire resulted in sexual relations—not always consensual—between French, African, or Indian men and Asian women. The resulting Eurasian, Afro-Asian, and Indian-Asian children were typically orphaned or not legally recognized by their fathers. Colonial law considered nonrecognized children "indigenous" colonial subjects; as such, they lacked access to the privileges of French citizens. Further complicating the matter, when the battalions moved on, fatherless *métis* children were left to grow up in rebel country.

Both Vietnamese society and Catholic nuns developed welfare systems to care for orphaned children, systems that potentially included *métis* children. During the colonial wars, Vietnamese village society had three means of caring for orphan children: adoption by a Vietnamese couple, village-based protection systems known as *Nhà dưỡng tế*, and mutual aid societies. Adoption was a common practice in Vietnamese society. Childless married couples or parents who had lost a child could adopt orphans from hospitals or impoverished parents.[10] Orphaned and impoverished children who were not adopted could seek aid through *Nhà dưỡng tế* and mutual aid societies. The *Nhà dưỡng tế,* which were developed from the state level by Emperor Gia Long in 1814, were community-funded relief houses that provided temporary shelter and aid for orphans as well as children who were infirm or impoverished. Unlike French orphanages, orphans and other residents of the *Nhà dưỡng tế* were not required to pay a fee. Mutual aid societies were organized at the village level and were based on a system of reciprocity: members paid dues on a regular basis or pledged to provide aid as needed. Individuals who failed to fulfill their social responsibility brought shame to their families. Two types of mutual aid organizations, *giáp* and *phúng,* assisted families and orphans in the aftermath of the colonial war. The *giáp* assisted members in emergencies, such as family deaths or a loss of crops; the *phúng* attended to more thematic concerns, including care of descendants.[11]

In the late nineteenth century, French nuns opened orphanages in Vietnam—part of the French mission to promote colonial expansion and imperial grandeur through church-related humanitarian aid.[12] In 1862, the sisters opened an official orphanage to care for the numerous orphaned, abandoned, and impoverished children near the Saigon citadel. In the early years of French colonialism, most *métis* who were abandoned by both parents were initially sent to Catholic orphanages.[13] While the state was limiting direct financial support to the missions, it continued to underwrite Catholic health institutions and schools, as these programs supplemented the colonial infrastructure.[14] Even during the separation of church and state, the French colonial government supported church-run orphanages. These orphanages opened throughout the countryside and were administered by Catholic nuns. From the late nineteenth century through World War I, the order of Les Soeurs de Saint-Paul de Chartres was the major French caretaker of Vietnamese orphans and impoverished children, including *métis* children.

In 1874, an orphanage in Saigon welcomed Eurasian girls along with their Vietnamese wards.[15] The official history of Les Soeurs de Saint-Paul de Chartres reports that wards were either orphaned or brought by their parents. According to this history, dying parents left their children with the nuns to ensure their children would receive food and shelter after their death; rich parents sent their children to the Catholic orphanages to educate them and teach them French manners; and poor parents deposited children at orphanages when they could not afford to feed them. Sainte Enfance orphanage sometimes even offered parents monetary payment in exchange for depositing their children.[16] Some may have understood this as an incentive for parents to abandon their children. The official history does not indicate that any of these children were forcibly separated from their mothers, and some parents left their children in Catholic orphanages with the understanding that they could reclaim them whenever their health or financial situation improved.[17] Yet as it turned out, the orphanage of Sainte Enfance sometimes forced parents seeking to retrieve their children to repay the cost of raising them.[18]

Nuns raised their charges to speak only French and to follow French cultural norms. They converted the children to Catholicism, as the nuns understood French identity to "involve religion as much as race. . . . Religious difference was as important as biological difference."[19] They prized the practice of French culture, declaring that they had "never seen anything so beautiful as fifty little boys and girls dressed as though they were in France that day."[20] In 1886, the sisters created an agricultural colony outside the gates of Saigon, where they would care for and instill discipline in the children, as well as train them to be economically productive members of society, while maintaining the costs of the mission.[21] Agricultural labor would remain a theme in colonial discussions of fatherless *métis* children through the end of World War II.

FOUNDING THE *MÉTIS* PROTECTION SYSTEM

While the colony's Catholic orphanages accepted the *métis* children of European as well as African soldiers, a separate institutional system was created specifically for Eurasian *métis*. At the beginning of the twentieth century, the colony's French population was far outnumbered by its indigenous population, and the *métis* population was small but growing. Records from 1906, the first year that official statistics were taken for Indochina, show that there was one *métis* for every four Europeans.[22] The *métis* population had the potential to explode, as more than twelve thousand French troops roamed the countryside.[23] Yet the birthrate among Europeans remained low. In Cochinchina, home to the largest population of military and permanent French settlers, there were only 157 children whose parents were both European. That year, in Cochinchina, there were only thirty-nine marriages among European couples, and six divorces.[24]

While altruistic in the minds of protection society administrators, child removals also functioned as preventive politics. French administrators and permanent colonists feared that the growing *métis* population would one day rebel against the colonial government, as had occurred in the Caribbean colonies. Concerned French citizens warned the colonial government to do what it could to prevent the formation of a hostile class of *métis*—"and hostile for good reason," as one administrator wrote—who resented that their French fathers had neglected to recognize them. As protection society administrators in Cambodia reckoned, unless the state acted "quickly" to create a program for fatherless *métis* children, the French government risked "substantiating . . . the prejudices of class and race that had created the misfortune of the Antilles," where the mixed-race population's persistent demands for inclusion caused much anxiety among French officials.[25]

French colonists who were permanent residents of Indochina began forming child protection societies for fatherless *métis* in the 1880s. The *métis* protection societies began as independent, civilian-led organizations, and by the turn of the century, multiple orphanage institutions had opened in each of the five *pays* of Indochina. Protection societies drew their membership from French socialites and colonial officials, including customs agents, high-ranking postal officers, and, by World War I, the resident superiors of Annam and Tonkin, all participating in a civilian capacity. Members were wealthy, moderately liberal Republicans who believed that *métis* should be assimilated into French colonial society. Indeed, many had indigenous wives and *métis* children themselves. Unlike the private child protection societies of the concurrent American progressive movement, the *métis* protection societies of Indochina were operated largely by French males. Only after World War I would protection societies include women or wealthy Vietnamese and Cambodians in their ranks.

For an institutional model, protection societies looked to the Netherlands Indies. The French colonial government drew from, and modified, Dutch policies on nonrecognized Eurasian children and patterned its *métis* protection system after that of the Netherlands Indies, a colony that had managed its sizeable *métis* population since the seventeenth century.[26] The governor general of Indochina solicited the French consulate in Batavia for reports on

Dutch policies towards its Eurasian population, specifically policies on citizenship for fatherless Eurasian children, statistics on adult Eurasian poverty, and welfare policies pertaining to fatherless Eurasian children.[27]

As in Indochina, Dutch law in the Indies did not have a distinct category of citizenship for Eurasians. According to Dutch law, *recognized* Eurasians of the first generation were "European," and those of the second generation (i.e., those with three Dutch grandparents) were "of the white race" (*la race blanche*). As for *nonrecognized* Eurasians, the Dutch state considered them indigenous colonial subjects; only Eurasians recognized by their Dutch parent inherited Dutch citizenship.[28] As per an 1848 Dutch law, once a Dutch father recognized his child, the Indonesian mother lost all of her legal claim to the child; even upon the father's death, she could not claim guardianship.[29] However, the French consulate in the Indies also alerted the governor general to a failure in the Dutch policy towards its "mixed-race" (*sang mêlé*) population. As the French consulate saw it, Eurasians, who constituted the majority of the impoverished Europeans in the Netherlands Indies, greatly exacerbated the problem of a European underclass.[30]

Métis poverty had already become a major concern among colonists in Indochina. Journalist Albert de Pouvourville warned of the sorry spectacle of "sons of French colonials . . . pulling rickshaws,"[31] and protection society administrators predicted that "Asians, *indigènes* or even Chinese (the horror!)" would pity the French.[32] Since the French government could not feasibly monitor all of the colony's *métis* adults, administrators attempted to forestall *métis* poverty and deviant behavior by placing as many fatherless Eurasian children as possible in French orphanages patterned after the Netherlands Indies model of nongovernmental, private protection societies and prepare them for skilled labor or professions in agriculture.

While concerned French colonists worked with the colonial government to develop a formal *métis* institutional system based largely on the secular Dutch colonial model, the French gradually restricted church influence over Eurasian welfare. Similarly, the colonial government in French West Africa also took greater control of the *métis* protection system and laicized *métis* education.[33] In Indochina, the schism between the church and the colonial state dated back to the 1880s. As most missionaries' first loyalty was in theory to the church, rather than to French imperial designs, some colonists denounced missionaries as "agents of the Vatican."[34] In the 1890s, Republicans in the colonial administration demanded that Indochina's Catholic mission be dismantled. While anticlerical measures had been largely successful in France, the anticlerical laws did not achieve full jurisdiction in the colony.

The protectorates of Tonkin, Annam, Cambodia, and Laos applied only a few such measures; although Cochinchina was officially subject to the laws, for political reasons officials rarely enforced them. Moreover, as even some Republicans in the colonial administration admitted, the laicization of medical services and orphanages would be "an expensive indulgence," given that nuns and clergy were already willing to care for the ill and poor for no salary whatsoever.[35]

Nevertheless, with the official separation of church and state, colonial officials began removing *métis* from Catholic care. The laicization of the protection societies is perhaps unsurprising, given that many of the protection societies were linked to the anticlerical movement. For example, Camille Paris—an ardent Freemason and well-known anticlerical voice in the colony—headed the Society for the Protection of Abandoned Métis Children and argued fervently to rid it of church influence.[36] The bylaws of the Local Committee for the Protection of Abandoned Métis Children in Annam forbade any intervention in the religious matters of a child's upbringing unless specifically requested by the father.[37] Likewise, the resident of Bắc Giang ordered all Eurasian orphans placed in laic institutions.[38] There, *métis* would be educated under the Third Republican system, which, as Pierre Albertini writes, "incontestably reinforced a feeling of membership in the French nation."[39] The removal of Eurasians from church influences, regardless of the costs this entailed, speaks to the importance the colonial government placed on a loyal fatherless *métis* population. Laicized Eurasian care also enabled the state to take a larger role in *métis* policy and to regulate the wards' upbringing by controlling the purse strings.[40]

Colonists founded Eurasian protection societies to prevent Indochina's fatherless *métis* from contributing to an impoverished European class, as had occurred in the Netherlands Indies, or even rebelling, as had occurred in the Caribbean colonies, where rebellion vanquished the region's slave economy. The colonial government guided protection societies to develop along the model of those of the Netherlands Indies, resulting in nonreligious institutions where fatherless *métis* children were taught skilled labor and agriculture to help them seamlessly integrate into the colonial economy.

GENDERED ANXIETIES AS A CAUSE FOR REMOVALS

The protection society system's primary objective was to place fatherless *métis* children in French-run institutions. Protection societies obtained wards in multiple ways. They used agents or police to search for children in areas formerly occupied by the French military. *Métis* children were likely to stand out, as there were few French children in rural areas.[41] Protection societies took in children who were orphaned or who had been abandoned by both parents and were often found wandering the streets. Mothers entrusted their children to the protection societies when they could not or did not want to care for them, or when they felt the societies offered better opportunities for their children. Protection societies even recompensed the mothers who had been willing to entrust their children. As one journalist reported, the protection societies were, among other things, an effort by generous French colonists to right the wrongs of the Frenchmen who had refused to recognize their children.[42]

In cases in which mothers refused to relinquish custody of their children, protection society administrators drew from *métropole* child welfare laws to justify removing the children from their mothers. Among those laws, the July 24, 1889, law on the divestiture of paternal power was the driving force—both ideologically and legally—behind the colony's *métis* protection movement. This law enabled *métropole* authorities to claim paternal rights over children who had been physically or morally abandoned by one or both parents. The 1889 law marked a turning point in French child welfare in several respects: it allowed the state to intervene in the family and take custody of children, it regulated female parental power, and it created the concept of parents' "moral responsibility"—a concept authorities invoked to rescind parental rights when they deemed such responsibility lacking.[43] Yet officials rarely acquired evidence for claims of moral abandonment, instead basing their judgments of incompetence on mere presumptions.[44] The decree of May 7, 1890, made the 1889 paternal divestment law applicable to French citizens in Indochina and to all residents of Cochinchina and certain designated urban zones in Tonkin and Annam.[45] Until 1924, the law was technically inapplicable in the other areas of Indochina, including Tonkin, Annam, Cambodia, and Laos, because they were protectorates,[46] yet that did not stop authorities from using the rhetoric of the 1889 law to justify removing fatherless *métis* children from their mothers. In 1904, the president of the Society for the Protection and Education of Abandoned Young French Métis in Tonkin acknowledged that although the 1889 law was inapplicable to indigenous children, he promised the governor general that with "proof of danger," the society "will make sure to intervene."[47]

A second *métropole* law, also introduced in 1889, provided another means by which protection society administrators justified intervening in mixed-race families. This law, promulgated in Indochina in 1897, stated that a person born of two unknown parents (meaning that neither parent had legally recognized the child) was a French citizen. The law, however, stipulated that "nothing changes the condition of *indigènes* in French colonies." In other words, a child whose two indigenous parents did not legally recognize her or him had no claim to French citizenship. As for children of mixed parentage, the law was ambiguous, allowing protection society members to make the case that fatherless Eurasian children whose mothers had not done the paperwork to register their births with the state—as was frequently the case in the countryside—were legally French and thus under the jurisdiction of the 1889 parental divestiture law. Thanks to this legal sleight of hand, *métis* protection societies had stronger legal grounds for removing fatherless *métis* children from their Vietnamese, Cambodian, or Lao mothers' care and raising them in French institutions.

Not all administrators approved of the use of the 1889 paternal divestiture law to justify the removals. In 1904, a colonial public prosecutor warned the governor general that this law applied only to French citizens and not to Vietnamese mothers or nonrecognized *métis* children.[48] The resident of Bắc Giang—who was something of a political renegade on the issue of *métis* families—concurred. He insisted that the 1889 paternal divestiture law did not apply to Eurasians because *métis* children had not actually been abandoned by their mothers. He reminded his colleagues of the difference between the common and legal understandings of the term "abandoned child"; only in the legal definition could an abandoned child still live with the mother. *Métis* protection societies, he implied, risked overstepping their jurisdiction. He also insisted that the state only separate Eurasian children from their mothers with maternal consent—even if the mother in question was a concubine. A concubine, he wrote, was the equivalent of a legitimate wife, and "What right would we have to take the child from the mother and oversee [the care of] the children that she had with a European?"[49]

But these two colonial officials were in the minority. As Gregor Muller observed, as early as the 1880s, *métis* children in Cambodia were routinely separated from their mothers.[50] Protection society administrators made the case that *métis* children were being raised in immoral environments, thereby justifying the use of the 1889 paternal divestiture law. Protection societies targeted Eurasian children because they lived with their indigenous mothers in the absence of a French father and thus supposedly suffered from the lack of moral guidance that only a European parent could provide. Just as officials in the *métropole* condemned the lifestyles of single mothers,[51] colonial officials in Indochina condemned the lifestyles of mothers with *métis* children—particularly those who had never married—and operated on the assumption that these mothers were morally base and hence unfit to care for their children.

The mother-as-prostitute image would dominate protection society rhetoric on *métis* children all the way through 1975, when *métis* protection societies were forced to leave after the Vietnam War. During the early years of colonialism, Charles Gravelle, a protection society administrator in Cambodia, called mothers of *métis* "prostitutes."[52] Administrators of the Association for the Protection of and Assistance to Franco-Annamite Children claimed that mothers were prostitutes before meeting the French fathers and then "returned to their vices" after the men's departure.[53] A protection society in Tonkin accused mothers of having multiple, successive relationships with French men for the sole purposes of ensuring financial support.[54]

Administrators insisted that *métisse* daughters would be corrupted by witnessing "the spectacle of [their mothers'] trade."[55] Officials cautioned of a cyclical nature of prostitution: "The Vietnamese woman who consents to live with Europeans is a veritable prostitute. Once the European man leaves, she returns to her vice and the child is exposed to the debauchery.... [Because] there is no maternal direction, the child does poorly in school and the girls often go on to become prostitutes. If not taken care of they are potential dangers for the colony."[56] Mothers would "compromise their child's morality" and "prostitute her the moment they could."[57] Another administrator warned, "They parade [their Eurasian daughters] everywhere and adorn them with beautiful clothing and jewelry."[58] Administrators cited rumors about a widespread *traite des métisse,* a human trafficking scheme of mixed-race girls that had supposedly taken root in Indochina.[59] According to these claims, a typical Eurasian trafficking scenario involved mothers selling their *métisse* daughters to Vietnamese pimps, who would subsequently pay the mothers a monthly salary from their daughter's prostitution earnings.[60]

Authorities accused *métisse* girls of sex work and forcibly removed them from their mothers. In a 1904 case, French civilian J. F. Montagne alerted the Society for the Protection of Abandoned Métis Children of two girls who—according to Montagne—were on the verge of being sold by their mother. Montagne wrote off the fourteen-year-old daughter, Noelle Phượng, as "already lost," likely referring to her alleged sexual activities. He advised authorities to "let her be sold" so that they had reason to take her twelve-year-old sister, Jeanne.[61] Another case that year in Bến Tre involved the two Eurasian daughters of a woman named Hoa. Officials assumed that Hoa had prostituted her seventeen-year-old daughter out to a European man even though the daughter insisted that she was in a consensual relationship with him. Hoa's younger daughter implored authorities to let her older sister stay with her mother, whom she insisted loved her daughters and provided them with an education. In the end, the children remained with Hoa, and the state (for unlisted reasons, perhaps because she was not sufficiently "bad") did not apply the 1889 law to their case.[62]

Protection society members were likewise preoccupied with the prospect of *métisse* girls marrying Asian men. One administrator warned the governor general of a dire situation that he believed was playing out: "When the *métisse* [matures], a wealthy Chinese man wants to marry her and he offers the mother money. It is not prostitution, but the girl goes with him."[63] The Society for the Protection and Education of Young French Métis of Cambodia warned that *métisse* girls who married indigenous men would become "déclassé" and assimilate into the Cambodian population. Assimilation was a concern to many protection society administrators, who took the long view that *métisse* girls were French women and, as such, should marry European men, who would give them decisive access to the French milieu.[64] If they fell into native society, this would—administrators believed—reflect poorly on the colonial mission.

When it came to fatherless *métis* boys, French administrators and protection society members focused on the potential danger they posed to colonial security rather than issues of sexuality. Fearing that *métis* boys were destined to become "vicious" "rebels and enemies of France," who would potentially "take up arms against their fathers,"[65] protection societies advocated separating the boys from their mothers and placing them under French care.[66]

A few administrators made the case that Eurasian child removals would not only serve as preventive measures but would provide tangible benefits to the colonial state. Camille Paris made the case that "the *métis* of both sexes should be considered a precious element of [colonial] domination. It is they who will form the stable and definitive French population of Indochina.[67] Insisting that the *métis* protection system was "patriotic," one administrator called on the colonial state to raise *métis* children in the "national milieu"—meaning the French milieu—where they would be taught "love and respect for our dear France."[68]

After separating fatherless Eurasian children from their mothers, protection societies provided shelter and education at schools such as the elite Lycée Chasseloup-Laubat in Saigon. The aim was for the state to serve as a surrogate parent for the hapless children who had been abandoned by their French fathers. Speaking to what Françoise Vergès identifies as the myth of the colonial family romance, one administrator bragged to the governor general, "The [protection] society replaces the family.... They have [French] men and women visit, and they are tender towards the children. What the *métis* needs is a family."[69]

THE PROBLEM OF *MÉTIS* EDUCATION AND THE COLLÈGE AGRICOLE DE HƯNG HÓA

The French educational system became a means by which administrators integrated male *métis* wards, both by preparing them to integrate into the higher sectors of the colonial economy and by cultivating their loyalty to the French state, thereby presumably eliminating their motivations for rebelling. For the most part, fatherless *métisse* girls were left out of colonial debates over education, even as Vietnamese language presses engaged in heated debates over the question of female education.

The strategy of educating fatherless *métis* boys through the French educational system developed just as French parents in the colony were pressuring authorities to racially segregate colonial schools. French parents feared that educated Vietnamese would undermine colonial racial and class boundaries. From their inception, elite colonial schools had admitted the children of French parents as well as the children of privileged Vietnamese. Since the schools had limited admission, they required applicants to take entrance exams. By the first decade of the twentieth century, many Vietnamese children were scoring higher than French children, and colonists feared that Vietnamese students would soon outnumber French students in the schools. French parents' complaints were threefold: that the growing Vietnamese student body would come to overshadow their French counterparts, that Vietnamese graduates would demand equality in colonial society upon graduation, and that the presence of Vietnamese students would lower the standards of the schools. This last point was, of course, ironic, given that it was the higher test scores of Vietnamese students that had led them to be admitted in larger numbers and thus given rise to French concerns in the first place. One can infer that by "standards," critics were most likely referring to social, rather than academic, standards.[70]

Some colonial administrators called on schools to reject fatherless Eurasians as well. In one early case, the Commission of Education in Hanoi ad-

vised the mayor to forbid fatherless Eurasians to attend the Écoles Munici-
pals, which admitted not only French children but also the "few Asian
children who could demonstrate aptitude."[71] In other words, some schools
that admitted Asian children actually rejected fatherless Eurasian children.
In 1904, the director of public education in Tonkin suggested assimilating
nonrecognized Eurasian children as Vietnamese and enrolling them in Vietnamese schools.[72] The matter reached the Hanoi City Council, where one
(unnamed) council member acknowledged that the schools in question admitted wealthy Vietnamese children and *métis* recognized by their fathers but
rejected nonrecognized *métis* children.[73]

For those fatherless *métis* who were permitted to attend colonial schools,
they faced many cases of discrimination. For example, in a 1907 case at the
École Primaire Elementaire, *métis* wards complained that a teacher was ex-
cessively violent when disciplining *métis* student Marc Baudin. The teacher
discredited the boy with claims that he was a homosexual and dismissed
métis children in general as lazy students who made no progress, showed up
late to class, and were a nuisance at the school. After an investigation, the
protection society concluded that it was the teacher who was "overly strict"
and harbored "prejudices" against *métis* children.[74]

Challenges aside, protection society authorities decided that a French
education was the solution to preventing *métis* from rebelling against the
colonial state. In 1907, colonial administrators created an isolated educational
system for *métis* children—recognized and fatherless alike. Within this isolated track, *métis* would receive a French education but be separated from
French children. The Collège Agricole de Hưng Hóa was one such school.
Established in January 1908, the school opened in fall 1909 to twenty-seven
fatherless Eurasian pupils (the *métis* children of African and Indian fathers
were excluded). Georges Michel, whose story opened this chapter, was one of
the students at the school.

The Collège Agricole de Hưng Hóa was one of many agricultural colonies that were established in the early twentieth century in Indochina and
that drew from a long tradition of agricultural schools and agricultural colonies in the *métropole*.[75] Metropolitan agricultural colonies had emerged in the
mid-nineteenth century with the famous Mettray institution, a prison colony where inmates were rehabilitated through agricultural labor. Stemming
from nineteenth-century beliefs that bodily discipline begot cognitive discipline, authorities at Mettray served as "technicians of behavior: engineers of
conduct, orthopedists of individuality. Their task was to produce bodies that
were both docile and capable."[76] The metropolitan government developed

agricultural colonies all over France as a means of reforming criminals and other people who were considered menaces to society. Agricultural colonies also transformed the countryside by reducing poverty, subduing revolutionary potential, and reeducating and assimilating immigrants into local French society.[77] Agricultural work at the Collège Agricole de Hưng Hóa, colonial authorities hoped, would instill discipline in fatherless *métis* wards and reeducate them to embrace French cultural norms.[78]

Located in Hưng Hóa, Tonkin, the Collège Agricole occupied a former military barracks. Consistent with fin de siècle concerns about the corrosive influence of modern life and the importance of working the land in building moral character, the colonial administration chose Hưng Hóa to "shield the pupils from the influences of the big city." Yet because of its remote location, the chief of educational services lamented, "the necessary surveillance in this type of scholarly establishment is very difficult for the responsible authorities."[79] The area had only been under French control since April 1884, when the French defeated the Black Flag rebel army in the Battle of Tonkin. Even as late as the 1890s, the pacification of the North was still under way, with Black Flag units still roaming Tonkin; it was not until 1895 that authorities arrested Phan Đình Phùng, a top leader of the anticolonial Cần Vương (Save the King) movement. This raises the question of why colonial authorities placed *métis* adolescents whom they were trying to prevent from rebelling in areas in which rebellion had been a problem. It is possible that authorities saw the Collège Agricole as a means of contributing to the pacification of the Tonkin countryside in much the same way as agricultural colonies had transformed the metropolitan French countryside, thereby deterring rebellion.[80]

The school admitted pupils between the ages of eight and twelve, consistent with metropolitan educational practices designed to reach students before they reached the psychologically turbulent phase of adolescence.[81] Younger pupils received an elementary education; at twelve years old, children entered the agricultural and professional trade track. In addition to providing a French education, the Collège Agricole educated its wards in skilled agriculture to prepare them for entrance into the colonial economy. Teachers instructed in French even though many students lacked the necessary linguistic aptitude; in some cases, administrators—the French delegate to Hưng Hóa, for example—had to rely on a Vietnamese interpreter to convey an important point.[82]

According to French administrators, before arriving at Hưng Hóa, the fatherless *métis* boys had led the "existence more or less of vagabonds, during which they picked up more vices than virtues."[83] Almost all the children who became students at the Collège Agricole had previously lived in *métis* protection society institutions. The 1910 records from the school indicate that the families of sixteen students (out of twenty-six total) had voluntarily enrolled their children in *métis* protection societies. It appears that these families had relinquished custody of their children largely for financial reasons. The remaining ten students enrolled in 1910 "did not have families," indicating that some may have been abandoned by both parents or forcibly removed from their mothers by colonial authorities.[84]

Like metropolitan boarding schools (*internats*) and the Indian boarding schools in the United States, the agricultural school effectively eroded the family structure and replaced it with the state.[85] Documents from the Collège Agricole's archives frequently invoke the rhetoric of family in describing the school's mission. The director of public education at Tonkin wrote that school authorities developed a new atmosphere for the wards, many of whom who had been removed from their own families:

> The school is like a large family in which the director is the father with the task of raising the boarders to the point that they can take care of themselves. . . . He follows them like the father of a family . . . until the day that the students are grown up enough to no longer need a guardian.[86]

The director of the school reiterated the paternal metaphor: "I consider myself to be the father of this large family."[87] Subordinate to him were two teachers, one male and one female. Along with teaching general education, the female teacher did laundry and, with the help of two Vietnamese female aids, provided the children with "maternal care."[88] The use of women as teachers to impart maternal influence was a cornerstone of French Third Republic policy.[89] Consistent with Republican ideals about fostering masculinity in schools to stabilize society,[90] the Collège Agricole, designed specifically for boys, emphasized masculinity in a school curriculum designed to prepare students for integration into French colonial society. The school, according to one colonial administrator, would supplement protection society institutions insofar as "all the protective philanthropic projects for abandoned *métis* have only succeeded in saving the children; they have not made men."[91] By "men" he presumably meant culturally French men.

The Collège Agricole had the twofold goal of transforming fatherless *métis* boys into Frenchmen as well as productive members of society. Accordingly, the agricultural education provided at the Collège Agricole was designed to discourage *métis* boys from slipping into the colony's impoverished European class; instead, the young men would presumably become part of an elite class of French farmers who would command a high salary. In the words of the resident superior of Tonkin, the school would "provide the means to ensure the *métis* orphans and abandoned children first a means of subsistence, and second an education—one that would make them educated workers."[92] Likewise, the director of the Collège Agricole claimed that "the transformation at the Collège Agricole, a manual labor school, would be not only advantageous to the future of the *métis* but would also provide the colonial economy with apprentices who have a basic education and sufficient skills, and are capable of becoming workers."[93]

Although authorities designed the school to create young men who were culturally French and loyal to the colonial state, their ambitions were thwarted from the beginning. Some of the colony's administrators, including school administrators, rejected the governor general's notion that these children should be treated as French or develop a French identity. Instead, school administrators dismissed these children as irredeemably Vietnamese. There was, consequently, a disparity between the colonial administrators' intention and the school administrators' execution. Administrators designed the school to educate students in the sciences of agriculture and mold them into young Frenchmen. In reality, however, school authorities required them to perform strenuous agricultural labor—a duty usually reserved for Vietnamese—and treated them, in the students' words, "like [Vietnamese] coolies."[94]

The school's financial problems only exacerbated the harsh treatment of the students. From the start, the school barely subsisted on the funding it received from the colonial government and protection societies. Even before the school opened, the director of public education in Tonkin lacked the funds to feed and house the school's prospective wards. To make matters worse, in distributing the school's meager funds, school administrators prioritized their own standard of living—and that of the French teachers—over the students' well-being.

The students' relationships with the local Vietnamese population varied. A few wards had actually wanted to remain in the indigenous milieu and participated in school activities only reluctantly.[95] More frequently, students reproduced colonial racist attitudes and made a practice of intimidating the locals. One example of the violence perpetuated by certain students occurred during village theater performances in Chuc Phê. *Métis* wards would sneak off school grounds to attend the festivities, then bully locals and "push around and brutalize the Annamite members of the audience."[96] On at least one occasion, some of the older, "strong and muscular" *métis* "inspired a veritable terror among the population"—so much so that the school director instructed local Vietnamese police to arrest them. Ironically, the police themselves were so intimidated by the *métis* boys and their bullying that they refused to carry out the orders.[97]

Students resented the school's squalid living conditions, which they considered more befitting of indigenous people. In fall 1909, the school's students issued a formal complaint to the administration. They accused the director of feeding them cheaper, lower-quality food than had been budgeted and pocketing the change.[98] They cited many other examples of administrative abuse. For instance, the director had fed the students rancid meat, and they had fallen ill after being fed tainted dried fish. School officials sometimes denied them food for days at a time. The situation was so bad that the private cook of one of the French instructors, concerned that the students were malnourished, offered to feed them at his own expense. Perhaps tellingly, the school director, M. Rouilly, refused his offer. Rouilly initiated an investigation into the matter of student living conditions, but the students sensed manipulation. When the director of education for Phú Thọ arrived to investigate, the students were, they claimed, given "the best meal ever," and the director of education dropped the investigation.[99]

A few months later, in January 1910, the school director's wife caught Georges Michel, whose story opened this chapter, and his classmates preparing a second letter of protest. Among other things, the students wrote that they were "unhappy at the Collège, we work a lot and eat miserably. This question is the most serious of all." Moreover, they complained, the director forced them to perform labor befitting a Vietnamese person, and "detained [them] like prisoners." As punishment for their persistent complaints, the director starved the students for a day and a half.[100] At this point, a riot broke out, led by Georges Michel. Ten students fled the school in search of help from the resident of Phú Thọ. They never made it to the resident's house, however; instead, they retreated into the jungle, where they subsisted on wild berries. Five days after their disappearance, a teacher found them sleeping in a pagoda and urged them to return to the school. One by one, they made their way back. Upon their return, Rouilly punished the children with a night in a prison cell at the Garde Indigène, after which point the French delegate at Hưng Hóa dispatched police to the Collège Agricole to keep order.[101]

A representative from the office of the governor general held both students and administrators responsible for the "mutiny." The mutineers, he wrote, had set a bad example for the younger students. More generally, the governor general denounced the students for their resistance to performing labor. As for the school, he wrote, the administration had also failed in focusing on agriculture in a region where farming the land was difficult and in allowing a conflict of interest whereby the school's director was in charge of its finances as well as its overall operations. Moreover, administrators had made the mistake of admitting adolescents who had never received an elementary school education. Adolescents, he implied, were rebellious and too old to absorb French culture.[102]

When investigating the riots, the chief of education in Tonkin, for his part, made the case that the Collège Agricole had been doomed from the start. Part of the responsibility, he wrote, lay with the school's administration. Like the governor general's representative, he noted a conflict of interest in the fact that the school's director was responsible for its finances.[103] The chief also found that school administrators had fundamentally misrepresented the Collège Agricole to prospective students: the school had presented itself as teaching the science of farming but instead forced students to perform manual labor. Moreover, he said, even if the school had fulfilled its mandate, its trajectory for the students was fundamentally flawed. The graduates would find themselves in a no-win situation. On the one hand, they would lack the funds to start their own farms; on the other hand, if they sought employment on someone else's farm, employers would reject them in favor of cheaper Vietnamese labor.[104]

In the end, however, the chief of education held the students themselves responsible for the school's demise. His remarks on this subject reflect the school administration's inherent racial bias against Eurasians. The chief viewed their racial hybridity as freakish, describing a typical Eurasian child as "an albino [with] a deformed head, a beast-like figure . . . [he has] all the faults of the two races, without any of the good qualities." Underscoring the importance of removing them from the indigenous milieu, he wrote, "they become what their education makes them, a product of the environment within which they live. [Eurasian] students in France can become good Frenchmen; [however], residing in Tonkin in the Annamite milieu, they have the same ideas as the Annamites and, moreover, an excessive vanity as a result of their origins."[105]

The chief of education's explanation suggests that he understood race as a mixture of nature and nurture, with an emphasis on the latter. The riots seemed to confirm the common assumption that fatherless *métis* were of low moral caliber and predisposed to delinquency and anticolonialism. In his opinion, the school had had no choice but to discipline its rebellious charges in order to show them their place. He concluded that with its corrupt student body, the school had no chance of meeting its goal of creating young skilled farmers loyal to the colonial administration.[106]

The chief of education worried mainly about the students' sense of entitlement. He claimed that "since the children have been raised by their mothers since they were little to think they were better than Annamites, they do not want to do the work intended for an Annamite."[107] An administrator from the office of the governor general came to the similar conclusion that "the maternal education had given them, from their most tender childhood, the habit of considering themselves superior to the indigenous people, and they did not want to devote themselves to the same work as the latter."[108] Ironically, it was also the school's French administrators who had given students the idea that they were French and suggested that Frenchmen were above manual labor.[109] As a result, the students "did not want to work the land; for them it was degrading."[110] This administrator scoffed at the Eurasian wards for presuming they were superior to Vietnamese and hence entitled to the benefits of Frenchness: "The rioters bristled at the thought of manual labor and felt they were being lowered to the rank of coolies, and they thought that by virtue of the couple drops of French blood in their veins they should be treated like French students, not having to do anything but their schoolwork."[111]

In response to the microrevolution at Hưng Hóa in 1910, the colony's governor general closed the school. The state sent some of the students to the École Professionnelle de Hanoi and guided others into alternative professions. Some of the students returned to their families (if their families were still around), others to the *métis* protection society. Authorities sent two of the ringleaders—Georges Michel and another boy named Bardel—to China, where they were placed in employment with the Companie de Yunnan. In summer 1912, the colonial government initiated plans for another agricultural school for *métis* children, this one to be situated on the Black River in Sơn Tây, but there is no evidence that the school ever opened. Evidently the colony's high-ranking administrators regarded the Collège Agricole as a failure only in practice, not in theory. Despite the riot and ensuing closure of the school, these administrators persisted in their endeavors to transform the social categorization of fatherless Eurasian children to French.

The failures of the Collège Agricole de Hưng Hóa speak to the more general problems afflicting the colony's program towards fatherless *métis* children in the early years of establishing French rule in Indochina. The school failed because of competing ideas about whether fatherless Eurasians should be treated as French or indigenous. Through their infighting and mixed messages, school administrators inadvertently created the very danger they had sought to avoid: rebellious, ambitious half-white adolescents who resented their place in the colonial racial order and the colonial government itself. Until protection society leaders and their allies in the colonial administration could succeed in convincing the French colonial public that illegitimate *métis* children should be considered French, the French public would continue to reject them.

It would take the bloodshed of World War I to change the way that French colonists regarded fatherless Eurasian children. With long-standing fears of French population decimation exacerbated by the mass carnage of the war, French colonists in Indochina would have a vested interest in perceiving fatherless Eurasian children as part of the French race. During World War I, protection societies would win the support of the French public in the endeavor to separate fatherless *métis* children from their indigenous mothers and integrate them into the colony's French social circles.

2

Frenchmen's Children, 1909–1929

In 1927, colonial authorities in Indochina sent François Marcel, a fatherless Eurasian boy, to the *métropole,* where he would live with a French family, work as an apprentice, and presumably integrate into French society. François was one of 139 fatherless Eurasian children sent to the *métropole* from 1919 to 1929 as part of a national program to alleviate the *métropole's* rural labor shortages and repopulate the country after the devastating losses resulting from World War I.[1] An additional goal was to eliminate any political threats such children might pose if they remained in the colony.[2]

Five years after he arrived in France, François recalled that he had initially refused to leave Indochina because he did not want to be separated from his family. The protection societies shipped him off nonetheless. "In France," he wrote, "they sent me to Coutances (Manche), [where] the climate did not suit me." Young François also "deplored the separation from [his] family," the change of food and customs, and the fact that "[the new family] did not give [him] enough to eat." The experience, he wrote, was so traumatic that he "was very sad and . . . became a little mentally ill." Protection society administrators "thought [he] was crazy and sent [him] to an asylum with crazy men."[3]

The program to send fatherless *métis* children to the *métropole* was one of two programs developed during the post–World War I period to remove *métis* from the indigenous milieu and integrate them into a French cultural environment. In the other program, wards remained in the colony, where protection society officials placed them in land settlement programs around Annam. The Coutances and Annam population settlement programs emerged during a period (1914–1929) in which France sought to rebuild its population in response to wartime losses. French administrators and civilians in the colony, like those in the *métropole,* sought to reassert the glory of the French nation and race by increasing the French population. The goal of the *métis* projects was not only to uproot fatherless *métis* children from the influences of Vietnamese, Lao, and Cambodian culture but also to use them to address some of the demographic problems in the empire. This chapter will show how *métis* protection societies appropriated metropolitan rhetoric on depopulation to make the case that fatherless *métis* children of French (or other European) fathers should be considered French.

DEPOPULATION, RACIAL OWNERSHIP, AND THE EURASIAN SOLUTION

The death toll from World War I shocked the French public. On average, 930 Frenchmen were killed per day between August 1914 and November 1918.[4] The large number of casualties resulting from World War I fueled a resurgence of French pronatalism, whose proponents called for increased births to solve the social, economic, and political problems plaguing the country. Metropolitan administrators considered importing nonwhite laborers from the colonies, but pronatalists feared that *métissage* with nonwhites would lead to the degeneration of the white race.[5] Some metropolitan pronatalists looked to the diverse geography of the French empire as a means of fostering the reproduction of the French race. They believed that the white French population grew more rapidly in the colonies than in the *métropole* and attributed this fecundity to a simpler, agriculture-based lifestyle. The long-term goal of these pronatalists was to cultivate white populations in the colonies and then repatriate them to the *métropole*.[6] This plan, of course, hinged on France's ability to attract metropolitan French families to the colonies— hardly an easy task.

To support the settlement and growth of French families in Indochina, pronatalist organizations sprang up throughout the colony as World War I–related French death rates rose. Pronatalists called on the colonial government to fight French depopulation, aid needy families, and provide child care, so as to encourage large families.[7] The Indochina chapter of the Popular League of Mothers and Fathers of Large French Families argued that an increase in the colony's French birthrate would prevent "the disappearance of our race" and ensure that "France, our dear *Patrie,* will be strong and powerful."[8]

Contrary to what pronatalists thought, the French population in the colony was not actually dwindling; rather, it was thriving. The French population of civilians and military grew from 17,499 in 1921 to 30,040 in 1929.

Marie-Paule Ha attributes this 40 percent increase to postwar economic development. The growth of the mining and rubber industries required more European business managers and more French colonial civil servants. Considering that more white women were coming to the colony, there was potential for more "pure" white births. In 1922, there were 26,890 French civilians and military personnel in Indochina, 6,192 of which were children, indicating potential for growth. The population of French females, meanwhile, had increased to 5,395, evening out the gender ratio of French adult females to males to 1:2.41; excluding military personnel, that ratio was 1:1.67. By 1929, the colony's French population had swelled to 40,093 civilians and military personnel. By that point, the colony's adult female population had reached 9,004, bringing the gender ratio of French adult females to males to 1:2.41; excluding military personnel, that ratio was 1:1.46. Although the colony's French population was growing throughout the 1920s, the rhetoric of the pronatalist movement was so strong that colonial administrators and protection society administrators were convinced there was a dearth of French in the colony.[9]

Métis protection societies joined the patriotic effort to rebuild the French nation. To solve the perceived population problem, protection society members and colonial administrators appropriated metropolitan rhetoric about white French population reproduction but rewrote fatherless Eurasian children into the plan to reproduce the French race. "At a time when the *Mère Patrie* is losing a little more of the blood of its children every day," the Committee for the Protection of Abandoned Eurasian Children of Annam asserted, "it appears to us that, from a patriotic and social point of view, our obligation is to increase efforts to save all those related to our race, even if it [the relationship to them] is minimal."[10]

That *métis* played a role in the plans to reproduce the French race in Indochina reflects the differences between the way that race and demographic theories developed in the *métropole* and Indochina. The colony's different trajectory for understanding race grew out of its distinct racial demographics. For one thing, the white French population in the colony was far outnumbered by Asians. Given that the French equated population size with political and military might, French colonists in Indochina experienced considerable anxiety over the possibility that the colonial government might eventually lose control of the colony.[11] A second demographic difference between the colony and the *métropole* was the prevalence in the colony of interracial sex and *métis* families, both of which normalized racial hybridity and called into question the boundaries of whiteness. Finally, the relative ubiquity in the colony's urban centers of recognized Eurasians raised by their French fathers and, for the most part, socially accepted as French made the acceptance of *métis* children as French that much easier in the colony. Protection society members came to see fatherless Eurasian children as a means to bolster the colonial French population—an idea that would gain currency through the end of World War II.

The contrasting racial formations of the colony and *métropole,* in turn, yielded contrasting ideas about the role of mothers. Although metropolitan society considered the patriarchal family the ideal as well as the norm, the pronatalist desire to support any woman willing to be a mother helped validate single motherhood as a family model.[12] In Indochina, on the other hand, the French government and protection societies, who regarded the influence of unmarried Vietnamese, Cambodian, and Lao mothers as an assault on the development of the French race, tried to regulate maternal authority.

French authorities had reason for concern. Within the context of growing nationalist and feminist movements, Vietnamese-language newspapers presented a new role for mothers. Like their counterparts in the *métropole,* Vietnamese feminists asserted their unique role in reproducing the nation and supported reforms that would strengthen women's roles as mothers. The popular women's newspaper *Nữ Giới Chung* educated female readers about "rules for raising children," pregnancy, and prenatal care.[13] Nationalist Phan Bội Châu and Đạm Phương, leader of the Women's League (*Nữ Công Hội*), likewise championed women as "mother of the nation" (*mẹ quốc dân*).[14] Other journalists referred to women as the producers of the nation,[15] the implication being that Vietnamese mothers were to act as cultural reproducers of the Vietnamese nation by raising their children to be nationalists.

While single indigenous mothers undeniably played a significant role in reproducing the French as well as Vietnamese nations, these mothers transgressed French colonial morals by raising their children "*à l'indigène.*"[16] The resident superior of Annam made the case that it was "necessary for the prestige of France in the colonies to care for the [Eurasian] children."[17] The removal of fatherless *métis* children from their mothers by colonial officials evidenced a considerable disregard for the legitimacy of maternal-led *métis* families.

THE EXPANDING LEGAL REACH FOR *MÉTIS* PROTECTION SOCIETIES

During World War I and the following decade, laws designed to help the *métropole* and colony recover from the war inadvertently expanded the legal reach for *métis* protection societies. With the pronatalist movement in full force, protection societies were able to exploit these laws to incorporate *métis* children of Frenchmen into the French nation.

Just before the war started, two metropolitan laws were enacted in the colony that allowed illegitimate *métis* to claim French citizenship whether or not their fathers had legally recognized them. On June 19, 1913, the November 16, 1912, law that permitted research into the paternity of unrecognized children was promulgated in the colony. Under the new law, the state could force men to recognize their children in cases in which the child was conceived out of rape, the parents were known to live together, the father had tricked or "seduced" the mother, or there was written evidence that the man had fathered the child. The law, however, was only applicable to French citizens and foreigners—not colonial subjects or *protégés*.[18] As a result, women who were colonial subjects or *protégés* and had been impregnated by French citizens found themselves in a legally ambiguous state—and hence unable to win French citizenship for their children. However, thanks to their political clout and teams of experienced lawyers, *métis* protection societies used the 1912 decree to secure French citizenship for some fatherless *métis* children. As for *métis* who grew up outside the protection societies, they rarely obtained citizenship even if they wanted it.

Notwithstanding their use of the 1912 decree, colonial administrators had initially been reluctant to apply the law out of concern over what they believed to be a "lucrative industry" in which Frenchmen accepted money from Vietnamese, Cambodian, or Lao mothers in exchange for falsely claiming paternity and thereby winning French citizenship rights for the mothers' children.[19] Indeed, in a 1915 list of paternal recognitions requested by the governor of Cochinchina, certain Frenchmen conspicuously recognized the children of multiple mothers, leading authorities to doubt that they could have juggled so many relationships in such a short span of time.[20] The French Public Ministry eventually corrected the problem with a 1918 law to annul false paternity declarations. Through the 1920s, colonial police pursued false paternity cases—and false claims to French identity—with zeal. In cases found to be fraudulent, such as the 1928 case of a Monsieur Benjamin, the state stripped his two purported children, Phạm Văn Hải and Vincent André—themselves unrelated—of their citizenship status.[21]

As Emmanuelle Saada has shown, the fraudulent recognition of children undermined the rigid colonial system of legal classification that distinguished French citizens from colonial subjects. False paternity declarations establishing a fictive familial relationship between citizens and subjects blurred juridical statuses. Administrators, however, only concerned themselves with rooting out cases that transgressed racial categories; the fraudulent recognition of a white French child was not a colonial preoccupation because such a child would not transgress racial barriers.[22] That the colonial government became so absorbed in such a small-scale industry reveals a disproportionate concern about protecting the racial integrity of *Frenchness*.

In 1913, the colonial government announced new conditions for applying for French citizenship. Among the terms were two articles that applied to nonrecognized *métis:* Article 1 allowed colonial subjects or *protégés* over the age of eighteen who could speak and write French to apply for citizenship, and Article 6 permitted those who had French ancestry or had been raised for five years in a *métis* protection society before reaching adulthood and graduating from a French school or professional institution to apply.[23] In the years following, *métis* protection societies would invoke the 1913 citizenship law to petition for French citizenship on behalf of their wards.

The need for more soldiers to fight the war led the metropolitan French government to enact laws offering new means for foreigners to access French citizenship. An August 5, 1914, law offered French citizenship to people of the Alsace-Lorraine region and foreigners who enlisted in the French military. Noting this opportunity, Charles Gravelle of the Society for the Protection of Childhood in Cambodia encouraged *métis* wards from Phnom Penh to serve in the military as a path to naturalization. During the war, protection societies sent sixty-seven male wards, aged sixteen to twenty, to fight for France in Europe.[24] The military rejected these wards, however, after a medical examination, deeming them too young to participate in war.[25] In another case, Nguyễn Văn Lộc, also known as Georges Palin, was also rejected. Born at the turn of the century to a Vietnamese mother and a French father who never recognized him, Georges entered a protection society at the age of fifteen and received a French education. He was sent to the *métropole* during the war and stayed on. In 1922, he applied for but was denied French citizenship on the grounds that he had not "risked" himself for France during the war.[26] It is not clear what criteria French authorities used to determine whether a draftee had sufficiently risked himself for France.

In 1922, Gravelle tried again to make the case for naturalizing eighteen *métis* wards who had fought for France in the war.[27] This time, evidently, he was successful. In 1923, Jacques, the nonrecognized Eurasian son of Monsieur B., petitioned for naturalization. Upon his father's death in 1908, he entered the Society for the Protection of Métis Children, where he received a French education. In 1915, he went to France as a wartime specialized worker. In his naturalization application, he described France as his "true homeland."[28] After proving that he could read, write, and speak French, he was granted citizenship.

Métis soldiers created a small stir among metropolitan authorities when they partnered with French women, often resulting in interracial pregnancies. While interracial relationships were not uncommon in the *métropole* during the war, state officials aimed to prevent indigenous men from returning to the colony with a French wife and child, because a white woman with an Asian man was taboo in the colony. In such cases, the metropolitan government tried to halt marriage plans or forbid the couple in question from returning to the colony.[29] In 1916, the protection societies sent Yves Nicolas to Paris as a volunteer worker. There he met and became engaged to a French woman. In 1918, he requested a marriage license and expressed his intent to return to the colony. Officials "raised objections that a *métis* should marry a French woman" and shelved his request indefinitely, purposefully denying his right to due process to protest what would have been a negative response to the marriage license.[30] In 1923, he requested permission and a passage to return to the colony but was denied on the grounds that his wife would find herself in a "difficult" situation[31]—an allusion to the colony's social taboo against white women marrying Asian men. In the end, Yves Nicolas never married his French fiancée; instead, he returned to Tonkin alone.[32] To prevent interracial relationships like this from being transported back to the colonies, the colony's *métis* protection societies encouraged Eurasian war workers to remain in the *métropole* after the war, and in 1919, the protection societies appointed a representative to oversee wards in the *métropole*.[33]

As the death toll from the war increased, the minister of colonies demanded a head count of the Eurasian children in Indochina whose French fathers had died in the war;[34] in 1917, administrators estimated that the number of fatherless Eurasian children had quadrupled as French fathers left for war.[35] Concerned that Vietnamese widows and girlfriends of fallen French soldiers had become the primary socializers of their children, protection society administrators sought to limit the mothers' influence. Authorities got their break in 1917 when two laws pertaining to soldiers' children passed in the *métropole*. The first law, which retroactively legitimated the illegitimate children of French fathers killed in the war, was enacted on April 7, 1917, in the *métropole* and promulgated in the colony three months later. Once legitimated, the children became French citizens and received citizenship benefits. Protection societies invoked this law to obtain citizenship benefits for wards and to declare those *métis* still living with their indigenous mothers to be French citizens, thus making it easier to justify removing these children from their mothers. The metropolitan government enacted a second law on July 27, 1917, called *pupille de la nation,* which established the special status of "state ward" for the children of fallen French soldiers.[36] The *pupille* law was part of an early twentieth-century view that society was linked by interlocking connections among "family," "nation," and "race," and that it was necessary to maintain these connections to protect the honor of both individuals and the community.[37] The *pupille* law applied to children whose father or mother had been killed or injured in the war as a soldier or a civilian. A *pupille de la nation* was "a child adopted by the Nation"; however, the booklet describing the law carefully noted that *pupilles* were not adopted in any legal sense and that families did not lose rights over their children. In this case, "adoption" was simply an affirmation of the government's support for the children of fallen soldiers.[38]

That said, the *pupille* law did in some cases serve as a means to remove the colony's fatherless *métis* children from their mothers. The 1889 law regulating unfit parents had only been applicable in cases in which a child had French citizenship or lived within French legal jurisdiction (Cochinchina and major cities). By assigning the state guardianship of children of fallen French soldiers, the *pupille* law, however, provided the state with the necessary jurisdiction to remove the newly minted citizens from their mothers' custody and, not incidentally, the native milieu. In cases in which mothers cooperated with protection societies, the *pupille* law allowed them to choose to institutionalize their children or raise them at home with state financial assistance—and surveillance. In cases in which mothers refused to comply with the state, the state seized custody of the children.

The ministry of colonies enacted another policy that specifically addressed the *métis* children of fallen soldiers and effectively regulated the cultural environments in which these children were raised. In June 1917, the minister of war and the minister of colonies decided that both recognized and nonrecognized *métis* children whose fathers had died in the war would be raised by their Indochinese mothers until the age of ten, provided that the mothers submitted to regular home inspections. At this point, the state would institutionalize them.[39] These three closely related laws—retroactive legitimation, *pupille de la nation,* and the Eurasian application of *pupille de la nation*—expanded the jurisdiction of the colonial government's intervention in *métis* families and the removals of fatherless Eurasian children from their mothers.

As Emmanuelle Saada has shown, on November 8, 1928, a decree was issued that tied French identity to race.[40] Based on a 1926 court decision, this decree offered citizenship to *métis* who demonstrated fluency in French culture, regardless of formal education.[41] A decree of December 22, 1928, declared that anyone born in Indochina of unknown parents could apply for citizenship—so long as they could prove that at least one parent was "presumably of the French race."[42] This decree marked the first time that the French government had used the term "race" in a legal document since 1848, when French law declared that it made "no distinction of race among people in the human family." Similar decisions were later passed in French West Africa (1930), Madagascar (1931), New Caledonia (1933), French Equatorial Africa (1936), and Togo (1937).[43]

The 1928 decree legitimated a Eurasian *métis* named Lòng, also known as Bourdieu. Born in 1900 to a Vietnamese mother and an unknown French father, Lòng served as a wartime artillery worker. Upon liberation from service in 1920, he married a French woman, and the two later had children together. Lòng applied for French citizenship and promised to stay in Marseille and not return to the colony, where his interracial marriage might upset the social order. Authorities granted him citizenship on grounds that they wanted Lòng's *métis* children to be French, and citizenship passed through the father.[44]

The postwar laws in the empire pertaining to citizenship sent a complex message about race as well as citizenship. In 1917, the colonial government retroactively recognized and granted citizenship to the Eurasian children of fallen French soldiers, and the 1928 law demonstrated an increasing inclusivity in legislating Frenchness through cultural criteria. On the other hand, the 1918 fraudulent paternity law, which was implemented through the remainder of the colonial era, indicated that race was still an impediment to French citizenship. By vigorously pursuing fraudulent paternity cases and making parents' race a criteria for the 1928 law, the government was not offering inclusive and universal citizenship but was instead protecting Frenchness. In the post–World War I period, the definition of "Frenchness" included not just cultural characteristics but also racial biology.

"FRENCH BY HEART AND BY BLOOD": RACIAL OWNERSHIP AND REMOVALS

The legal changes described in the previous section gave protection societies leverage with which to assert the French citizenship of their wards. Meanwhile, the pronatalist trends of the World War I era provided a new language with which to talk about fatherless Eurasian children. The argument that national strength was determined in part by demographic ratios allowed the colonial state to claim racial ownership over fatherless *métis* children, and this notion of ownership in turn elicited a sense of cultural and racial belonging for *métis* who lived in the margins of French society. Although the rhetoric of ownership and belonging did not supplant the rhetoric about the dangers posed by *métis,* it did provide an alternative rationale for removing fatherless Eurasian children from the native milieu—a rationale that would in turn serve as the ideological grease needed to integrate Eurasians into French colonial society.

Métis protection societies, whose administrators by the 1920s included a few females and wealthy Vietnamese in their ranks, continued to express anxiety about the purported threat posed by fatherless *métis* children. Indeed, stress from the war meant Indochina was plagued with political unrest in the form of rebellions among soldiers, workers, and students. In 1916, the colonial state thwarted an anticolonial plot involving the seventeen-year-old Emperor Duy Tân, who was subsequently exiled to Réunion. Meanwhile, youth in Tonkin and Cochinchina protested the colonial draft, mistreatment at school, and broader injustices throughout colonial society.[45] In 1920, Charles Gravelle, president of the Society for the Protection of Childhood in Cambodia, warned the governor general that fatherless *métis* children could turn against France, much as Emilio Aguinaldo, a Chinese *mestizo* and leader of the revolution against the Spanish in the Philippines, had turned against Spain,[46] and Eurasian radical Douwes Dekker and his Indische Partij, a nationalist party consisting of Eurasian and indigenous people, posed a significant challenge to the Dutch colonial government in the Netherlands Indies.[47] The resident superior of Cambodia warned the governor general: "It is necessary for the prestige of our French in the colony that the charitable institutions intervene and take in these abandoned ones and prevent them from quickly becoming depraved or rebels who are rejected even more by Vietnamese society than by French society."[48]

In the 1920s, two *métis* journalists—Henry Chavigny de la Chevrotière and Eugène Dejean de la Batie—emerged in the Cochinchina political scene to become household names and sharp political thinkers. De la Chevrotière was the recognized son of a *métis* from a prominent Franco-Antilles who migrated from Martinique to Indochina in the mid-nineteenth century. Educated in France, de la Chevrotière came to identify with his French heritage, but his multiracial background influenced him to lead the *métis* identity movement to consider an identity beyond that of Eurasian—that of a multiracial French population in the colony.[49] By contrast, Eugène Dejean de la Batie, also known as Eugène Lien, identified with his Vietnamese heritage. He was recognized by his father, a prominent doctor who was well connected in Saigon politics in the 1890s and a member of *métis* protection societies, but the younger de la Batie was raised with his mother and identified with "the race from which my mother comes,"[50] exactly the type of sentiment that the protection societies aimed to thwart among other fatherless *métis* children. A reformer in the spirit of French republicanism, Dejean de la Batie had a strong sense of justice and close ties to Nguyễn An Ninh and Phan Chu Trinh, who in turn were linked to the radical Nguyễn Ái Quốc, who would later be known as Hồ Chí Minh. Dejean de la Batie used his French citizenship to serve as the director and writer for the popular newspapers *L'Echo Annamite* and *La Cloche Fêlée*. Yet for all his critiques of the French colonial government, de la Batie limited his arguments to constitutional reform, never calling for full independence. In 1926, de la Batie was briefly arrested along with Nguyễn Anh Ninh for anticolonial activities.[51] Both de la Chevrotière and de la Batie would go on to be major players in *métis* politics, demanding more rights for *métis* in the 1930s and 1940s.

Although the reasons for colonial anxiety about fatherless *métis* children's potential for rebellion remained the same as in the previous eras, the rationale for removing them from their mothers was quite different during World War I and its aftermath. Protection society administrators and allies appealed to colonial officials by highlighting fatherless *métis* children's biological connection to the French population. The president of a protection society in Cambodia insisted that Eurasians were "French from the heart and blood,"[52] and military commander Donnat urged his superiors to provide material aid for "children who have French blood in their veins."[53] The president of the Society for the Protection of Childhood wrote to the governor general: "A new race has been created. . . . In Indochina [this race] could be a powerful link between the *métropole* and the colony. It would be the surest, and best, element of French influence in this land."[54]

Protection society members urged colonial administrators to use more inclusive language acknowledging the European heritage of *métis* children. In 1924, protection societies in Tonkin eliminated the name "*métis,*" which they considered pejorative.[55] They proposed *"Eurasien"* as an alternative, following the British example, because, unlike the term "Franco-Annamite," it accounted for children of all European parents, not just those of French origin.[56] Yet the term "Eurasien" notably excluded the biracial children of African or Indian fathers, most of whom were soldiers in the colonial army.[57]

The legal developments of the World War I era broadened the reach of protection society administrators. Along with the 1917 *pupille de la nation* law and the law to retroactively legitimate the children of deceased soldiers, protection society administrators could, following a January 22, 1924, law, apply the 1889 law regarding the divestiture of paternal power beyond its previous jurisdiction in Cochinchina and the major cities to all of Indochina. Under the 1924 application of the 1889 law, the state had the official power to forcibly remove children whose parents had "morally abandoned" their children.[58]

Equipped with the legal armor of the 1924 law, protection society administrators and colonial officials renewed their searches of the countryside for fatherless *métis* children. The resident superior of Annam suggested that "only a complete and early uprooting [*déracinement*] from their environment is recommended."[59] The protection society in Hanoi warned that if not removed in time, "the *métis* will build relationships with the native element that are too close and permanent."[60] In 1916, the resident superior of Annam advised protection societies "to remove (*soustraire*) [a child] as early as possible from the milieu in which he lives and from the situation of his mother."[61] "It is best," he wrote, to "confine *métis* children to Public Assistance as soon as they are ready. . . . That means around four or five [years old]."[62]

Protection society officials were hardly unaware of the controversy generated by the issue of separating children from their mothers. The resident superior of Annam acknowledged the "difficulties" resulting from the "brusque separation of the child and the Annamite mother."[63] He complicated the question of maternal consent in a letter to the governor general of Indochina, writing, "Properly speaking, abandoned [*métis* children] do not exist in this country."[64] The bulletin of the Society for the Protection of Childhood in Annam further acknowledged that "everyone who has cared for *métis* knows that mothers do not entrust their children to us [except] when . . . misery forces them there."[65] The protection societies, in short, did acknowledge that Vietnamese, Cambodian, and Lao mothers rarely abandoned their *métis* children, except in times of crisis.

Most protection society administrators nonetheless agreed on the need to raise *métis* children as French. They did not, however, agree on removal strategies. In 1917, the Society for the Protection of Abandoned Métis in Hanoi wrote to the resident superior of Annam requesting that the latter pressure the Society for the Protection of Childhood in Annam to remove the Felipi children from their mother, Lê Thị Quynh. The president of the Hanoi protection society took issue with the Annam protection society's policy of taking only those children whose mothers had voluntarily given up custody or had physically abandoned them. Instead, the Hanoi protection society pushed for more removals. In the end, the societies agreed to invite Lê Thị Quynh and her children to live together at one of the protection society establishments, where the children's environmental influences could be regulated.[66]

The French colonial government learned of the existence of fatherless *métis* children through word of mouth, often via military personnel living in the provinces. The societies advertised their project in villages in the hope that village residents or desperate mothers would hand over fatherless *métis* children. In Tonkin, the Red Cross assisted the protection societies' search for Eurasian daughters of fallen soldiers. The Red Cross offered mothers a stipend with which to raise their children according to French cultural norms, with the stipulation that protection societies regulate the household.[67]

During the war, families of deceased soldiers contacted the colonial government seeking custody of the soldiers' Eurasian children. The late Marc Legrand's family back in France, for example, called on the state to send his Eurasian children to the *métropole*.[68] After the 1915 death of André Delaporte—an interpreter in Luang Probang, Laos—his paternal aunt demanded government aid to force his children's Lao mother to relinquish custody to her. The mother refused,[69] but it is not clear whether she succeeded in fighting the aunt's claim or whether authorities removed her children.

Some French fathers entrusted their children to the *métis* protection societies before returning to the *métropole*. Frenchman Laroche entrusted his son Vincent to a protection society and left an endowment with which to raise Vincent in his absence. As it turned out, the protection society mismanaged the money by using the endowment to pay not only for Laroche's son but also for his daughter, whom the father had not included in the trust. In a bureaucratic snafu that developed into a "near scandal," authorities returned Vincent to his "crazy mother" to live among the native population "*à l'annamite.*" Taken with his physical characteristics (he stood out as "a beautiful adolescent . . . absolutely of the European type") and fearing that he would grow up to become a revolutionary or "street urchin," protection society administrators ordered his removal.[70] Archival records indicate that the young Laroche boy was eventually sent to the *métropole* as a specialized worker during the war and remained there after his service.[71]

In a few exceptional cases, mothers themselves requested aid from protection societies, though this did not necessarily evidence a willingness to relinquish custody of their children. These mothers were attracted to the home-stay programs that had been created to prevent "the little wives who come to us with suckling *métis* infants" from becoming sex workers.[72] The programs offered financial aid to mothers who raised their children at home but agreed to send them to French school and to submit to regular inspections to ensure that the child was being raised according to French cultural norms. Nguyễn Thị Bé—mother to two young *métis* who had been abandoned by their French father, Paoli—received a ten-piastre-per-month allocation but fell into poverty nonetheless. In 1928, she appealed to the mayor of Hanoi for an increased stipend but made it clear that, although she wanted her children to go to protection society schools when they were old enough, she was unwilling to relinquish custody of them: "I would be sad if I were condemned to live alone, without my sons who give me comfort."[73] It is not clear whether Nguyễn Thị Bé genuinely wanted to send her children away to school or whether she was merely telling authorities what they wanted to hear in order to receive the allowance. The 1939 records from the Society for Assistance to Franco-Indochinese Children indicate that at least one of the Paoli children was eventually confined to a protection society institution.[74]

Although the French minister of war claimed that "mothers did not protest when their children were institutionalized,"[75] some mothers did resist the forcible removals. When authorities went looking for the Eurasian child of Lê Thị Ngọc and Georges Rossi, a Corsican soldier who was sent to fight in Europe, they learned that the mother had fled with the child to escape protection society officials.[76] In 1915, a military commander alerted the resident superior of Tonkin to the situation of the unrecognized Eurasian child of a Monsieur Costa, who had recently died. The child's mother had little in the way of resources after being robbed by rebel forces. The society attempted to take the child and his siblings from the mother, but she resisted. Archival documents indicate that the protection society eventually took custody of three of her children and separated them from one another in different institutions.[77]

Although not the primary public justification for removals, racial phenotypes certainly influenced administrators' decisions to take custody of fatherless *métis* children. The Society for the Protection of Childhood in Cambodia described young Etienne Lacroix as a "deserving boy whose white race is incontestable."[78] In Cao Bằng, authorities removed another Eurasian boy named Corso on the basis of his white skin and blond hair.[79] Conversely, protection society administrators rejected children who did not look sufficiently white, even when the mothers requested aid. In 1916, the resident superior of Tonkin wrote a "very confidential" note directing the protection society to reject Nguyễn Thị Lan's Eurasian children because "elsewhere in the country, they would not pass for being the children of Monsieur Mercier."[80] This obsession with white racial phenotypes also led authorities to reject Afro-Asians and Indian Asian *métis* children. Racial phenotypes would dominate the discourse about the forcible removals of fatherless Eurasian children through 1945.

During World War I, as authorities investigated mixed-race families of mobilized French soldiers, they continued to judge these mothers by their perceived sexual morality, their marital status, and the cultural environment in which they were raising their children.[81] In 1917, the president of the pronatalist People's League of Fathers and Mothers of Large Families of France lobbied the resident superior of Annam to intervene in the case of the Lambert children. In the absence of Monsieur Lambert, the mother had "returned to her *nha-que* ways." French colonists used the Vietnamese term *nhà quê,* meaning "peasant" or "hick," to refer to Vietnamese people whom they believed could never be civilized according to French standards. The police cited Madame Lambert's cultural practices as a major justification for the forcible removal of her children.[82]

Colonial police further denounced Madame Lambert on the basis of what they considered her sexual immorality. Having found Madame Lambert eating lunch with two Vietnamese males, authorities questioned her relationship to the men, insinuating that they were her lovers. She responded defiantly: "I am an Annamite above all, and I eat with whom I please." Colonial administrators initially decided to remove her children, but changed their minds when they learned that Monsieur Lambert would soon be returning from war, deciding that he would not approve.[83] Their decision shows the extent to which the societies privileged a father's opinion—in this case, above and beyond their own personal judgment about the mother's supposed moral corruption.

Métis children themselves also resisted being institutionalized in the protection societies, albeit infrequently. In 1920, the Society for the Protection of Métis Children in Tonkin reported that two Eurasian boys had run away from the institution. Colonial police later located one of the boys, who had returned to his mother. As punishment, as well as a deterrent for the other wards, the society decided to expel him and, by default, leave him with his mother—the implicit message being that expulsion from school and exclusion from one's peer group amounted to the greatest punishment. Yet the protection society did not wish him to remain with his Vietnamese mother in the native milieu, which they believed was unsuitable for a French-looking boy and might even influence him to join the ranks of anticolonial rebels. To resolve their conundrum, administrators waited until the runaway boy's punishment had likely had its deterrent effect on the other wards, then forcibly removed him from his mother's care a second time—undoubtedly traumatizing him yet again—and returned him to the protection society.[84]

Once the protection societies had gained custody of fatherless *métis* children, the societies pursued gendered strategies for integrating the wards into French colonial society. Officials guided fatherless *métisses* towards stereotypically female jobs, such as European-style chambermaid service, tailoring, ironing, candy making, and cooking.[85] Girls who showed the most intellectual aptitude attended school, where they earned degrees and went on to become teachers, nurses, or midwives. The colonial government even created jobs specifically for *métisses*.[86] Girls lived at the protection society institution until they reached marriageable age and were "protected" by the societies even after they were married.[87] Marriage, itself, was held in high esteem; in their annual reports, the protection societies frequently announced news of female wards' marriages. While protection society members preferred that their Eurasian wards marry Europeans, the low number of Europeans in Cambodia made such marriages infrequent. The protection societies of Cambodia therefore "settled" for Vietnamese and Cambodian suitors for their female *métisses* wards to make "honest mothers of these girls."[88]

Protection societies rarely reported on male wards' marriages and instead focused on their education and professions. The societies educated or guided fatherless *métis* boys towards more traditionally masculine jobs and negotiated their entry into either academic or trade schools. The majority of *métis* wards in Cambodia attended the elite Collège Sisowath or French schools in Saigon on scholarships provided by the king of Cambodia.[89] Some attended the École des Arts to learn the craft of reproducing Angkorian models—a skill that would presumably assure them an "advantageous job."[90] The less stellar wards took positions as apprentices for ironworkers, engineers, woodworkers, sculptors, or cobblers at the École Professionnelle in Phnom Penh.[91] During World War I, some male wards were sent to work in factories in the *métropole;* the stronger students enrolled in Paris's top schools, where they studied to become doctors or schoolteachers.

INTEGRATION TECHNIQUES: EURASIAN AGRICULTURAL INSTITUTIONS IN ANNAM AND THE *MÉTROPOLE*

During the post–World War I era, *métis* protection societies developed plans to place Eurasian wards in land settlement programs in Annam as well as in the *métropole*. These programs served three purposes. First, administrators hoped that placing Eurasian children in strategic areas would help solve, however minimally, postwar labor shortages in Annam and the *métropole*. Second, as had been the case with the Agricultural School of Hưng Hóa in 1908–1910, administrators aimed to use the land settlement programs to transform the Eurasian wards into productive French citizens loyal to the French government. Third, like the Agricultural School of Hưng Hóa, these programs allowed protection administrators to regulate the behavior of fatherless Eurasian children, thereby discouraging them from joining the ranks of the Vietnamese anticolonial movement.

Eurasian settlement programs were popular panaceas among colonial states in Asia. In British India, under the Andaman scheme to alleviate urban poverty, authorities sent Anglo-Indian Eurasians to the Andaman Islands to perform agricultural work and isolate them from what colonial officials believed to be the degenerating influences of the city. This scheme had the additional function of hiding impoverished Eurasians from public view.[92] Similarly, in 1923, Dutch colonists proposed a plan to use New Guinea as a settlement for the colony's Eurasian population, a "Eurasian homeland" intended to become a "tropical Holland." By 1938, the Dutch colonial government was subsidizing the settlements; however, the majority of them failed because the Eurasian settlers, most of whom were urbanites, lacked the proper training to run agricultural ventures.[93] In 1926, wealthy Eurasians of Malacca, Malaya, created a "Portuguese settlement" as a charitable project for lower-class Eurasians of Portuguese decent.[94]

In Indochina, the agricultural settlements developed as an alternative means of integrating the colony's *métis* into French society. As in the prewar period, many of the colony's French schools continued to reject fatherless Eurasian wards. In 1919, the inspector of education in Indochina denied requests that fatherless Eurasian boys be permitted to take entrance exams for, or receive scholarships to, elite schools on the grounds that the boys were colonial subjects. Scholarships were reserved for French citizens.[95] Government officials considered a range of other options for fatherless Eurasian boys. Officials ruled out directing *métis* wards to join the French Foreign Legion, a contingent of the military that awarded French citizenship to foreigners who had served France, because they feared that the association with the Foreign Legion would highlight the *métis* wards' outsider status. Colonial officials toyed with the idea of building their own military school for the *métis* children of veterans, an École des Enfants de Troupe.[96] They also discussed the possibility of creating penitentiary establishments for fatherless *métis* children with disciplinary problems. Both ideas would be revisited in the late 1930s.

As early as 1916, the colonial government considered establishing agricultural settlements for fatherless Eurasian *métis* children in the Dalat-Langbiang area of Annam, where the state cultivated coffee—one of Indochina's major investments. Agricultural colonies in Dalat-Langbiang were supported by the People's League of Fathers and Mothers of Large Families, as well as by the Society for the Protection of Abandoned Métis Children of Annam. Colonial administrators also proposed settlements in the Thái Nguyên, Lạng Sơn, Thanh Hoá, Phú Hoan, and Nhã Nam areas of Tonkin. Whereas the Dalat-Langbiang settlement plan eventually came to fruition, it is not clear whether the Tonkin agricultural settlements ever did. The colonial government did set up agricultural settlements in Phú Hoan and Nhã Nam, but these were for Vietnamese orphans.

The Eurasian agricultural settlements in Annam fit into a larger plan to develop Dalat into the colony's summer capital. Under this plan, which was set in motion in 1904, Dalat would serve as a "European Center" and a "counterweight to Vietnamese power."[97] The Eurasian settlement plan would not only advance the development of the Dalat-Langbiang area but, as it turned out, provide an optimal white French presence in the proposed colonial capital by World War II. The British in India likewise believed high-altitude settlements to be advantageous for mixed-race children—among them the St. Andrew's Colonial Homes in Kalimpong, 4,500 feet above sea level.[98]

Indochina's protection society workers believed that placing fatherless *métis* children in agricultural colonies would prevent the development of "a caste of *métis*," and colonial officials expected that, with proper guidance, these children would go on to integrate into French colonial life. At the settlements, *métis* children aged fourteen and older learned to cultivate the land and attended French schools. Authorities planned to release the wards at the age of twenty-one to settle the highlands of Annam. Institution administrators believed that the settlements would "not only serve the *métis* of Annam but also serve all of Indochina" by populating the settlement with newly minted French men and women who would contribute to colonial agricultural production.[99]

Protection society administrators also developed a second plan, one that would send fatherless *métis* wards to the *métropole*. Young François Marcel, whose story opened this chapter, was one of the children sent to Europe under this program. Planning began as early as 1916, and the first group of *métis* wards was shipped out in 1919, soon after the armistice. The primary aim of this program was to prevent fatherless *métis* children from joining anticolonial rebellions. By "uprooting" these children from Cambodian society, the resident superior of Cambodia argued, French administrators would prevent further exposure to "pernicious" Cambodian influences. This was, he argued, "the only way to get a result." He concluded that sending fatherless *métis* children to France would eliminate any political threats they posed, which could "seriously inconvenience the French administration."[100] The protection society authorities thus resolved to send the wards to the *métropole* when they were thirteen years old—still too young to revolt but mature enough to handle the transition.[101] Time in the *métropole* would "make French souls" out of the children; they would develop a love for France, and adopt the "ambitions of whites."[102]

The belief that orphans and poor children could be "reformed" through labor and a change of environment was consistent with orphan-related policies in the *métropole*. In the late nineteenth century, metropolitan reformers had planned to send revolutionaries and urban paupers to help settle the colonies, with the additional goal of preventing them from destabilizing metropolitan society.[103] The general counsel of the Seine region had, for example, proposed sending metropolitan children on public assistance, whom he considered to be the products of "promiscuity among beasts," to settle areas of North Africa, where they would exploit the land and "propagate the race and solid virtues."[104] In 1922, the department of Seine likewise proposed sending French orphans from the *métropole* to Indochina to cultivate the land. The governor general declined on the grounds that metropolitan orphans would not survive life in the colony because they lacked the requisite agricultural and local language skills.[105] In enumerating his excuses (the last of which was dubious given that few French settlers spoke any Southeast Asian languages), the governor general was likely seeking to prevent metropolitan orphans from increasing the colony's population of impoverished whites.

While most metropolitan officials loathed the idea of using nonwhite immigrants—especially *métis* people from the colonies—to solve the population problem in metropolitan France, the minister of colonies differed.[106] He argued that "[if] raised in France without any connection to the *indigène* mentality, the young *métis* of a French father is more qualified to become French than [is] a foreigner in whose veins runs not a single drop of French blood and who only becomes naturalized by a more or less prolonged stay in France."[107] His comment bespeaks a belief that fatherless *métis* Eurasians more legitimately "belonged" to the French nation than did white immigrants with no French heritage.

Some colonial authorities questioned administrators' decision to send *métis* children to the *métropole*. Acknowledging the violence of separating fatherless *métis* children from their families, the president of the Society for the Protection of Métis Children in Hué argued that it would be preferable to send wards to the Dalat-Langbiang settlement because "the mothers can rest easy knowing that their children are still in Annam." He rejected the plan to send children to the *métropole,* as it "brutally transplants these sickly children . . . from a warm climate to that of our country, which is relatively cold. We risk seeing them contract pulmonary problems from which they will not recover. Moreover, how can one force the mothers to separate themselves from their little girls and boys when they are still so young? Who will accompany them and take care of them during their voyage?"[108] The resident superior of Annam concurred—but for logistical reasons only, recognizing that there would be difficulties transporting the children to the *métropole* and that the children might not adapt to the colder climate.[109]

The preceding reservations notwithstanding, the governor general of Indochina, by a decree of May 8, 1919, entrusted the vice president of the Society for the Protection of Métis Children to accompany Eurasian wards, many of them *pupilles de la nation,* to the *métropole.* The metropolitan apprenticeship program lasted from 1919 through 1929; in 1928, the societies sent girls as well as boys, to "ensure that [the girls] have an honorable existence."[110] *Métis* protection societies advertised the program throughout the Indochinese countryside in French, Vietnamese, Lao, and Khmer languages. Most of the wards were between the ages of eight and fourteen; administrators reasoned that after the age of fourteen, which marked the beginning of adolescence, one's character was presumably already formed and thus not receptive to molding. By 1929, there were 139 fatherless *métis* children living and working as apprentices in metropolitan France.

The *métis* wards arrived in Marseille and then traveled by train to Coutances or Lorient, where two former protection society members, Charles Galuski and Henri Desnoyer, met them. The wards eventually settled in Coutances, Landes, Villefranche, and villages along the Rhône, among other areas, and were placed with French farming families, "who offered them a guarantee of the best morality."[111] Older boys went to trade schools and took apprenticeships in such fields as agriculture, mechanical trades, pastry making, and the flour-milling industry. At least three children reunited with their French fathers.

The metropolitan apprenticeship program was not without problems. Metropolitan administrators accused their counterparts in Indochina of sending sickly children. Of the thirty-nine children sent in 1925, twenty children arrived in metropolitan France "in a deplorable state," displaying symptoms of trachoma, a contagious infection of the eyes that can result in blindness.[112] (Two other children, whose symptoms were discovered early on, had been left behind in Tonkin.) Authorities hospitalized those sickly wards immediately upon arrival in the *métropole,* and some remained hospitalized for at least six months. By the time the hospitals discharged the children in the south of France and sent them to Coutances in the North, winter had set in, and the children had a difficult time acclimating. Young François Marcel, whose story opened this chapter, endured psychological trauma from the separation and culture shock. Some of the French guardians complained that their charges were too young and needed motherly care. The society insisted that, however young the wards were, they had already become accustomed to institutional life and thus no longer needed their mothers. [113]

The protection societies' plan to integrate fatherless Eurasian *métis* children into metropolitan French society proved difficult. The metropolitan French did not always accept the *métis* wards as legitimate French boys, instead rejecting them as "young Annamites."[114] Trade schools, for their part, rejected wards for their indigenous legal status. In one case, both the minister of the colonies and the minister of the navy had to pressure a mechanics school into admitting *métis* wards.[115] As for the children themselves, some were unwilling participants. François Marcel resisted the trip because he feared leaving Vietnam and being separated from his mother.[116] The former protection society administrator Charles Galuski spoke of another student who was very intelligent but had a "very regrettable deviation towards extremist ideas," meaning anti-French ideas. As this rebellious student was one of the three who had been reunited with his father, Galuski was only too happy to support the reunion, thereby ensuring a French male presence in the student's life and separating him from the other students.[117]

Overall, protection society administrators considered the metropolitan apprenticeship program a success. Due to the global economic collapse, 1929 was the last year that Indochina sent children to metropolitan France, although the original transplants remained there through at least World War II. Throughout the 1930s and 1940s, colonial administrators would repeatedly request that colonial officials resurrect the program.

The massive death toll of World War I convinced many French in the *métropole* and colony that a demographic crisis was under way and that robust initiatives were required to regenerate the French race. Colonial officials saw fatherless *métis* children as one solution to this problem—a means of bolstering the colony's white French population. This, of course, meant that *métis* had to be racially reclassified. During the interwar years, colonial protection societies appropriated the rhetoric of pronatalism and their understanding of the relationship between French identity, race, and blood lineage to make the case for Eurasian whiteness, and they justified the removal of fatherless Eurasians from their indigenous mothers by claiming a sort of racial ownership over the children. This rationale amounted to an inversion of the one employed before World War I. No longer did protection societies remove fatherless Eurasian children out of a *fear* that they would be mistaken for French; instead, protection societies removed Eurasian children *in hopes* that they would be mistaken for French—at least after being properly acculturated in protection society institution programs.

Invoking reinterpreted metropolitan laws, *métis* protection societies greatly expanded their reach and used Eurasians as a resource for bolstering the white French race with plans for *métis* settlements in Annam and the *métropole*. Like the prewar agricultural school at Hưng Hoá, the World War I–era programs demonstrated that fatherless *métis* children could, through labor, learn to be productive citizens and contribute to metropolitan as well as colonial society, thereby proving their worthiness as young French men and women. Protection societies would pursue these sorts of strategic population programs through World War II.

The economic collapse in 1929 put an end to the program to send wards to France. Moreover, mass poverty resulting from the Great Depression led mothers and even *métis* children themselves to request state aid. Orphanages were flooded with children, leading the colonial government to expand poverty relief programs for fatherless *métis*. With pressure from a *métis* political group and representatives from the metropolitan government, in the late 1930s the colonial government overhauled the *métis* protection system and centralized its operations under the direction of the colonial government.

3

The Great Depression and Centralization, 1929–1938

In 1938, fifteen-year-old Paule Lý wrote a letter to the resident superior of Tonkin pleading for financial support. Paule had no doubt heard about the benefits offered by *métis* protection societies given that they advertised their services throughout the countryside. Her letter, written in Vietnamese and riddled with spelling errors, was addressed to "Your Excellence" and chronicled young Paule's life of hardship. Born in 1923 in Lai Châu, Paule was the *métisse* child of a Vietnamese mother and a French father who had never legally recognized her. In 1924, the father returned to France, leaving Paule and her mother without financial resources. During the Great Depression and its aftermath, Paule's mother was too poor to afford to send her daughter to school. "Please, your generous excellence," she begged, "love me like a *métis* child, let me go to the *métis* school, eat there, free of charge, and issue me a stipend for clothing." Anticipating the difficult future that lay ahead for many fatherless *métis,* she pleaded, "When I get older, please your excellence, find work for me to do, so I can feed myself and escape the destitute life. I will be eternally grateful for your favor."[1] There is no record indicating that Paule was ever admitted to the protection societies; her chances would no doubt have been hindered by her age and by her inability to write in French.

Paule Lý's story speaks to changes that swept colonial society during and after the Great Depression. Mass poverty led the French government and indigenous charities to develop poverty relief programs, including child-care institutions that opened in most of the provinces of Indochina. As institutionalized child care became normalized, an influx of mothers of *métis* children—and, as in the case of Paule Lý, sometimes even the children themselves—began requesting aid. Protection society orphanages of the 1930s swelled with wards.

Meanwhile, an organization called Les Français d'Indochine criticized the colonial state for failing to extend French privileges to nonrecognized *métis* and pressured the state to increase aid for fatherless *métis* children. In 1937, the Mission Guernut, a metropolitan-directed study of the state of the colonies, warned the governor general of Indochina of an impending political crisis arising from the *métis* population and advised the colonial state to take *métis* protection out of the hands of private welfare organizations and to centralize it under the control of the office of the governor general of Indochina. In 1939, the colonial government opened the Jules Brévié Foundation for fatherless *métis* children and established a military school called the École des Enfants de Troupe Eurasiens.

THE GREAT DEPRESSION AND POVERTY RELIEF

The economic boom that Indochina experienced in the 1920s had gone bust by the end of the decade. The crisis hit Indochina in two waves. In 1929, the first wave dealt a blow to the rice, rubber, and mining industries. By 1931, when the second wave of the Depression hit, a large number of landowners had defaulted on loans, and many companies went bankrupt. In 1931, up to one-third of the population was unemployed; meanwhile, the cost of living skyrocketed. Residents of Saigon, Indochina's economic capital, felt the crisis through 1934, and the city's poor suffered through the end of the 1930s.[2]

The privations of the Great Depression led to mass poverty, homelessness, famine, and the orphaning of children. The inability of the French state to provide relief belied the empire's *mission civilisatrice,* the claim that colonial rule protected and aided its colonized populations. France's failure was not lost on Vietnamese intellectuals, who saw poverty relief as a moral obligation of the state.[3] Indigenous charity organizations sprang up all over Indochina to care for the impoverished. Among other things, these private charities, which were ostensibly apolitical, helped the poor, orphans, and lepers.

Poverty relief quickly became politicized. As Van Nguyen-Marshall shows, Vietnamese elites and the French state vied for moral authority over Vietnam through welfare programs. The Vietnamese intellectual elite addressed the issue of poverty relief in terms of Vietnamese survival and national independence. Citizens had a patriotic duty to care for the poor, especially impoverished children; child-care institutions, in turn, had a duty to teach children to be patriots.[4] Articles published for children in the Vietnamese press instructed them to become nationalists, urged them to work hard at school to benefit the nation, and equated loving the family and loving the nation: "We know how to love our family; [now] we must know how to love our country."[5]

The colonial state sought to mitigate the nationalist bent of indigenous welfare programs by organizing them under a central office, requiring organizations to apply for charitable status, and regulating their endeavors.[6] Louis Marty, head of the colonial police force known as the Sûreté, was the driving force behind the colonial government's plan to open a child-care facility (nhà nuôi trẻ) in every neighborhood of Saigon to help working as well as unemployed parents.[7] By the early 1930s, as nurseries, day-care centers, and orphanages opened up all over Indochina—particularly in famine-stricken areas, plantations, and mines—institutionalizing child care became a normal practice, rather than a foreign concept. As child welfare advocate Hoàng Trọng Phu remarked in 1933, "Little by little Ho Sinh—daycare [and maternity] centers—are entering the customs of the villagers."[8]

Vietnamese language women's newspapers published extensively—and mostly favorably—on the subject of the colony's new child-care institutions.[9] Vietnamese women's newspapers communicated to readers that the institutions had been developed to solve women's problems, including finding employment outside the home and dealing with illegitimate children—perhaps a veiled reference to fatherless métis children.[10] Some journalists, however, had reservations. For one thing, the institutions, according to the journalists, made it easy for mothers to abandon unwanted children or at least neglect them. The nurseries (crèches) closed before many domestic workers finished work, potentially leading some mothers to reject them in favor of longer-term institutions.[11] Notwithstanding these concerns, institutional child care became a popular solution for many working mothers, especially the desperate mothers of métis children. The Vietnamese media, which as a general rule was unconcerned with métis children, did not take on the thorny questions raised by the institutionalizing of these children.

ATTITUDES ABOUT LOVE, SEX, MARRIAGE, AND MÉTISSAGE

During the 1930s, questions about love, sex, marriage, and métissage were discussed within the context of debates about tradition and modernity in Vietnamese culture. Raised with a completely French education, the generation of Vietnamese that came of age during the 1920s and 1930s began questioning the traditional Vietnamese social order. Among the issues debated—in

Vietnamese popular culture as well as in Vietnamese literature—was whether young adults had a duty to accept a marriage arranged by their parents or whether they should enjoy the freedom to choose their own spouse. This was expressed through the discourse on romantic love, which posited traditional society, filial piety, and social obligation as symbolized through arranged marriage against new ideas of individualism and modernity as symbolized through romantic love. The discourse on social obligations and romantic love became a common theme in Vietnamese literature.[12] Within this context, as Quang Anh Richard Tran's research shows, Vietnamese youth explored new modalities of sexuality. Stories of homosexuality, prostitution, and experimentations in dress and gender expression appeared in the Vietnamese presses.[13] Girls and young women followed French trends for makeup and tighter clothing, both of which scandalized the older generation. Western-style dancing, previously deemed too provocative, became popular among young people.[14]

With Vietnamese youth contemplating romantic love and pursuing different forms of sexual expression, interracial relationships grew more common—although not necessarily more accepted. A new wave of Vietnamese-language reportage took an unblinking look at the darker elements of society, including *métissage* and *métis* children.[15] Citing language barriers and the fact that interracial couples rarely married, authors concluded that these relationships were inherently problematic. Interracial relationships, journalists declared, could only be successful when the French man and Vietnamese woman spoke a common language and understood the other's customs and "soul."[16] Newspapers printed sensationalistic stories about Western men breaking up Vietnamese relationships.[17] Perhaps the most famous accounts of *métissage* in the colonial period were written by journalist Vũ Trọng Phụng, who investigated what he called an "industry of marrying Westerners." Phụng interviewed dozens of interracial couples in a village outside the city of Bắc Ninh. (The presence of some three hundred French legionnaires in Bắc Ninh, and countless counterparts in Thông, Tuyên Quang, and Việt Trì, led locals to nickname them "the international provinces.") Phụng portrayed women in *métis* relationships as shrewd, mercenary, hardened women. The women he interviewed spoke candidly of their ambitions, admitting, "of course we got involved with them for money, never for love." Mothers bragged about their trick of obtaining support for a single *métis* from multiple European "fathers."[18]

Colonial officials were long aware of this "industry of marrying Westerners." In 1931, following a series of venereal disease outbreaks among troops, military authorities issued a directive to police that wives of soldiers were believed to be clandestine prostitutes in areas surrounding military garrisons.[19] The issue came to a head in 1936, when a venereal disease outbreak led the head of the gendarmerie to register wives and girlfriends of European soldiers as prostitutes. Police marched to the barracks where military wives lived, arrested more than 124 women, registered them as prostitutes, tested them for venereal disease, took photographs, and issued them prostitution identification cards.[20] The women were humiliated. They lodged a formal complaint declaring themselves to be the soldiers' legal wives and the mothers of their Eurasian children, and that they were dishonored by the photographs and venereal testing. The women pointed out that the gendarmerie had no business arresting them, as they had already interviewed with the police when they got married.[21] In a letter to his superiors, the head of the gendarmerie explained his rationale: because these women were "at the service of European soldiers," who gave them food and shelter, "it is useful to consider them as prostitutes." If they were not prostitutes, he reasoned, they would have chosen "proper love," meaning marriage to Vietnamese men.[22] The resident of France and military superiors agreed to keep European soldiers' wives and lovers under surveillance from that point on.[23] As we shall see in chapters 4 and 5, this policy would come in handy for protection societies when looking for women impregnated by European soldiers.

French men, as portrayed in the Vietnamese press, disrespected their Vietnamese partners by addressing them in diminutive terms like *ma congaie* (my girl) instead of the more respectful *ma femme* (my wife), which was how they would have addressed a French woman. The men whom Vũ Trọng Phụng interviewed about the "industry of marrying Westerners" were shockingly candid, not to say arrogant, about their sexual exploits, which included the humiliation, dehumanizing, and even raping of Vietnamese women. Newspapers chronicled the exploits of conniving French men who seduced naïve, romantically minded women and robbed them and their families.[24] Newspapers portrayed African men resorting to cunning and even violence. An African soldier convinced seventeen-year-old Đặng Thị Chắt to steal money from and assault her mother before running off with him.[25] Another African kitchen worker made the news for abusing his Vietnamese wife.[26] Several newspapers covered a 1937 story about Hoàng-thị Sửu, the twenty-seven-year-old wife of an African man who beat her severely.[27]

The Vietnamese-language media pitied the children of *métissage*. Blaming irresponsible fathers and manipulative mothers, articles warned that "the beautiful *métis* children" were damned. Because French fathers "rarely recognize their own children," the *métis* are treated like "pariahs" in Vietnamese society.[28] As Suzanne, the *métisse* daughter of Mrs. Ách, told journalist Vũ Trọng Phụng: "The Europeans do not entirely respect us; the Annamites will not fully love us. In the respectable Western society, a drop of Annamite blood is a disgrace, and to the noble Annamite society, a drop of French blood is not quite an honor either. Oh, my God! That means I don't have a country!"[29] Phụng lamented that "the innocent children" received a "bitter punishment" for their parents' actions, adding, "Those pitiful children truly deserve love."[30]

MÉTIS PROTECTION DURING THE GREAT DEPRESSION

During the Great Depression, protection society administrators continued to obsess about global French depopulation and to pursue pronatalist policies in the colony. In reality, however, the French population in Indochina was growing, not declining. By 1930, there were 43,789 French civilians and military personnel in Indochina, and because 10,477 of these individuals were children, there was a growth potential. The population of adult French females, meanwhile, had increased to 9,113, bringing the gender ratio of French adult females to civilian French adult males to 1:2.66; excluding military personnel, that ratio was 1:1.5. As Marie-Paule Ha has shown, notwithstanding officials' assumptions that importing metropolitan French women would decrease the number of mixed-race births and encourage French births, it turned out that greater numbers of French women were not enough to deter French men from falling in love—or lust—with indigenous women and fathering more *métis* children.[31] Seeing fatherless *métis* as one solution to French depopulation, protection society administrators continued the World War I–era trend of referring to fatherless *métis* children as "French by blood" and "French by race and pride" to make the case that "French born in Indochina of fathers who are French voters" deserved to be treated better than "veritable pariahs on the social map of Indochina."[32]

Yet the fact remained that most *métis* children were not recognized and thus could not enjoy the same privileges as French men and women. Many officials continued to fear that these fatherless *métis* would come to resent the French colonial government and rebel against the colonial French, echoing early twentieth-century metropolitan French fears of adolescent rebelliousness in general. Former resident superior of Laos and deputy mayor of Hanoi, Honoré Tissot—argued that there was a "danger" that if not removed from indigenous elements and allowed to "take their rightful place" before they reached the "threshold of their life," meaning adolescence, the colony's fatherless *métis* would rebel.[33]

Indeed, colonial officials had reason for concern considering that motherhood was increasingly becoming politicized. The most popular mainstream woman's magazine, *Phụ Nữ Tân Văn,* urged women to adopt a nationalist stance when raising their children.[34] Articles drew an analogy between the family and the nation, portraying the family as the means by which to both reproduce and strengthen the nation. In the most fundamental sense, this meant increasing population numbers and raising children to be nationalists.[35] Meanwhile, the nascent Indochinese Communist Party (ICP) was likewise appealing to mothers. The ICP used women—mothers in particular—as powerful symbols of the oppressed worker and colonized nation. Among other things, the ICP promised to fight for maternity leaves, maternal rights in cases of divorce, the prohibition of polygamy and forced marriages, and infant care at the workplace. According to party historiography, child-care institutions served as a conduit for many mothers—and their children—to learn about and join the communist movement.[36] The ICP, however, limited its calls for women's liberation only to those issues that pertained to class equality. It neglected many important issues—such as male privilege and female victimization in the home—that occurred among all classes, the working class included. The party went so far as to denounce calls for gender equity as an idle concern of elite women.[37]

Protection society administrators resolved to act quickly to remove the colony's fatherless *métis* children from negative influences. Tissot directed the protection society to "tear them from the often unhealthy environment of their first years, before they contract an unfortunate mentality and customs that we will later be powerless to uproot." He insisted, "We must make the *métis* part of our civilization" and "fill (*imprégner*) them profoundly with our civilization, to the point where they will not become pariahs" and can be conveyed "directly into French cadre."[38] Fatherless *métis* children would then be placed in a "hygienic environment . . . [because] it is a healthy life [style] that makes healthy men."[39] With the word "hygienic," protection societies referred both to sanitary cleanliness and to the supposed cultural cleanliness of a French cultural environment uncontaminated with indigenous influences. The societies carefully regulated the children's diets, as a French diet was believed to make a Frenchman. In some institutions, children were fed French food for all but three or four meals a week, when they were permitted to "eat like Annamites, to save money."[40] Protection societies concerned themselves with the healthy development of the children's bodies. They encouraged boys to follow daily exercise regimes and play team sports, such as basketball or soccer. During the summers, protection societies sent male wards to *colonies de vacance*—state-run French summer camps designed to transform sickly young men into healthy, productive citizens.[41] *Métisse* girls were prized for their beauty and celebrated as the physical embodiment of the French empire. The 1937 Paris Exposition even included a beauty pageant in which *métisse* women from all over the empire were paraded before the metropolitan public.[42]

POVERTY AND THE QUESTION OF MATERNAL CONSENT

A new phenomenon developed out of the privations of the Great Depression: a surge in the number of mothers requesting financial aid from, or admission for their *métis* children into, the colony's *métis* protection system. Emboldened by the normalization of institutionalized child care and motivated by a desire to escape not just poverty but the discrimination associated with *métissage,* these women had abundant reason to solicit aid. Some of these mothers intended to institutionalize their children only temporarily; others intended to permanently relinquish custody of their children. The latter were driven by a variety of motives: a belief that the protection system would offer their children a better life and social mobility; an inability, financial or otherwise, to care for their children; a resistance to the challenges of motherhood; or a desire to profit from the subsidy money that often came with entering one's children into the *métis* protection system. In 1938, a protection society in Cambodia offered mothers five piastres per month, per child; on average, mothers received twenty piastres per month.[43] Certain cases of mothers who solicited aid suggest that financial hardship was a key motivator. Nguyễn Thị Công, who was unemployed and had no savings, requested funds to underwrite the cost of raising her son, Charles Cardini.[44] The mother of Pierre Gautier sent her son to a protection society because she could not afford to care for him.[45] It is unclear whether these mothers were aware that after accepting protection society aid, the society would force them to relinquish custody of their *métis* children when the child came of age.[46]

Drawing on the 1912 law permitting research on paternity, some mothers contacted protection societies to help them track down deadbeat fathers—not realizing that the mere act of alerting protection societies to the existence of their children put them at risk of losing custody. Lê Thị Binh, who in 1931 gave birth to a son after an affair with Antoine Chevalier, was one such case. After Chevalier's return to France in 1932, he initially supported the family, but eventually the payments ceased and the couple lost contact. Binh asked the military to help her find her former lover, and authorities managed to track him down. However, instead of forcing Chevalier to support his son, French authorities honored his request to have the child removed from the mother and sent to France.[47]

Some women requested aid from the protection societies because they found motherhood burdensome. Journalist Vũ Trọng Phụng wrote about one mother who wanted to relinquish custody of her daughter to a protection society because she felt daughters were worthless, especially those who did not have French citizenship or the privileges it afforded. She hoped that once her daughter reached adulthood, the protection society would give the daughter a job or send her to France. While Phụng's portrayal of a selfish mother indifferent to her child's welfare may have been accurate in this case,[48] it was almost certainly not the norm; many other mothers most likely legitimately loved their children.

In cases in which mothers agreed to enroll their children in *métis* orphanages, each society had its own policies for limiting maternal influence. The Society for Assistance to Franco-Indochinese Children allowed mothers who had consented to relinquishing custody of their children to see their children only on scheduled days.[49] Another protection society required that mothers renounce all rights over their children and, in most cases, prevented them from seeing their children at all.[50]

The stories of women who solicited aid from the protection societies raise complicated questions about maternal consent. It is possible that mothers did maintain some degree of agency in relinquishing their children to the protection societies, but it is also possible that under better financial circumstances these mothers might not have been so willing to do so. Colonial administrators themselves were conscious of this ambiguity: "The complete abandonment of a child today is rarer in the Annamite countries than one would believe; it is only in times of famine or epidemic that they sell their children. We are not speaking about what they call the *traite des jaunes*."[51] Complicating the financial question was the role of cultural taboos in mothers' decisions to abandon their *métis* children to the protection societies. Given that *métissage* was considered shameful in the colonial period, some mothers may have given up their children in response to the pressure of social stigma, while others may have done so in a proactive effort to avoid such stigma.

A final factor that may have complicated mothers' decisions to relinquish custody of their *métis* children was the sharp rise in the number of new child-care options for Vietnamese children. On the one hand, the Vietnamese press coverage of the *crèches* and orphanages may have made permanent institutionalization of *métis* children seem like an acceptable alternative to home care. On the other hand, mothers may have confused the mission of protection societies, which took permanent custody of their children, with that of the new colonial Vietnamese child-care system, which was only a temporary care system. Along with extreme poverty and cultural taboos, this possible confusion over the nature of child-care facilities calls into question what was ostensibly maternal consent.

The objections of mothers—and some children—to the removals were clear in other cases. For example, with the consent of the father who was living in metropolitan France, the state forcibly removed young Françoise Dumas against the wishes of her mother, Trần Thị Ngọc Anh. The protection societies claimed that Ngọc Anh was unfit on the grounds that she had a bad reputation, was unemployed, and engaged in prostitution, yet they provided no evidence of such behavior.[52] Needless to say, authorities never even considered the children's wishes. Some *métis* themselves resisted state care and rejected the prospect of becoming part of French colonial society. Jean-Pierre Brun, the child of Nguyễn Jeanne and a deceased French public works engineer, had lived with his Vietnamese grandmother until the protection system institutionalized him when he was thirteen. As Jean-Pierre was a strong student, the protection society provided him with good educational and employment opportunities once he had graduated. Yet Jean-Pierre chose to leave the French milieu, cut ties with protection society officials by giving them a false address, and evaded colonial police until the Sûreté found him living with his mother and integrated in the Vietnamese cultural milieu.[53] Suzanne, the *métis* child of Madame Ách, whom journalist Vũ Trọng Phụng had interviewed, also left the care of a *métis* protection society in Hanoi. Suzanne observed to Phụng that had she stayed with the society, she could have married a Frenchman and gone to France, or taken a job that would have improved her social and financial status. Instead, she left the protection society—and French colonial society—out of love for her mother and an affinity for Vietnamese culture. She told Phụng that she would rather live with her Vietnamese mother even if it meant suffering poverty and hardship.[54] Such cases, however, were likely rare.

LES FRANÇAIS D'INDOCHINE

In the mid-1930s, a *métis*-led political group called Les Français d'Indochine rose to prominence in Cochinchina.[55] The emergence of a unified, politicized group of *métis* and colony-born Frenchmen was exactly what protection society administrators and the colonial government had been trying to prevent since the 1890s. Indeed, the French had much to fear, given that Eurasian political groups had challenged other colonial governments in Southeast Asia, the most notorious being the Insulinde, a political organization of Eurasian nationalists in the Netherlands Indies established in the 1930s.[56]

During the mid-1930s, Les Français d'Indochine became a viable political force, using their newspapers *Blanche et Jaune* and *Les Nouvelles de Dimanche* to disseminate their ideas. The group counted important *métis* political figures among its members, including Henri Chavigny de la Chevrotière and Eugène Dejean de la Batie. (By this point, Dejean de la Batie's politics had become considerably more conservative than they had been in the 1920s.) While the members of Les Français d'Indochine remained steadfast in their support of French colonial rule in Indochina, they did aim to shift the reins of political and economic power from the *métropole* to the colony itself. Les Français d'Indochine, in other words, sought to privilege the rights of French citizens in the colony over the rights of the metropolitan French who held temporary posts in the colony.

The writings of Les Français d'Indochine reveal tensions between a colonial administration dominated by metropolitan-born French and the local-born Les Français d'Indochine. The group criticized the colonial government for giving the best jobs and higher salaries to metropolitan-born French, "people who never set foot in the colony, who ignore . . . the customs of the aborigines."[57] Metropolitan French were considered mere "birds of passage," who worked in Indochina only temporarily before moving on to another colony, and never invested themselves in the future of Indochina as Les Français d'Indochine would.[58] Les Français d'Indochine urged the colonial government to invest its resources in *métis* and colony-born French, as Indochina "also has its unemployed. It is irrational to neglect them for the benefit of metropolitan French."[59] Instead, argued one member, the colonial state should give employment preference to "children of the colony," who were bilingual, bicultural, and better acclimated to the climate.[60]

Les Français d'Indochine championed *métis* children, whom they considered "more French than the French themselves,"[61] the implication being that they were more patriotic and invested in the colony than were metropolitan French. One author conspicuously avoided referring to *métis* people by the common terms of the day—*eurasien, métis, Franco-Indochinois*—all of which marked the *métis* as the colonial Other by highlighting their mixed ancestry and their relationship to indigenous culture. Instead, he used terms that emphasized their belonging in French society: "the French of Indochina," "sons of Frenchmen," "Frenchmen born in this country," "French of the country," "the progenitor of Frenchmen," "children of the colony," "these Frenchmen," and "our children."[62]

Les Français d'Indochine criticized the colonial government for failing to provide unrecognized *métis* with access to the privileges of French citizens.[63] Considering how sparing the administration was in granting naturalizations, unrecognized *métis* had a slim chance of gaining any of the rights of French citizens.[64] Fed up with these injustices, Les Français d'Indochine member Henri Bonvicini warned that nonrecognized *métis* would "[never] stop protesting against the jurisprudence that refuses them French status" and warned that "revolutionary, nationalist, or communist propaganda" was targeting *métis*.[65] Another member warned that disenfranchised unrecognized *métis* could become rebels.[66]

As many members of Les Français d'Indochine themselves served in protection societies, their ideas echoed protection society plans for integrating fatherless *métis* children into the French milieu. The group called on the government to remove these "accidents of colonization" from the indigenous milieu,[67] where "they are literally drowned in the masses of 25 million natives."[68] Another *métis* member even suggested that members "steal" [*voler*] abandoned *métis* children from their mothers, who were considered a corruptive influence.[69] Their plan was to leave suckling children with their mothers until the age of three, after which the protection societies would remove them. The protection societies would then educate them in the colony's French schools, train them to be skilled workers, and eventually send some to the *métropole* to develop their loyalties to France by "ending this anomaly of French who do not know France."[70] It is worth noting that few if any of Les Français d'Indochine's largely *métis* membership had themselves been removed from indigenous influences or placed in the *métis* orphanage system. Most had been raised by their French fathers as well as their indigenous mothers and thus integrated into French colonial culture and educated at elite colonial institutions.

Les Français d'Indochine offered a plan for a "micro-colonization" model, similar to the one being planned for Dutch Eurasians in West New Guinea.[71]

One member suggested following the Italian model, under which the Italian government shipped homeless Italians to Ethiopia and gave them land to cultivate.[72] The Ethiopian model had the twofold benefit of enabling homeless Italians to earn a living while facilitating Italy's colonization efforts. Under a comparable plan proposed by the same author, the colonial government of Indochina would use the agricultural schools of Bến Cát and the Gressier plantation in Xano, Cochinchina, to train fatherless *métis* boys in agriculture. The schools, according to his plan, would then aid in populating southern Annam and Cochinchina, consistent with the Annam settlement policies of the 1920s.[73] Another member suggested that the colonial government train fatherless *métis* children to become colonial administrators.[74] These suggestions both to use *métis* to colonize Indochina's key agricultural areas and to train them to become future colonial administrators would be realized during World War II, when, as we shall see, the colonial government established *métis* settlements in strategic areas of the colony.

THE GUERNUT COMMISSION AND THE INQUIRY INTO THE SITUATION OF EURASIANS IN INDOCHINA

The 1936 election in the *métropole* led Indochina's colonial government to take control of the *métis* protection system. That year, Leon Blum's left-wing Popular Front government was elected in the *métropole*. As the Popular Front was an alliance government that included socialists and communists, its political platform initially found support among left-wing republican Vietnamese intellectuals who hoped France would consider granting independence to its colonies. This prospect evaporated as Germany accelerated its militarization, and the Popular Front pursued ways to keep a stronger grip on the colonies.[75]

The Great Depression had ended by the time the Popular Front came to power. Yet there remained a large percentage of impoverished people in the colonies, where recovery was slower than in the *métropole*. Indochina, after all, had been plagued during the 1930s not only with economic crises but also with famine, strikes, and revolts, all of which had led to a struggle among colonial authorities to maintain political control.[76] The Popular Front government introduced social changes throughout the empire, yet these reforms remained limited in that they neglected the more fundamental problems of colonial rule and race relations.[77]

Popular Front prime minister Leon Blum launched an empire-wide investigation called the Guernut Commission into the social and political problems afflicting the colonies. Between January 1 and March 14, 1937, Justin Godart oversaw the collection of data on the social, political, and economic problems of Indochina and explored solutions to these problems.[78] The commission interviewed high- and low-level government administrators, military officers, and nongovernmental organizations, as well as French, Vietnamese, and *métis* civilians, on a wide range of subjects.

One of the areas of inquiry was the condition of the colony's *métis*. Researchers gathered press clippings and interviewed protection society members, orphanage administrators, and veterans' organizations that were known to include deadbeat fathers among their members. Revealing their bias, the researchers neglected to interview any mothers or maternal family members of fatherless *métis* children, let alone the children themselves. The methodological bias of the commission prevented researchers from identifying some of the key problems facing the fatherless *métis* population: colonial poverty, racial hierarchies, and gender discrimination. Instead, the mission's findings merely justified further state intervention into *métis* families.

Respondents to the Guernut Commission identified interracial sex as the root of the *métis* "problem." One respondent wrote: "The question of *métis* is a consequence of the expansion of the white race across Asia. . . . The French came to Indochina and created a new decadence. They are responsible for it."[79] The French resident from Kratie, Cambodia, warned that "*métissage* should not be encouraged. The race, in spite of everything, is bastardizing itself; now, we should, without being racist, enforce ourselves to conserve [the race] as pure."[80] The resident from Kampong Chhnang demanded that the government take precautions to discourage interracial sex, as "Franco-*Indigène métissage* cannot be anything but accidental and exceptional."[81] At this point, statistics from 1937 show that there were 28,101 French civilians in Indochina, 11,575 of whom were children. When counting the military, the total swelled to 42,345. Excluding the military, there was a gender ratio of one French civilian adult female to 1.02 French males; when factoring in military personnel, that number became one French female to 2.05 French males.[82]

Respondents gave wildly varying estimates on *métis* population numbers and never explained their methodologies. One Tonkin report to the Guernut Commission estimated that in 1938 there were four thousand to five thousand *métis* in Tonkin, and predicted that by 1948 there would be ten thousand *métis*.[83] Another report estimated that in 1931, the population of recognized *métis* constituted 5 percent of the French population in Tonkin; by 1936, according to the report, *métis* had increased to 19 percent.[84]

Yet, as another respondent to the commission's questionnaire cautioned, the "numbers of non-recognized [*métis* children] are much higher in reality than has been indicated. . . . It is extremely difficult to obtain precise results on this subject."[85] From my research, I estimate that there were likely ten thousand to twelve thousand unrecognized *métis* children and adults in Indochina by that point.

Respondents to the Guernut Commission inquiry warned that *métis* would soon outnumber French residents of the colony. One respondent claimed that by 1938 the population of recognized and nonrecognized *métis* in Tonkin would surpass that of the 11,575 European children currently in Indochina.[86] Another respondent invoked examples of other communities with sizable *métis* populations in Manila, Batavia, and Brazil to warn of the dangers associated with *métis* fecundity.[87] To complicate matters, French women were beginning to seek nonwhite partners. Respondents from Cochinchina cited examples of what they believed to be a new phenomenon of French women marrying, or engaging in relationships with, Vietnamese men, and predicted that this new relationship pattern would lead to an exponential growth of the *métis* population.[88] The French resident in Bạc Liêu explained that marriages between French women and Vietnamese men were increasing as a function of economic prosperity. Now that Vietnamese parents were sending their boys to the *métropole* to study, the young men "[came] back in a state of mind that prepared them for marriage to a French woman."[89] The subtext of the predictions about sex between French women and Vietnamese men was twofold: not only was the *métis* population growing, but France was losing a valuable resource for producing white babies.

Respondents warned commission investigators that fatherless *métis* children were outcasts in Indochina, as they were accepted by neither the French colonial population nor the indigenous population. Respondents blamed the colony's French women for racism against the *métis* population: "the sentiment of disapproval [of *métis*] on the part of whites is aggravated by an instinctive feeling of jealousy on the part of European women."[90] This speaks to a myth common at the time: that white women had introduced racism into the colony insofar as they allegedly ended the era of concubinage and *métissage*.[91] Yet even as administrators accused white women of harboring racist attitudes towards *métis*, they acknowledged that the indigenous communities likewise rejected fatherless *métis*: "The French do not consider [fatherless *métis*] as their own," wrote the French resident from Bà Rịa. "The Annamites, in the environment within which the [*métis*] live, also treat them as foreigners."[92] The resident of Bạc Liêu claimed that "Annamites consider *métis* to be too 'crafty.'"[93] Indeed, judging by the articles on *métis* published in Vietnamese newspapers, they were marginalized by Vietnamese society.

Having been raised without French cultural influences in what many French administrators considered to be a morally repugnant environment, fatherless *métis* children, according to Guernut Commission findings, would grow up to resent their place in colonial society and potentially form *métis* political groups or even join the ranks of anticolonial rebels. The administrator from Vĩnh Long warned, "Rejected by us, [fatherless *métis*] become embittered and do not hesitate to look to harm our [endeavor in Indochina]."[94] The official Guernut Commission report warned that fatherless *métis* children would become Vietnamese patriots and turn against the French empire. Indeed, the deposed Prince Cường Để, an anticolonialist, was rumored to have already issued a directive for Vietnamese revolutionaries to ally themselves with the colony's *métis*. Citing comparative cases from the Netherlands Indies, where the colonial state "conserves its property through loyal *métis*," and San Domingue, a colony lost by France because its colonial government failed to win the loyalty of the *métis* population, the resident of Bén Tre assured the Guernut Commission, "The political importance [of *métis*] has not escaped me."[95]

Even if *métis* did not resort to revolution, the Guernut Commission advised, their growing population could potentially tip the voting balance of the colonial councils. Colonial administrators worried that *métis* council members would establish policies that would benefit Les Français d'Indochine at the expense of the metropolitan French or the colonial government.[96] Justin Goddard, head of the Guernut Commission, wrote that *métis* posed a particular political threat because, by 1937, *métis* adults with French citizenship already held a majority of French votes in some of the municipal colonial legislatures; accordingly, Goddard suggested that it was in the colonial government's best interest to foster *métis* loyalty to the colonial state.[97] Administrator Marinette told commission investigators: "[Fatherless *métis*] risk forming—and the risk is growing more and more serious—a class of Frenchmen led astray, fallen into the hands of characters whose job is to make an electoral enterprise, and [they will become a source of political] agitation that would have regrettable repercussions for the stability of Indochina."[98]

Although Guernut Commission respondents warned the government about the potential problems that the colony's fatherless *métis* population could cause, they also regarded these children as a potential demographic benefit for the colonial French population, an argument also made by Les Français d'Indochine. After all, the resident of Bạc Liêu wrote, *métis* were "already

French by blood";[99] the resident superior of Tonkin likewise described *métis* as "carrying true French blood."[100] This belief that fatherless *métis* were French "by blood" contradicted the fascist theories of racial biology that, by the mid-1930s, had gained credence throughout much of Europe; according to these theories, a person who did not have two white parents was not considered white.[101]

The more liberal respondents to the Guernut Commission survey thus urged the colonial administration to use *métis* to solve what they believed to be a declining French population in the colony. It is worth noting that in recommending solutions to the problem of depopulation, respondents could just as easily have urged that naturalization laws be relaxed in order to increase the number of indigenous French citizens. But this political solution was never even proposed; instead, respondents homed in on the issue of race. One respondent wrote, "In a country with a low birth rate it is not opportune to reject children who would be half French by race."[102] The resident superior of Annam warned the governor general: "Our country does not have a [sizable enough] birthrate to [neglect] a contribution of truly French blood and people who are easily assimilated."[103] Another respondent to the inquiry wrote that France "needs children," and the colonial government should look to those "in whom half their circulating blood is French."[104] "Healthy" miscegenation, another respondent argued, makes "good Frenchmen, who are useful to the country and are physically and morally good."[105] Some respondents believed *métis* had a unique ability to adjust to various climates, in contrast to the intolerance for tropical heat that had inhibited French population growth in Indochina.[106] According to the French resident from Qui Nhơn, these advantages indicated that *métis* "are likely to constitute a solid framework for colonization if they are well directed."[107] Invoking the precedent of *métis* populations in the Netherlands Indies, one respondent to the Guernut Commission inquiry contended that Indochina's *métis* were likewise politically indispensable for maintaining the empire. In the Netherlands Indies, the respondent wrote, the *métis* population had "conserved the colony for the Dutch" and ensured "the durability of the empire." To prove his case, he cited the esteemed General Van Daalan, the superior general commander of troops, himself a *métis*. Without *métis*, he concluded, Dutch "colonial society would not be able to maintain itself."[108]

Echoing the calls of protection society members and Les Français d'Indochine alike, survey respondents demanded that the colonial government take a leading role in policies towards fatherless *métis* children. The French resident of Hà Tĩnh insisted that the *métis* "problem" had implications for the "honor and dignity of the French state," and that Indochina needed "an official solution, a solution of the French government"—not a solution on the part of private citizens, who had run protection societies heretofore.[109] The French resident of Kiến An wrote that "it would be eminently desirable for the government of Indochina to follow a . . . policy in this matter."[110] Their goal was to upgrade the status of the *métis* protection system from multiple small grassroots, civilian-led organizations to a single state-directed protection system centralized under the direction of the governor general, because, as one administrator wrote, "it seems that, without doubt, the future of this colony belongs to *métis*."[111]

Most respondents to the Guernut Commission inquiry encouraged the colonial government to take the lead in removing fatherless *métis* children from their indigenous mothers, thereby demonstrating the government's commitment to solving the *métis* question. The French resident of Kampon Chhnang urged the French government to "search for these unhappy people, take them into its charge at a young age, and make good citizens of them, who are particularly apt . . . to be agents in the connection between the *métropole* and colony."[112] The Association of Legionnaires in Indochina, many of whose members had fathered *métis* children, lobbied government officials to take the children from their mothers, who were presumed to be corrupting their children with "*indigène* ways." The association's reports urged the government to remove "morally abandoned" children from Vietnamese maternal care and place them in child-care institutions.[113] The resident superior of Annam wrote that although removing *métis* from their mothers "obviously poses a difficulty of conscience . . . in the majority of these cases, we have to separate the child from a mother unwilling to abandon [him or her]."[114] Henri Plante, president of the Amicale des Français d'Indochine in Cambodia, suggested a twofold requirement that indigenous women declare their fatherless *métis* children to the French *État Civil* and that "from the age of five, all *métis* children be taken in by a public institution."[115] An administrator from Bạc Liêu urged the government to "take charge of the children, educate and instruct them to raise them effectively within the ranks of French citizens."[116]

Respondents to the Guernut Commission inquiry considered the World War I–era *pupille de la nation* law—which protected the right of children of fallen French soldiers—insufficient, as it was limited to recognized children. Instead, respondents advised the state to create a *pupille de la nation* law specifically for *métis*—and offer it to all *métis* children, even those who were not recognized or did not have soldier fathers. One respondent suggested "imitating" what the French understood as Dutch government policies towards *métis:* "All *métis* children for whom the father is failing should be adopted by the state, raised and educated at [the government's] expense. The [state] will guide them towards a profession according to their aptitude and physique."[117] After "adopting" fatherless *métis,* another respondent wrote, the government should take financial responsibility for raising and educating them.[118] Survey respondents also urged the colonial government to establish programs to integrate fatherless *métis* children into the French colonial population. Again citing examples of policies towards *métis* populations in the Netherlands Indies as well as those in Portuguese Macao and many South American nations, one respondent argued that the government must provide *métis* with employable skills and access to public service jobs.[119]

To integrate fatherless *métis* children into French society, respondents suggested reviving the 1920s policy of sending them to the *métropole.* Tissot, the resident superior of Tonkin, who would later take a leading role in *métis* protection programs, wrote that the only way to ensure a complete removal of fatherless *métis* children from the "maternal" milieu was to send them to metropolitan France.[120] The exclusively French cultural environment would "strip the children of their peasant ways," Tissot wrote.[121] Sending them to France, another respondent wrote, "permits them to know the country of their fathers and, above all, lose the indigene mentality that they have a tendency to conserve."[122]

A second proposed solution for the *métis* question was to provide opportunities for fatherless *métis* children to establish themselves in Indochina's agricultural sector, a suggestion also proposed by Les Français d'Indochine. Underscoring French concerns about a demographic crisis, one respondent to the Guernut Commission's inquiry wrote: "The colony needs [*métis*] to populate and exploit it."[123] Respondents repeated earlier suggestions that the colonial government prepare fatherless *métis* children for a future in agriculture by establishing *métis*-specific agricultural schools.[124] This idea was consistent with the colonial *métis* protection policies exemplified by the 1908–1910 Hưng Hoá Agricultural School and the agricultural settlements established in the central highlands in the 1920s. The municipal counselor of Saigon suggested that the colonial government follow the model used to solve indigenous overpopulation in Tonkin, particularly in the Red River Delta. To foster population balance and relocation, the Tonkin policy offered Vietnamese residents of the Delta small land concessions in the central highlands. Once released from protection society orphanages, *métis* would likewise receive small concessions to farmland in the central highlands. The resident superior of Annam urged the Guernut Commission to set up a " 'petit colonization' in the Highlands of Annam." He specifically suggested a site at Blao.[125] Such agricultural concessions would, he hoped, fulfill the wards' material needs while preventing them from "bloating the classes of the unhappy and embittered."[126] The French resident from Gia Định suggested that *métis*' bilingual skills would help the colony insofar as they would enable the *métis* to become "masters" over the indigenous workers.[127]

A third suggestion offered by respondents to the Guernut Commission inquiry was to create a military academy for fatherless *métis* boys.[128] After completing the proposed academy program, *métis* would join the colonial military as noncommissioned officers.[129] The military academy would serve as a sort of boot camp for disciplining wards and building national loyalties. The wards would thus form a much-needed leadership segment of the colonial military—a segment that would be loyal to France yet, thanks to its bilingual skills, able to communicate effectively with the troops.

Taking all of these responses into consideration, the Guernut Commission's official conclusion for "the *métis* problem" recycled familiar paradigms about the threat of a rapidly growing *métis* population. Justin Goddart wrote that *métis* children in Indochina posed a serious "moral" and political problem for the colony, as they were social outcasts among both the French and indigenous populations. He warned that the children lived in a morally repugnant environment and, given their marginal status, were predisposed to rebel. The Guernut Commission, however, suggested that if the colonial government could find a way to integrate fatherless *métis* children into French colonial society, they would become a valuable resource for the French endeavor in Indochina.[130] The colonial government decided three avenues through which to facilitate the integration of fatherless *métis* into (or out of) French colonial society: a *métis* penitentiary program, a *métis* military school, and a unified protection society centralized under the control of the colonial government.

Agricultural Penitentiaries for Métis *Children:* The idea for agricultural penitentiaries developed out of metropolitan disciplinary models that aimed to rehabilitate criminal bodies by returning them to the pure influences of nature.[131] Indochina already had multiple agricultural penitentiaries for colonial subjects, but none specifically for *métis*. The protection societies suggested that the colonial government develop a "recovery institution" for *métis* boys who had been deemed "depraved." Although nominally dedicated to "recovery," this would be a penitentiary institution in practice. It would follow the model of a Tunisian penitentiary institution or the agricultural institution developed in Bắc Giang for Vietnamese boys.[132]

Agricultural penitentiaries would function as a holding ground for wards who were not good enough to eventually be integrated into French colonial society yet whom protection societies did not want to return to the native milieu. The protection society considered sending *métis* children to existing agricultural penitentiaries for minor crimes, like stealing. Fatherless *métis* children like Gaston Dubois, the child of a French citizen "of the black race," who was caught stealing in 1938, was condemned to three months in a penitentiary colony.[133] In another case, twelve-year-old Pierre Charles, child of a French Foreign Legion soldier, was removed from his mother and placed in a protection society orphanage. Once there, the child proved to have a "deplorable attitude": he was "not disciplined, a liar, a thief, lazy, [and] mean." Authorities decided not to expel him because they wanted to prevent him from reuniting with his mother.[134] In 1938, the protection society of Tonkin called on the resident superior of Tonkin to condemn a young *métis* child named Adam to a penitentiary, but for unnamed reasons, the resident superior refused.[135] From the documents available, it appears that the *métis* agricultural penitentiaries never came to fruition.

École des Enfants de Troupe: The second proposed program for *métis* children that developed out of the Guernut Commission report was the École des Enfants de Troupe, a military school for *métis* children of French soldiers. Run by the military, the school would train loyal citizens and skilled soldiers. The idea was first raised in 1915 by the resident superior of Cambodia,[136] and in 1938, Tissot suggested sending *métis* wards to the École des Enfants de Troupe in the *métropole*. The minister of war, however, rejected the idea out of concern that children from the colony would take the spots reserved for sons of "legitimate military."[137]

The colonial government and military decided to send *métis* to military schools within the colony. Colonial officials found a temporary solution by designating an "annex section" for *métis* children in the Écoles des Enfants de Troupe for Vietnamese children in Phủ Lạng Thương and Cap Saint Jacques.[138] The problem with situating the *métis* in a predominantly indigenous environment, said the governor general, was that the *métis* "certainly will not develop into young Frenchmen, in spite of the French citizenship that will be conferred on them when they reach adulthood. They will also come to resent the public powers and the military authority if they can grow up thinking that they are admitted in the same establishments as [Vietnamese children]."[139]

The governor general of Indochina created the École des Enfants de Troupe for unrecognized *métis* who were "presumably of French race" in the outlying areas of Dalat,[140] an area targeted by the Guernut Commission for white French settlement. There, wards would be protected from Vietnamese influences and raised in the French milieu.[141] Along with a military education, the school would provide a "social education," from which wards would learn that their "primary role is [their] responsibility to the civilizing French [nation]."[142]

The decision to create an École des Enfants de Troupe for *métis* children renewed calls to remove children from their mothers. The resident superior of Annam immediately demanded a census of *métis,* urging his minions to search first in areas of current or past military garrisons.[143] General Martin demanded immediate action because the *métis* "live in a dangerous promiscuity and the only contact they have with European civilization is with the soldiers who live in concubinage with their mothers"[144]—essentially the situation described by Vũ Trọng Phụng in *The Industry of Marrying Westerners.* Administrators removed *métis* children, like thirteen-year-old René Pierre, from Hà Giang on the basis of their white racial phenotypes. The mayor of Hanoi advocated for René Pierre's admission to the school, confirming that he "presents the ethnic signs permitting us to establish the presumption that his progenitor is of French race."[145]

The school opened its doors in September 1939. Cadets were twelve to fourteen years old at the time of admission. The student population was drawn from all over Indochina. Children were placed at the school by protection societies, churches, and in some cases willing parents. At the school, cadets wore the uniform of the colonial infantry: a beret, khakis, a cotton cardigan, and a white hard hat for military exercise. Students pursued the traditional French baccalaureate program, as well as a military education, courses in indigenous languages, and physical education, which was designed to improve their physical development while promoting a spirit of camaraderie.[146]

The Jules Brévié Foundation: In their suggestions to Guernut Commission representatives, respondents pressed the government of Indochina to revamp its *métis* program. The League of Human Rights called on the colonial government to provide education and job placement for wards.[147] The Federation of Frenchmen of the Colonies and Former Colonies also lobbied the minister of colonies to send fatherless *métis* children to France, where "these *métis,* who, in reality, are French, [will] contribute physically and intellectually to the new power of our nation." Echoing World War I–era fears of integrating "nonwhites" into French society, member Monsieur Corsil wrote, "I won't go so far as to say that the problem of depopulation could be [completely] regulated by this method, but . . . [this policy] permits us, little by little, to repel foreigners and to substitute [*métis*].[148] To ingratiate the minister of the colonies, Corsil offered to call the initiative the G. Mandel Foundation, after the minister himself.[149] This plan was never realized, and it would not be until after World War II that programs to send *métis* to the *métropole* were revived.

Governor General Jules Brévié presented a new solution in which the colonial government would take swifter action to remove *métis* from their mothers. Brévié, who arrived in Indochina in 1936 from French West Africa (AOF), was likely influenced by AOF policies towards fatherless *métis* children and its protection society system, which was designed to educate and train Eurafrican children to become auxiliaries to the colonial state.[150] Brévié directed the colonial government to take control of and expand the *métis* removal program. He predicted that any increase in colonial military troops in Indochina would only result in an exponential growth of the fatherless *métis* population and further warned of "sizable debaucheries that wait to eat away at the youngsters as they leave the orphanage."[151] Invoking the ubiquitous family metaphor, the governor of Cochinchina, Pierre Pagès, warned the governor general that in order to "make [*métis*] an honorable figure in the grand French family," and to make them "stay deeply attached to France," the colonial government "must not hesitate to remove [*enlever*] them from the indigenous milieu as soon as possible (around the age of five)."[152] Brévié assured his superiors that "no ethnic element is better prepared to receive this natural impregnation [of French culture] that is the foundation of colonial politics."[153]

Predicting potential complications when breaking up families, Pagès warned: "Without a doubt, we will have to overcome the resistance of the Annamite families, for reasons that are not difficult to understand." Shedding light on the methods authorities used to obtain maternal consent before removing children, Pagès suggested that it would be the role of the colonial government to persuade the mother that "the interest of the child requires this separation and it is to her advantage to accept it." Mothers were more likely to accept this idea, he wrote, if the colonial government offered a stipend immediately after the child was born or after the father had left the family— presumably their moments of greatest vulnerability.[154] Pagès admitted that the maternal stipend program was imperfect. He warned that the public might get angry if the government gave stipends to the mothers of *métis* children and not to the mothers of indigenous children. On the other hand, if the government gave stipends to the mothers of indigenous children as well as the mothers of *métis* children, then "certain unscrupulous [indigenous] fathers" would likely neglect their children on the assumption that the state would take care of them. After all, he wrote, the mothers of indigenous children could seek child care through the new *crèches* and orphanages.[155] Sister Rosalie, the superior principal of sisters in Cù Lao Giên, Cochinchina, promised that "we will do our utmost to replace the mothers of these children."[156]

After more than a year of discussion with metropolitan French officials, fellow colonial administrators, military officers, protection society administrators, and heads of colonial welfare organizations, on March 20, 1939, Governor General Jules Brévié announced that the Council of Economic and Financial Interests of Indochina had called for the creation of a federation of secular and religious welfare organizations. Writing that he "[saw] only advantages in the larger participation of religious organizations in the education of Franco-Indochinese children,"[157] Brévié invited the church back into the *métis* education process—a process in which it had taken only a minor role after France was secularized in 1905. The foundation would hold central control over all *métis* orphanages. The foundation's plan included a main orphanage in Dalat, the French hill station in the central highlands that was slated to become the new capital of Indochina. There, *métis* wards would attend a small school next to the elite Lycée Yersin, where they would rub shoulders with the children of wealthy French families.[158] Upon graduation, male former *métis* wards would follow either a vocational or an agricultural education track. The Brévié Foundation had the added benefit of producing young French men and women who would eventually settle in the highlands. The governor of Cochinchina proposed reopening the Foyer des Femmes for newly graduated unmarried female wards as a means of discouraging them from engaging in prostitution.[159]

In preparation for the program, police searched the countryside for fatherless *métis* children. The resident superior of Tonkin alerted colonial officials and local military officers of two hundred fatherless *métis* children under the age of seven who had been raised by their mothers in the native milieu. He directed authorities to seek out more fatherless *métis* children. For the time being, he wrote, administrators "only [needed] to concern themselves with children who have been abandoned [by both parents] or whose mothers have consented to relinquish custody."[160] Within a few weeks, the Hanoi police compiled a list of seven *métis* children whose mothers had consented to entrust their children to the French government. The report categorized the children by skin tones of "white," "lightly tinted," or "colored" [*de coleur*];[161] the white and lightly tinted children were placed in the protection society orphanages. A week later, the resident superior of Tonkin alerted the governor general to another dozen girls, aged ten to eighteen and living with their mothers, and thirty recognized *métis* boys, aged one month to ten years old, abandoned by their mothers and living in poor conditions in Sơn Tây. The Sơn Tây provincial government implored the colonial government to aid the children for the sake of "French prestige."[162]

By a decree of August 2, 1939, Governor General Brévié announced to the colonial public his plan to open the Jules Brévié Foundation for fatherless *métis* children.[163] The creation of the foundation marked the beginning of complete state control over the *métis* protection system. The colonial government would continue to play a central role in *métis* protection through 1945.

The child-care programs that the colonial state developed in the early 1930s to deal with the widespread poverty of the Great Depression not only normalized institutionalized child care but, combined with political pressures from Les Français d'Indochine and the recommendations of the Guernut Commission, led the colonial state to take control of the *métis* protection program. Following the Guernut Commission report, colonial officials began viewing fatherless *métis* children as key to maintaining colonial rule. Since World War I, *métis* children began to be prized for their French blood and, in some cases, their "white" looking appearance, and officials believed they could be easily transformed into young French men and women. Accordingly, the newly consolidated and state-run *métis* protection society stepped up its efforts to remove fatherless *métis* children from the colonial milieu. During World War II, the colonial government would continue to aggressively search the Indochina countryside for fatherless *métis* who could pass for white French men and women, and use them to solve some of the colony's demographic problems.

4

War, Political Loyalty, and Racial Demography, 1938–1945

In 1942, Madame Aumont, a French librarian from Hải Phòng who worked part-time for the Jules Brévié Foundation, alerted colonial authorities to the existence of Robert Henri, a two-year-old fatherless *métis* child. At the time she filed her report, Madame Aumont had already forcibly removed Robert's older sister and brother from their mother, Nguyễn Thị Khai. Robert, an "intelligent, gentle" boy, had most likely been able to remain with his mother either because authorities were unaware of his existence or because he was still nursing. At this point, however, Madame Aumont declared Ms. Khai "incapable of raising" the two-year-old and ordered authorities to forcibly remove him from his mother.[1]

In a move that leaves little question about maternal consent, Ms. Khai tracked down her youngest son at the École Saint Joseph, an orphanage run by the Jules Brévié Foundation. When Ms. Khai demanded that the priest in charge return her child, he refused; she then took young Robert "in spite of the defense put up by the father superior." Mother and child went into hiding and, with help from local village chiefs, evaded authorities. The pair made it as far as Kiến An, until someone betrayed them. Aumont directed authorities to find and remove Robert once and for all from his mother. In a move designed to strip Ms. Khai of all remaining maternal rights, the Jules Brévié Foundation pursued a court order to appoint a soldier Robert's legal guardian. Aumont then separated Robert's older siblings and relocated them in orphanages in Nam Phap and Bắc Ninh to prevent Ms. Khai from tracking down and taking back her children.[2] In 1945, Madame Aumont would claim that Ms. Khai was "completely uninterested in her children."[3] Today, this is the only document referencing the separation in the official FOEFI files, which have been made available for former wards to research their personal history.

Although the French government maintained administrative control of the colony's domestic affairs, the Japanese occupation of Indochina in World War II and subsequent rise of Vietnamese anticolonial movements triggered a veritable panic among French administrators and colonists about maintaining a French presence in the colony. To colonial administrators in Indochina, naturalized indigenous citizens would not suffice; instead, they had a racialized image of French identity. Fatherless *métis* children who could pass for white would play an important role in this endeavor. Colonial officials cited racial markers like blond hair or blue eyes to justify the removal of fatherless *métis* children from their indigenous mothers. The perception of these children as white marked yet another shift in the colonial attitude towards the population of fatherless *métis*. Initially regarded with suspicion and dismissed as irredeemably Vietnamese, these children had come to be accepted as part of the French community since the 1920s; now, given the demographic crisis of whiteness that surfaced during World War II, they were increasingly relied on to make up a large portion of the future French community in the colony. The Brévié Foundation planned to raise fatherless *métis* wards to form a stable class of French men and women who would eventually form a permanent French elite in Indochina, settling in strategic areas of the central highlands and providing the white faces considered essential for the proposed new colonial capital of Dalat.

THE JAPANESE INVASION OF SOUTHEAST ASIA

In spring 1940, as the Nazi military prepared for a June invasion of France, Japan planned to make Indochina part of the Greater East Asia Co-prosperity Sphere, Japan's imperial vision for Asia. Given the significant oil deposits in the Netherlands Indies, Southeast Asia was essential to fueling the war in the Pacific. Indochina in particular was strategically valuable to the Japanese for three reasons: Tonkin was along the railway that allied forces used to supply Chiang Kai-Shek's military in China; the region was a source of crucial resources, including rubber, coal, and tin; and it could serve as a strategic starting point from which to invade other areas of Southeast Asia.

In June 1940, with a Japanese invasion appearing inevitable, the colonial government evacuated French and *métis* children from Hanoi to the countryside to keep them safe from the Japanese military and aerial bombings.[4] Cut off from France and lacking support from the United States or Britain, the French colonial government in Indochina signed a series of agreements with the Japanese military allowing Japan to station troops in Indochina, leading the French government to replace Governor General Georges Catroux with Vichy loyalist General Jean Decoux. The decision by Catroux to appease Japan probably saved Indochina from a violent invasion and enabled France to maintain a foothold on the colony, as Japan allowed the colonial government to continue to administer to Indochina. This concession, however, came with the rather severe stipulation that Japanese interests would predominate.

The Japanese military swiftly attacked other colonies in mainland Southeast Asia. Japan succeeded in part by striking an informal deal with the Thai government that allowed Thailand to reclaim provinces that France had taken during colonization. The brief Franco-Thai war of 1941 forced France to cede two Cambodian provinces and four Lao provinces to Thailand. On December 8, 1941, only a few hours after Japan bombed Pearl Harbor, Hawaii, the Japanese military invaded the Philippines, British Malaya, Singapore, and Brunei. In the winter of 1942, Japan attacked the remaining islands of Southeast Asia, including Portuguese Timor and the Netherlands Indies. That May, Japan invaded Burma.

The Japanese military's policies towards Eurasians in Southeast Asia were haphazard. France's agreement for peaceful Japanese occupation seems to have protected the colony's *métis* from the kinds of brutalities experienced by their counterparts in other areas of the Greater East Asia Co-prosperity Sphere.[5] Nonetheless, mothers of Indochina's Eurasians feared for their safety and disguised their children's European features by dying their hair black and painting their faces with ash. In British Hong Kong, the Japanese military initially spared Eurasians from the internment camps that imprisoned Europeans, instead courting Eurasians on account of their language skills and bicultural fluency.[6] In the Netherlands Indies, where the European and Eurasian communities were so integrated that they were nearly indistinguishable, Japanese authorities realized that it would be impossible to intern the more than three hundred thousand Eurasians who played a vital economic role. Japanese authorities lured Eurasians by permitting those who cooperated to avoid internment, which was forced on Europeans. This policy led many Eurasians who had once shamefully hid their Indonesian heritage to flaunt it. In Singapore, the southern capital of the Japanese empire, Japanese authorities interned first-generation Eurasians with the European population; second-generation Eurasians remained free. Exploiting their resentment of British racism, the Japanese military recruited Eurasian men for intelligence services and Eurasian women as secretaries in the occupying administration.[7]

The Eurasian experience in Malaya was perhaps the harshest, as they were the object of both Japanese and British hostility. British and Japanese alike suspected Eurasians of espionage. During the invasion, British officials refused to evacuate Eurasians with the European population, forcing mixed-race families to separate and thereby endangering Eurasians. Japanese authorities ordered first-generation Eurasians to wear badges identifying their racial status. The situation in Malaya changed in 1943, when a sympathetic Japanese general—himself a paramour of a Eurasian woman—set up the Bauhau Agricultural Settlement to protect Eurasians from police brutality and from being conscripted into the infamous "comfort system" of sexual slavery. More than two thousand Eurasian families resettled to what they considered a "promised land." But the settlement ultimately failed due to poor crop output, disease, and isolation. Roughly two thousand Eurasians died.[8]

JAPANESE OCCUPATION AND THE *MÉTIS* SOLUTION

The Japanese invasion threatened Indochina's political stability. The invasion emboldened nationalist and communist groups with its slogan "Asia for the Asians." The hope was that anticolonial groups would undermine French power and prevent the French from launching a counteroffensive. That said, Japanese military leaders often turned a blind eye to French brutalities against anticolonial groups, perhaps as a means of preventing such groups from becoming too powerful and rebelling against the Japanese themselves.[9] Some anticolonial groups worked with the Japanese, including the colony's most prominent noncommunist anticolonial groups, such as Vietnam's Phục Quốc Đồng Minh Hội, whose leaders had long-term ties to Japan. Likewise, factions within the armies of the Hòa Hảo and Cao Đài religious groups were rumored to have been working with the Japanese.[10] The Indochinese Communist Party (ICP), however, organized against the Japanese and gained important political traction by doing so. In 1941, the ICP founded the Việt Minh to pursue a unified front with all economic classes to liberate Vietnam.

To curtail political subversion among Indochina's youth, the colonial government introduced Vichy-style paramilitary youth groups to the colony, a strategy also employed in France. Sister Durand, one of the major actors in Indochina's Vichy youth groups, was also a member of the Jules Brévié Foundation for *métis* during this time.[11] By February 1944, the governor general claimed six hundred thousand Vichy youth group members in Indochina.[12] A key organ in the movement was the newspaper *Thể Thao Đông Dương*

(Indochina Sports)—unmistakably pro-Vichy, down to the pictures of Marshal Pétain that graced almost every issue. It regularly published articles on hygiene, sports, and health. Some articles even compared the Vichy regime to the Greek and Spartan empires.[13]

As Anne Raffin has shown, the Vichy paramilitary youth project backfired on the French. By encouraging youth to be patriotic to their *pays* (Tonkin, Annam, Cochinchina, Laos, or Cambodia), the Indochina Federation, and the French empire, patriotism towards the *pays* turned into Vietnamese nationalism—and anticolonialism. The Việt Minh easily recruited youth by taking advantage of the social networks formed through the organizational structure of the highly trained paramilitary groups. Phan Anh, a leader among Vichy youth programs, trained youth in his program to be Vietnamese nationalists. He would become the minister of youth under the Democratic Republic of Vietnam in 1945.[14]

The political instability brought about by World War II revived a pronatalist approach to addressing the perceived population imbalances. Colonial administrators and protection society officials looked to Eurasian *métis* children—whom they believed could be French if properly educated—to help maintain French dominance in the colony. The colonial vision of fatherless Eurasian *métis* as the colony's permanent French population contradicted a concurrent trend in racial categorization in the *métropole*. As pronatalism developed in France, "scientific" theories of racial hierarchy gained popularity. In the World War I era, theories of racial blood-typing, which categorized races according to presumed biological differences, had grown in popularity throughout the world; by the end of the war, these theories had stirred anxiety in metropolitan France over immigration and interracial marriages. During the 1930s and 1940s, racial blood-typing supported fascist theories of racial hierarchy and popular racist ideas.[15]

As the *métropole* moved towards *exclusive* biological racial categorizing during this period, the colony moved towards a more *inclusive* approach based on racial blood-typing. Two of the colony's foremost anthropologist-demographers, Philippe Huard and Đỗ Xuân Hợp, stressed the importance of mixed racial unions as a solution to the French population deficit, arguing that although biracial births "do not reach the importance of strictly white births, they are a distinctly fair way to increase" the white population.[16] Indeed, the annual rate of known *métis* nearly reached parity with that of the colony's European birthrate. In 1939, there were 894 European births and 598 registered *métis* births. In 1942, the number of European births rose to 970; there were 696 registered *métis* births. By 1943, there were 1,010 European births and 867 registered *métis* births.[17] Realizing that the rate of *métis* births was likely much higher than those registered, authorities searched the countryside for fatherless Eurasian children. In accordance with the arguments of Huard and Đỗ, colonial administrators turned to Eurasian *métis* to address the colony's perceived population imbalance during World War II.

Advocates of the Brévié Foundation's confidential Program for the Organization and Utilization of Eurasians in Indochina believed that *métis* could contribute to the white presence in the colony in one of three ways: as the colony's new permanent white French elite, as colonists in strategic areas of Annam, and as residents of the proposed new colonial capital of Dalat.[18] In short, if removed from their mothers as soon as they stopped nursing, fatherless *métis* children would constitute a kind of blank slate for the government's demographic agenda. The Jules Brévié Foundation drew from ideas proposed in the 1930s by Les Français d'Indochine to cultivate a *métis* elite class that would check the power of indigenous elite—a group towards whom Decoux's government pursued a complex strategy during the Japanese occupation. Decoux's regime effectively restored the social status of the traditional elite by celebrating local "traditions" and romanticizing peasant life. In addition, the colonial government's hardline policy towards communists "endeared" Vietnamese, Cambodian, and Lao elites to the colonial government.[19]

Concerned that indigenous elites would grow too powerful, the colonial government turned to the colony's *métis* population as a kind of buffer. In 1943, the Jules Brévié Foundation developed a plan to train fatherless *métis* children to become the permanent elite French political class. Jules Brévié Foundation president George Coedès—member of the École Français d'Extrême-Orient, one of the most famous historians of mainland Southeast Asia, and himself husband to a Cambodian woman and father to six *métis* children—anticipated that this new French elite would counterbalance the power held by Vietnamese, Cambodian, and Lao elites.[20] In his vision, fatherless *métis* children would eventually take over administrative positions formerly held by metropolitan French, thus ensuring that the colony would never again lack for white French administrators.[21] Fatherless Eurasian children would be "made Frenchmen" and educated to form a class of "future colonists,"[22] or a *"classe spéciale de 'Français de l'Indochine,'"* who would remain in the colony as a permanent French population.[23]

Given that the goal of the Brévié Foundation was to raise fatherless *métis* children *"à la français"* and transform them into "little Frenchmen,"[24] it steered wards towards professions deemed suitable for middle-class whites.

Male wards were guided towards professional schools, l'École des Enfants de Troupe, or apprentice schools, with the intention of making them into administrators, civil servants, customs officers, secret police, public works officers, skilled workers, and teachers.[25] Female wards were encouraged to earn a primary school degree (*certificate d'etudes primaire*).[26] The young graduates would take jobs as either saleswomen in local shops or teachers, and live in dormitories for single women (*foyers des femmes*) until they married.[27]

In addition to the plan to use fatherless *métis* as the colony's administrative elite, the second part of the Jules Brévié Foundation's plan was to use *métis* children to settle strategic areas of Annam. This plan fit into a larger program to reconfigure the colony's demographics. The privations of the Great Depression had stirred anxiety about a native overpopulation in areas of Tonkin; moreover, a long-standing labor shortage in certain areas of Annam and Cochinchina—the "rice basket" of the colony—left Indochina vulnerable to food shortages and rebellion.

Since World War I, the colonial government had hatched multiple demographic plans to address indigenous overpopulation and undercultivation. A 1917 plan sent workers from Tonkin to agricultural settlements in the Mekong Delta. In 1936, French geographer Pierre Gourou devised a demographic plan to resettle workers from Tonkin to the Boloven plateau, Djiring, and the foothills of Biên Hoà—areas that would also be targeted for *métis* agricultural settlements. In 1937, Gregoire Khérian outlined a two-part program to, first, curb the native birthrate by discouraging polygamy, early marriage, and the desire for a male descendant and, second, to encourage population redistribution through incentives to move northern workers to Dalat-Langbiang, Blao, and other fertile and underpopulated areas of the South. Khérian's idea jibed with research conducted under the 1937–1938 Guernut Commission's empire-wide study on the state of the colonies, which likewise warned of a problem of "heterogeneous" populations in the highlands. By 1942, Khérian's idea had appeared in an issue of *Indochine Hebdomadaire Illustré,* which also included an article by René Robin decrying the population imbalance.[28]

While demographic arguments ostensibly focused on serious concerns about famine and agricultural production, they also constituted a metanarrative decrying the danger of indigenous overpopulation. This discourse echoed throughout the French empire. In 1943, Jean Paillard warned that with a population of forty million French in the *métropole* ruling over a population of seventy million colonized subjects, the metropolitan French were a minority in their own empire.[29] In addition, the Japanese invasion introduced a large presence of Japanese troops to Indochina, thereby increasing the demographic imbalance. The demographic problem was exacerbated in 1943, when maritime hostilities meant few metropolitan civil servants could make the voyage from France to Indochina to replace their colonial counterparts who had left the colony after completing their tours of duty. To fill their place, Governor General Decoux resorted to hiring indigenous administrators to fill the gaps created by the metropolitan French.[30]

The colonial government and the Jules Brévié Foundation turned to fatherless *métis* children as a solution to the political-demographic problems engendered by the exigencies of wartime. The Brévié Foundation revived a 1920s program calling for *métis* agricultural settlements that would augment the white French presence in strategic areas. In 1941, Jules Brévié Foundation member William Bazé, himself an orphaned *métis* who had become a wealthy planter in Cochinchina,[31] proposed *métis* settlements in strategic areas of Xuân Lộc, in Đồng Nai, along the old colonial road to Dalat, and near Núi Bà Rá.[32] During World War II, Bazé oversaw the Center for the Formation of Eurasian Colonists in Bến Cát, near Thủ Dầu Một. Under this program, prospective Eurasian colonists studied agriculture for eighteen months before settling in Xuân Lộc.[33] The colony's director of economic services expanded Bazé's plan to use *métis* children to cultivate underpopulated regions of Djiring-Blao, another region included in the Khérian study.[34] One colonial administrator predicted that the *métis* settlements in Lang Bian and Djiring-Blao had potential because "Eurasians, often of unstable character, have a marked inclination for agricultural work."[35]

The Jules Brévié Foundation also considered creating other agricultural settlements and a hill station settlement in Tonkin, similar to that of Dalat. The chief of veterinary services suggested creating a horse farm for Eurasian wards near the Chinese border in Tonkin, in the area inhabited by the ethnic Nung group, as well as settlements in Laos. By the end of 1944, after the colony's inspector general of agriculture conceded that the proposed settlements would fail due to the high cost of labor, necessary materials, and prophylactic medicines, Brévié Foundation administrators abandoned their plans to establish *métis* settlements in Tonkin.[36]

In the third part of the Jules Brévié Foundation's plan, *métis* wards would aid in the settlement of Dalat, the prospective new colonial capital. Colonial administrators envisioned the capital-to-be as a predominantly white city inhabited by white administrators: a piece of France in Indochina. Since Dalat's "discovery" by Dr. Yersin in 1893, various governors general had experimented with plans to transform the site into a French city. In 1897,

Governor General Paul Doumer finalized plans to turn Dalat into a French hill station. In 1937, administrators announced plans to make it the new colonial capital.[37] The new capital would be in "the heart of the ethnic minority country—without the ethnic minorities!"[38] By World War II, "Dalatophilie," as the mania for Dalat was popularly known, had taken over the colony; French colonists moved to the station in droves to enjoy its climate, which colonists believed would assuage many of the colony's mid-twentieth-century health problems.[39] Dalat, once an "isolated, hostile country," had been transformed into a "cozy little corner of France,"[40] complete with French villas, houses, and other buildings.

Yet Dalat continued to pose complicated demographic challenges for colonial administrators. However enchanting Dalat may have seemed to nostalgic Europeans—with its *chateaux* and *maisons*—it continued to lack the permanent French population that would satisfy colonial plans for the new capital.[41] Dalat, after all, was mainly a vacation spot and health resort for Saigon's French to recover from tropical illnesses. Moreover, the city's Vietnamese population was quickly growing, as colonial public works projects for the new capital and jobs working as servants attracted Vietnamese migrants. While colonial administrators initially assumed that an influx of Vietnamese migrants would contribute to the "evolution" of the "savage" hill tribes that inhabited Dalat, they quickly realized that a Vietnamization of the city would threaten its exotic appeal.

Colonial administrators turned to fatherless *métis* children to fill Dalat's perceived relative dearth of white inhabitants. Jules Brévié Foundation president George Coedès proposed resurrecting a 1920s plan to use *métis* to settle in Liangbian and Dalat.[42] Protection society administrators gushed that a *métis* settlement in Dalat would "not only serve the *métis* of Annam, but all of Indochina," by populating the settlement with children who could pass for white French.[43] Moreover, Dalat's geographic isolation would protect the children from the Japanese military—not to mention indigenous mothers looking to reclaim their children.[44] The Jules Brévié Foundation made the city its headquarters for *métis* orphanages, contributing to Dalat's reputation as the "city of youth."[45] The main orphanages were located in a building graced with a Nazarene star on its roof. On the other side of town, l'École des Enfants de Troupe occupied a bucolic campus where *métis* cadets practiced paramilitary exercises.[46] Wards from both the Jules Brévié Foundation and l'École des Enfants de Troupe attended the elite Lycée Yersin and Collège Adran, where they hobnobbed with the crème de la crème of the colony's white, wealthy French children.

Like their Vichy counterparts, authorities in Dalat obsessed over physical health and the importance of sports. The city was said to offer fatherless *métis* children a "good climate, indispensable to their physical formation," and "a French milieu that is no less necessary to their moral formation."[47] Administrators hoped that *métis* children growing up in Dalat would become fit and strong, learn to manage plantations, and attend French schools.[48] Children of both sexes in the Jules Brévié Foundation's Dalat institutions participated in basketball, gymnastics, and track and field.[49] The foundation sent children to summer camps (*colonies de vacance*) in resort areas, including Cap Saint Jacques, Kampot, and wilderness areas surrounding Dalat.

"QUICK AND SERIOUS TRACKDOWN" OF FATHERLESS *MÉTIS* CHILDREN

Concerned that Japanese military and anticolonial rebels would recruit among fatherless Eurasian children, the Jules Brévié Foundation found yet another justification for removing fatherless *métis* children from their mothers.[50] "The *métis* whom we do not take in will become outcasts who will seek vengeance on us,"[51] wrote one Brévié Foundation member. Foundation member R. P. Dupont suggested a "quick, serious track-down of children under 6 years of age."[52] General Decoux warned his administrators that "no *métis* minor in a position to be helped should escape this census . . . and the *métis* problem would be once and for all exactly quantified" and controlled.[53] By "helped" he meant removed from their mothers. General Decoux ordered resident superiors to "track down children, take their medical measurements, and do so quickly; do not allow the children to escape and do not inflict damage on the family."[54] Of course, damage of some kind was inevitable for those who refused to cooperate.

To expedite removals, authorities engaged in subtle legal acrobatics. In a 1941 letter to George Coedès, Governor General Decoux interpreted the decree of November 4, 1928—which provided a way for *métis* to get access to French citizenship—as a legal means for the government to automatically declare fatherless *métis* children French without a court decision. Colonial administrators went on to enact a form of coercive *parens patrie* that allowed them to take custody of fatherless *métis* children. Under Decoux's interpretation, if a French father had abandoned his child, and the indigenous mother had not legally recognized her child—a requirement of which many mothers were unaware—the state could proactively declare the child a French citizen and name the Jules Brévié Foundation as legal guardian.[55] Decoux ordered a search for all fatherless *métis* children with the potential for French citizenship and declare them abandoned by their mothers. Reverend Father Dupont told Jules Brévié Foundation members to take children from their mothers on grounds of moral abandonment.[56] One official warned, "The uprooting [*arrachement*] of children from their mothers poses a serious problem in cases not related to parental degeneration." To deflect potential political backlash, he advised the Jules Brévié Foundation to assign a French guardian to every fatherless *métis* child. The guardian would confine the child to a protection society and have the final say concerning the *métis* child's welfare—including the decision to keep the child in the institution.[57] This guardian-cum-middleman plan effectively eliminated any means for mothers to invoke maternal rights vis-à-vis their children.

Governor General Decoux's interpretation of the 1928 decree effectively changed the relationship between fatherless *métis* individuals and the state. Informed by a sense of racial ownership over fatherless *métis* children that dated back to the 1920s, Decoux's reading allowed for a more aggressive colonial state. Previously, the onus had been on individuals not registered in the État Civil to prove that they were French. By expanding the role of the state to render automatic French citizenship to fatherless *métis* children without a court decision, Decoux's interpretation of the 1928 decree allowed the state to assume that all fatherless *métis* children were French citizens, thus bypassing both the role of individual volition in the naturalization process and the complicated bureaucratic process typically required to prove French nationality.

Decoux's interpretation also increased the state's power vis-à-vis *métis* families. Giving birth to, raising, and having physical possession of a *métis* child was no longer grounds for claiming motherhood. According to Decoux's interpretation, indigenous women were not mothers to the very children to whom they had given birth until they registered these children with the colonial État Civil. Women who did not partake in this legal process of recognizing the children whom they had had with a Frenchmen held no maternal rights. Instead, these rights were usurped by the colonial state, which appointed a guardian and replaced the family environment with that of a protection society institution.

To ensure that the 1889 law on the divestiture of paternal rights and the 1941 interpretation of the 1928 citizenship law applied to all fatherless *métis* children, Lieutenant Colonel Belloc—whose wife helped the Brévié Foundation separate children from their mothers—discouraged the Foreign Legion soldiers under his command from recognizing their children. The logic was as follows: if legionnaires, many of whom were *not* French citizens themselves, were to recognize their children, the children would only be eligible for their father's citizenship, and for those not French, neither the 1889 paternal divestment law nor the 1941 reading of the 1928 court decision to bestow French citizenship to *métis* would be applicable in their case. The Jules Brévié Foundation, therefore, would have no legal means by which to remove a foreign *métis* child from its Vietnamese, Cambodian, or Lao mother. If, however, foreign legionnaires neglected to recognize their *métis* children, then, according to Belloc's plan, the Jules Brévié Foundation could assume that such children were French and remove them from their mothers using the 1889 paternal divestment law or a 1941 reading of the 1928 citizenship decision.[58]

In a second legal decision intended to "break the authority of the mother" and facilitate the establishment of French guardianship, the colonial government modified the 1917 *pupille de la nation* law, originally designed for the children of fallen soldiers. A November 24, 1943, decree announced the creation of *pupille de la nation Eurasien,* which offered *pupille* status to any Eurasian *métis*—notably excluding Afro-Asian and Indian Asian *métis*—who, regardless of the father's military contribution or vital status, had been physically or morally abandoned by their parents or who "did not receive an education or decent upbringing." The state placed such *pupilles* under the care of a guardian or public authorities on the condition that a medical exam could prove him or her to be of mixed race.[59]

In another subtle legal move in 1942, Governor General Decoux suggested simplifying the procedure for enacting the 1889 law on the divestiture of paternal power. Revealing his true intentions, he referred to it as the divestiture of *maternal* power—not paternal power as the law had originally stated.[60] Jules Brévié Foundation member Rival wrote that mothers who gave their children "insufficient" care could have their parental powers revoked—though he neglected to define "insufficient." Rival advised other colonial administrators to introduce an abuse case to the civil court, cautioning them to limit their proceedings "only to cases where the mother of the child . . . is native," implying that French mothers or fathers should not be prosecuted.[61]

Like their counterparts in the past, Brévié administrators obsessed about the sexuality of Vietnamese, Cambodian, and Lao mothers. "Many [mothers] are prostitutes," who raised their *métis* children in a "profoundly immoral environment" with a "minimum guarantee of morals,"[62] and exposed them to "crass conversations, obscene gestures," and an open sex life.[63] According to colonial administrators, most fatherless *métis* children lived in "terrifying conditions in accordance with the likings and liberties of the successive lovers of their mothers."[64] Those mothers who were "not true prostitutes," according to Brévié Foundation member Father Dupont, "live in concubinage with successive legionnaires, . . . few of them are honest."[65]

Those sympathetic to the protection societies proclaimed the "moral need" to raise Eurasian *métis* as French and "completely shield them from the Annamite milieu."[66] The Society for the Protection of Métis in Annam planned to remove children from the Vietnamese milieu—considered "dangerous for their moral education"—before they could "contract depraved customs."[67] "Take them away from their mothers [*enlever à leur mères*]," the resident superior of Tonkin ordered.[68] The only way "to obtain results that are certain and solid," Lieutenant Colonel Belloc argued, was to "take [*soustraire*] them as early as possible from the influence of the common [*vulgar*] Annamite milieu in which they live."[69] Brévié Foundation member Father Dupont concurred: "It is necessary to snatch [*arracher*] them from their mothers from the age of three."[70] Justifying the removals, Lieutenant Colonel Belloc claimed that the mothers of *métis* "sometimes love their children, but more often they are indifferent."[71]

The Jules Brévié Foundation, along with Tonkin resident superior Rivière, hired French women to act as the maternal allies of indigenous mothers and remove their *métis* children. Two women in particular appear regularly in the archival record. The first was Madame Belloc, the wife of Lieutenant Colonel Belloc. Madame Belloc used her military affiliation, knowledge of troop movements, and access to gossip about sexual liaisons to search for children nine months after soldiers had left the countryside. From her records, it appears that Belloc's searches focused on the Tuyên Quang area and other inland military bases, exactly the area where the military kept soldier's paramours under surveillance, as mentioned in chapter 3. The second French woman, a librarian from Tonkin named Madame Aumont, searched for fatherless *métis* children along the Tonkin coast spanning from Hải Phòng to Ninh Bình province. It was Madame Aumont who removed Robert Henri, his brother, and his sister—the children mentioned at the start of this chapter—from their mother, Nguyễn Thị Khai. As Madame Aumont reported to the resident superior of Tonkin, she deliberately placed apprehended *métis* children in orphanages in discreet locations, where the mothers could not find them.[72] While there are no statistics indicating how many children the French women forcibly removed, the 1944 records of the *métis* institution Maison de Nam Dinh, where Robert's older brother was held, listed all twenty of its wards as having "unknown" mothers—code indicating that the wards had been forcibly removed.[73]

Many mothers refused to relinquish custody of their fatherless *métis* children to the two French women. Such was the case for the Petit family of Tuyên Quang, watched by Madame Belloc. In 1939, Petit left his paramour and their young family to fight in Europe.[74] Madame Belloc took the children—Antoine (four years old), Bernard (six years old), and Alain (seven years old)—even though, as she acknowledged, "the mother is not uninterested in these three children whom she loves and she takes care of."[75]

The military often aided Madame Aumont and Madame Belloc in their searches and removals. In 1940, General Gazin submitted to the resident superior of Tonkin a list of children of former soldiers that the military was tracking for the purpose of removing them and placing them in a Brévié Foundation institution. Among those listed were the children of Nguyên Minh Huyên of Lạng Sơn. In the late 1930s, Minh Huyên lived with Jacques Duval—a French soldier—and gave birth to three children: Emma Anne, Amélie Renée Danielle, and Joseph. Emma was the only child to be recognized by the father before he departed for France in 1939. In 1941, on the advice of General Gazin, authorities removed Emma and Amélie and placed them in one of the institutions run by Notre Dame des Missions in Tonkin.[76]

Few mothers could escape Madame Aumont or Madame Belloc. Some, like Robert Henri's mother, Nguyên Thị Khai, did manage to reclaim their children and temporarily shield them from the authorities. In 1942, when the mayor of Hải Phòng sent Madame Aumont to find children eligible for protection society "scholarships"—that is, placement in protection society institutions and enrollment in French schools—twelve-year-old *métis* Marcel Marchand and his mother fled French authorities.[77]

Some French fathers invoked their "parental powers" to assist the Jules Brévié Foundation in removing children from their Vietnamese mothers.[78] While the colonial government held indigenous mothers—who had given birth to and raised their *métis* children—to strict rules about officially recognizing their children, it did not hold men to similar standards. Instead, the colonial government privileged the parental rights of fathers who had abandoned their children even though they had never legally recognized them.[79]

The phenomenon of fathers' involvement in the removal process indicates a cultural change in the role of fathers who had abandoned *métis* children. Historically, French men involved in extramarital affairs with indigenous women in Indochina were loath to admit to paternity, even if they were willing to pay for their children secretly. During World War II, however, men in this same position took their parental responsibilities seriously—albeit not seriously enough to actually raise their children. Ironically, this newfound interest in fatherhood reveals how little respect these men had for the women who had given birth to their children. Such was the case for Đỗ Thị Liên, who had a twelve-year-old *métisse* daughter, Đỗ Bích Hang, with Monsieur Leclerc, a retired soldier and father to multiple *métis* children with various women. In 1940, Leclerc demanded that authorities remove his *métisse* daughter, whom he abandoned without recognizing. Liên, however, had legally recognized her daughter. A mother's legal recognition should have cemented her rights to her child, but Leclerc's request to remove the daughter whom he had neither recognized nor raised proved sufficient grounds for the Jules Brévié Foundation to proceed with the removal. Authorities eventually removed and placed her with her father, who enrolled her at the École Sainte Marie. Hang, who expressed little interest in her new school, ran away from her father. Eventually, authorities captured the child and confined her to a protection society institution.[80]

In another case, Sergeant Benoit Lemaire abandoned his two-and-a-half-year-old *métis* son in Quy Nhơn after legally recognizing him. In 1943, Lemaire, who was living in Hanoi, asked the Society for the Protection of Métis Children in Huế to take the child from his mother. The mother, he wrote, was of "questionable morals" and had "inculcated in [the child] every possible fault."[81] The mother refused to relinquish custody of the child because, according to Lemaire, she wanted child support money from Lemaire's military pension. Lemaire requested the toddler be removed from his mother, but since Lemaire never intended to take care of his son himself, he requested the child be placed in a "preferable" situation—that is, under the care of nuns or an unmarried Frenchwoman. While it is possible that Lemaire may have been genuinely concerned for his son, the rhetoric in his letter suggests that he was more interested in protecting his pension and taking revenge against his former lover. The Jules Brévié Foundation advised Lemaire to exercise his "paternal power," which afforded him the "absolute right to have the child taken [from the mother] without the mother having the power to oppose."[82] In short, the Jules Brévié Foundation believed that the Lemaire child would be better off living with no parents than under the influence of his Vietnamese mother.

The threat of the Japanese military led mothers to request aid from the Jules Brévié Foundation. In 1940, when the colony was rife with rumors of a Japanese invasion, the widow of a Monsieur Fontaine allowed her children to enter the protection society on the following condition: "I ask that my daughter be returned to me two times per week or per month." It appears that the protection society accepted this condition.[83] In most cases, mothers could visit their children but were forbidden from taking them home, even for holidays.[84] In 1943, the heavy allied bombing of Tonkin that necessitated evacuations prompted mothers to request shelter for their *métis* children.[85] While it is possible that some of these women attempted to shirk the responsibilities of motherhood, others clearly thought they were doing the best for their children, especially given the proliferation of rumors that Japanese soldiers targeted *métis* children. Madame Aumont and Madame Belloc initially appeared to be helpful to such mothers. Aumont offered to place children in protection societies or give monthly stipends and free clothing to nursing mothers.[86]

As the war progressed, the threat of Vietnamese rebel forces led mothers to bring their *métis* children to the protection societies. These *métis* children had often been rejected from their extended families, villages, and Vietnamese society. Madame Aumont genuinely helped some indigenous mothers, such as Madame Bertrand, whose husband was hospitalized for tuberculosis. Madame Bertrand entrusted her thirteen-year-old son, Roger, to a protection society orphanage in Hanoi and requested a French education for her two younger children, aged six and seven. In 1944, after Monsieur Bertrand died, his widow also contracted tuberculosis. The resident superior of Tonkin ordered the children vaccinated and demanded authorities to "separate them from their mother as early as possible and save them from the moral and physical distress in which they find themselves." The colonial government proceeded to assign a guardian to the Bertrand children as per the *pupille Eurasien* law.[87]

Because Jules Brévié Foundation policies were classified as confidential, some mothers who entrusted their *métis* children to the organization may not have known that their maternal rights would be taken away permanently or that they would be permitted to visit their children only occasionally. The annual report of the foundation reveals that mothers demanded the return of the children whom they had handed over to the foundation to protect them from wartime violence.[88] Đỗ Thị Mao, motivated by a broken heart, implored the colonial government to return her children. In the late 1920s, Mao married a Frenchman named Muller, and together they had a son; but in 1930, Muller was repatriated. For the next ten years he neither contacted his wife nor sent money for their child. By 1940, Đỗ Thị Mao, impoverished and living "like a widow," was "obliged" to seek state aid to feed her child or place him in a protection society. The police commissioner summoned Mao and her child to a meeting, which turned out to be a ploy to take the boy and place him in an orphanage in Bắc Ninh. Upon visiting the institution, Đỗ Thị Mao "was amazed with grief." Looking back, she realized that she had given her son up "with great maternal and filial love" after having succumbed to "the shame of having a *métis* child like mine. . . . I was influenced by my neighbors' critiques." This mother's pain over losing her child is reflected in her letter to authorities: "I beg of you to return my son. . . . I can only continue to work with all my force day and night to get my child back."[89] The archival records give no indication that the protection society ever allowed Đỗ Thị Mao to reunite with her child.

REJECTED CHILDREN

A complicated picture of the colony's racial formations emerged out of the actions taken by the Jules Brévié Foundation during World War II. At the turn of the century, high-ranking administrators, who had long-term goals for the colony, had embraced an inclusive understanding of Frenchness that included fatherless *métis* children; yet when put into practice, their lower-ranking colleagues, whose outlook tended to be more myopic, had clung to a narrower vision that excluded fatherless *métis* children. This dynamic of rank and racial perception reversed during World War II. An obsession with increasing the white presence in the colony led high-ranking administrators to embrace an exclusive understanding of the French race that rejected Afro-Asian and Indian-Asian *métis* as well as Eurasian *métis* with health problems. Meanwhile, when put into practice, women who worked for the Jules Brévié Foundation tended to embrace a more expansive vision of Frenchness that included Afro-Asian and Indian-Asian *métis*. The women's view was likely influenced by their work following the French military troops, most of whom were from African colonies. These two dynamics highlight the inconsistency of racial formations over time, within a single period, and even among protection society advocates themselves, who were ostensibly working toward a common goal.

High-ranking Jules Brévié Foundation authorities focused on children's white racial markers. Madame Aumont petitioned removing nine-year-old François Bartoli on grounds that he was "very European in appearance."[90] Authorities debated removing Trần Văn Bao "if he clearly presents the physical characteristics of a Eurasian—if not, leave him with his mother."[91] The Society for Assistance to Franco-Indochinese Children, a satellite organization of the Jules Brévié Foundation, announced that it only accepted *métis* children who were "morally and physically healthy."[92] High-ranking foundation administrators Coedès and Dupont urged administrators to be attentive and to spot "abnormal" children within the target population. Internal Jules Brévié Foundation correspondence indicates that "abnormal" meant developmentally slow, handicapped, or born with birth defects.[93] In 1943, the governor general ordered Brévié Foundation members to "eliminate children of questionable *métissage,* those suffering from rickets, and the mentally disabled."[94] In 1944, Dr. Ravoux, a famous doctor who studied *métis* development, suggested creating a "home for the mentally retarded."[95] In one case, authorities used the potential for immigrating to France as a barometer for institutionalizing children. Those who were unfit to eventually immigrate to France—including the "abnormal, sick, deficient, or very degenerate"—would be left in the Vietnamese milieu, given a Vietnamese education, and steered towards agricultural work;[96] those who were "intellectually or physically deficient" would be sent to religious institutions.[97] When the mother of young Anne Bardot solicited aid, Jules Brévié Foundation president Tissot told her that the board members of the foundation had decided that "the federation [was] not qualified to allot aid to young needy *métisse,*"[98] the word "needy" suggesting physical or emotional problems. These children were to be left with their families and raised as Vietnamese.

High-ranking colonial administrators and the leadership of the Jules Brévié Foundation discouraged lower-ranking administrators from searching for or accepting maternal solicitation for *métis* children of African or Indian parents or even Eurasian *métis* who did not look sufficiently white.[99] A high-ranking administrator wrote that "black *métis* should, without a request expressed to the contrary, be left in the native milieu."[100] R. P. Dupont and George Coedès ordered officials to leave Asian-looking Eurasians with their Vietnamese families to be raised as Vietnamese.[101]

While high-ranking administrators obsessed about whiteness, lower-ranking employees, such as Mesdames Aumont and Belloc, took a very different view of what it meant to be French—one that included children with fathers from all corners of the French empire, including Africa and India. For example, in 1942, the widow of Senegalese soldier Ndoye requested help for daughters Agathe and Monique. Aumont deemed the girls "worthy" and attempted to place them in a Jules Brévié Foundation orphanage, yet higher-ranking foundation officials rejected them and suggested sending them to an orphanage for Vietnamese children.[102] Sympathetic to their case, Aumont placed them with another Senegalese, Sergeant Niang, and provided him with child support.[103] Two years later, the Ndoye sisters approached Aumont requesting more aid. Aumont took the request to her superiors, pleading that she could not consider "leaving these girls by themselves, idle," perhaps alluding to the threat of prostitution or betraying a small measure of empathy.[104] But Brévié Foundation member Rivière denied Aumont's request and directed her to "stop worrying about [the Ndoye sisters]."[105]

A similar disconnect occurred between Aumont and her superiors in the case of Thérèse and Bernard, the illegitimate *métis* children of Senegalese soldier Bonnet, who abandoned them. The children's mother had agreed to place them in a foundation orphanage on the condition that she could live near them. Learning that the children were highly intelligent, Aumont worked hard to place the children in a Brévié orphanage, even choosing an orphanage that would be convenient for the mother. But Brévié Foundation files show a disapproving note written in the margins of their correspondence with Aumont: "They are not Eurasians." Officials eventually convinced Aumont to drop the case, reminding her, "We do not concern ourselves with Hindu children."[106]

THE END OF THE WAR

Wartime fighting and bombings caused l'École des Enfants de Troupe Eurasien military school to be displaced multiple times throughout Indochina, but by the end of winter 1944–1945, the school returned to Dalat. After the liberation of Paris by Allied forces in August 1944, General de Gaulle focused some of Free France's efforts on liberating Indochina from Japan. As a preventive measure, the Japanese military launched a *coup de force* against the French colonial government on the night of March 8, 1945, through the morning of March 9. On the night of the coup, Japanese soldiers encircled l'École des Enfants de Troupe Eurasien, tied up school administers, and forced them at gunpoint to march to their imprisonment. According to later accounts, the students, using the drills learned at school, maintained formation, weapons in hand, while Japanese soldiers took over the school. In the coming weeks, the Japanese military forced students to do hard labor.[107]

During the chaos of the coup, a cadet named Pascal Esposito had secretly slipped out and taken the school pennant, a flag that symbolized "the true soul of the school." Young Pascal folded up the pennant and hid it in the lining of his jacket over the next few months. As allied soldiers came to liberate Indochina, Pascal escaped from the school and joined the ranks of the allied troops, brandishing the pennant to liberate the school. In early 1946, General Leclerc, the commander in chief of the French Far Eastern Troupes, awarded young Pascal the prestigious Croix de Guerre 39–45 and the Medaille Militaire for the symbolic patriotism of his risk. The pennant was returned to its place of honor, and the school reopened.[108]

The World War II occupation of Indochina left colonial officials preoccupied with fears of losing the colony to the Japanese, anticolonial rebels, or indigenous elite. One of the ways that they endeavored to prevent this was to maintain a visible French presence. Fatherless *métis* children who could pass for white French were one solution. The governor general ordered more searches of the countryside for passably white *métis* children to train to be the colony's permanent French population. Jules Brévié Foundation officials grew obsessed with children's white racial features, yet their subordinates interpreted "French" to include children of African and Indian soldiers. The result was conflicting ideas about what it meant to be French.

Yet policies towards fatherless *métis* children would change during the French Indochina War. The French military imported soldiers from all over the empire to defend French colonial rule in Indochina, resulting in a flood of Afro-Asian and Indian Asian *métis* births. As rebel forces strengthened and France negotiated the transfer of sovereignty to indigenous rule, the colony's adult *métis*—who, during the French Indochina War, ran the *métis* protection system—would use the specter of *métis* children left behind to dissuade the French government and French public from pulling out of Vietnam.

5

The Last French Island
in Indochina, 1945–1956

On January 28, 1946, a woman calling herself Nguyễn Thị Ân applied to the newly formed Democratic Republic of Vietnam (DRV) requesting that her French citizenship be annulled and replaced with Vietnamese citizenship. A fatherless Eurasian *métisse* whose legal name was Anne Ramolino, Ân was likely raised by protection societies. In 1933, the colonial courts had granted her French citizenship and a French name; as an adult, however, Ân had come to identify with her Vietnamese heritage. After the DRV was established in 1945, she applied for Vietnamese citizenship and a Vietnamese name. Upon confirming that Ân was proficient in the Vietnamese language and had a history of "good behavior," the president of the People's Committee granted her Vietnamese citizenship.[1]

During the French Indochina War (1946–1954)—in which France attempted to reestablish colonial control over Indochina while the DRV aimed to establish Vietnamese sovereignty—the colony's *métis* population became a potent and bitterly contested political symbol. To the DRV, *métis* like Nguyễn Thị Ân, who had voluntarily turned her back on her father state (France) in favor of her motherland (Vietnam), embodied the revolutionary spirit. To the French colonial government, by contrast, *métis* like Nguyễn Thị Ân were not only a cultural affront but also a political danger, given that they could easily defect and be drawn into the anticolonial movement. The French colonial government and the military continued to support the institutionalization of fatherless *métis* children in protection society orphanages so as to minimize the chances of their rebelling against the colonial government.

During the French Indochina War, a third interest group emerged that was likewise invested in the political symbolism of the colony's *métis* population: Saigon's wealthy and politically influential *métis* community. After World War II, the colonial government transferred the protection system to a civilian administration led by these influential adult *métis* community leaders.[2] The plight of fatherless *métis* children became an important political symbol for their community. Whereas other European powers in the region rescinded claims to their colonies and France signed treaties that gradually transferred sovereignty to the Vietnamese, *métis* leaders spoke against the agreements for fear that if France were to leave, the Vietnamese would punish *métis* for being children of colonizers. In their arguments against decolonization, *métis* leaders used the plight of fatherless *métis* children to criticize Paris for abandoning its colony in the same way that it had abandoned the *métis* children of Frenchmen.

Under the leadership of adult *métis,* the protection societies expanded their searches to include the *métis* children of African, and Indian troops who had been brought in to fight the war. This new policy bespoke an understanding of French identity that represented a significant departure from the Vichy-era obsession with whiteness. During the French Indochina War, French identity came to be understood in terms of one's relationship to the French empire, and as this empire began to slip away, Eurasian, Afro-Asian, and Indian-Asian *métis* children became increasingly potent symbols of France's fading empire. The *métis* protection system administrators of the French Indochina War era were driven by a desire to control and exploit the symbolism of fatherless Eurasian, Afro-Asian, and Indian-Asian children.

RETURN OF THE FRENCH

With the *coup de force* of March 9, 1945, the Japanese military deposed the French colonial administration of Indochina. Two days later, under Japanese direction, Emperor Bảo Đại declared independence and went on to lead a puppet government. The new state, beset with famine among other problems, lasted for only five months before the United States dropped the atomic bombs on Hiroshima and Nagasaki. On August 15, 1945, Emperor Hirohito announced Japan's surrender and, within days, the Việt Minh called for an August Revolution, a quasi-military campaign to fill the power vacuum left by the Japanese. On September 2, 1945, Japan surrendered to the allied forces, and Hồ Chí Minh declared Vietnamese independence under the new DRV government. The French colonial government would never be able to regain complete power in Vietnam. Instead, the DRV rapidly attracted political support, loyalty, and soldiers.

Its early successes notwithstanding, the new DRV government struggled to maintain its independence during the autumn of 1945. Even before Japan had surrendered, the allied powers had decided the fate of postwar Indochina at the July 1945 Potsdam conference. There, the allies agreed to allow European powers to reclaim their Southeast Asian colonies. The agreement stipulated that once Japan surrendered, the Vietnamese region of Indochina would be divided into two at the sixteenth parallel. The northern half was to be occupied by Chinese troops and the southern half by British troops, with the understanding that the French would eventually return to both regions.

A mere week after Hồ declared independence, the Chinese Kuomintang (KMT) forces entered northern Indochina to disarm the Japanese. A few days later, the British military and its 20th Indian Division invaded from the south. On September 23, 1945, French forces returned to Cochinchina and Annam. Meanwhile, the Việt Minh remained in KMT-occupied Tonkin through December 1946, when France took over.[3]

During this period, military troops flooded Indochina. The September 1945 British occupation of Cochinchina introduced a contingent of eighteen hundred Indian and Gurkha troops. France also increased its military presence. In addition to the 8,000 troops already stationed in the colony before 1945, France sent a total of 488,560 troops to Indochina between 1946 and 1954. Due to the tepid metropolitan support for reclaiming the colony, the military conscripted troops from the colonies. The Forces Français d'Extrême Orient was composed of 223,467 troops from the *métropole*, 122,920 troops from Algeria, and 72,833 troops from the French West African and Equatorial African colonies.[4]

Soldiers in Indochina frequently had relationships with Vietnamese women. The French military developed the Bordel Militaire de Campagne (BMC), a prostitution system exclusively for French and colonial military and designed to prevent the proliferation of venereal disease.[5] Yet troops continued to pursue relationships outside the BMC system. In one confirmed instance, Mohammed Ben, Mr. Gffacle, and other Moroccan soldiers deserted the French army and joined Hồ Chí Minh's army. They eventually settled in Sơn Tây (near Hanoi) and started *métis* families with local women.[6]

The increase in black African troops led to a rise in Afro-Asian *métis* births during the Vietnamese revolution—what one French general characterized as an "annoying consequence of miscegenation."[7] Vietnamese discrimination against these soldiers forced some to abandon their children. When the soldier Camara proposed to his pregnant Vietnamese girlfriend, her family and neighbors adamantly refused to allow her to marry an African man. Camara was forced to abandon his girlfriend and their future child when the French military transferred his unit to fight in Algeria. Some African soldiers did marry Vietnamese women and, after the war, brought them back to their respective home countries.[8]

Although the DRV officially opened its arms to *métis,* the central DRV government had little control over the many low-ranking Việt Minh soldiers who regarded *métis* as symbols of French colonialism. In the ethnic struggle and violence that were rife during the war,[9] *métis* were frequently targeted. Việt Minh soldiers arrested *métis* like Pierre Marie Roussel, accusing them of being French colonists.[10] Some soldiers saw them as a "treacherous race" and the "bad seeds" that France had spread across the country.[11] One grim episode would haunt French politics and the historical memory of the war into the twenty-first century: In the early hours of September 24–25, 1945, men disguised in Japanese military uniforms attacked the Cité Heraud, a complex that housed French, *métis,* Vietnamese, African, and Indian families in the Tân Định–Đa Kao area of Saigon. The attackers stormed the Cité Heraud in the early hours, before day broke. They raped women, blindfolded and slaughtered men, and threw the dead bodies into the river. The massacre lasted through daybreak and left almost two hundred people kidnapped, dead, or missing. Many survivors believed the attack had targeted *métis.*[12] Scores of *métis* children were orphaned and later transferred to protection society institutions.[13] While authorities never found the culprits, it is likely that the Bình Xuyên mafia ordered the massacre.[14] The Cité Heraud massacre became a rallying cry among French and *métis* protection activists throughout the rest of the war.[15]

While some low-level rebels targeted *métis* for being the children of Frenchmen, the upper echelons of the DRV officially welcomed *métis* into its new nation. As Frenchmen's sons and daughters who turned against the colonial government, *métis* could serve as powerful propaganda tools. Franco-Cambodian revolutionary fighter Bernard Thach was celebrated as a *métis* who supported the revolutionary cause.[16] Dương Bá Lộc, whose birth name was Jean Moreau, is still honored for his decision to support the Vietnamese revolution. Born in 1925 to a French father and a Vietnamese Italian *métisse,* Lộc was a French citizen. After his father died in the war, his mother petitioned for DRV citizenship and Vietnamese names for her Eurasian children. Jean Moreau became Dương Bá Lộc and joined the Việt Minh.[17] During the French Indochina War, some mothers used the symbolic potential of *métis* to ensure the survival of their children. Such was the case for Lê Văn Bảo, who was a mere toddler during the war. While caught in Việt Minh territory, his mother taught him nationalist songs to perform for Việt Minh soldiers. Entertained, the soldiers left the boy and his mother unpunished.[18]

To encourage *métis* loyalty to the revolutionary cause, the DRV allowed naturalized *métis*—many of whom had become French citizens through the *métis* protection system—to reclaim their Vietnamese citizenship. Applicants forfeited all documents identifying them as French citizens and formally declared their loyalty to the DRV.[19] The DRV followed the French ruling of May 26, 1913, for establishing criteria for *métis* citizenship.[20] Whereas the colonial government ruled on Eurasians who "lived like Frenchmen" and demonstrated French language proficiency, the DRV granted Vietnamese citizenship to *métis* Arnoud Bernard because he "lives like a Vietnamese person" and to Anne Ramolino, whose story opened this chapter, because she "speaks, reads and writes Vietnamese."[21] Some of these Eurasian individuals, including Anne Ramolino, pursued Vietnamese citizenship despite having undergone as many as fifteen years of French enculturation and having enjoyed privileges associated with French citizens in the colony. As the president of a protection society lamented, *métis* who defected to the Vietnamese side clearly "forgot where they came from."[22]

Privileges and enculturation notwithstanding, most *métis* applicants for Vietnamese citizenship had experienced a strong sense of rejection from French society. Henri André Kinh was the unrecognized child of Jean Brossard, namesake of the famous Brossard and Mopin construction company that operated throughout Asia. When Henri was young, his father deserted the family for "a woman of the same race." Although he provided a modicum of financial support for Henri, the father refused to recognize his son. Henri later lamented that by denying paternity, Brossard prevented him from having "a real last name." When Henri received French citizenship as an adult, the colonial government assigned him the surname of André. The substitution of what was typically a first name in place of the father's last name was a common practice by the French government for nonrecognized *métis* children. The "last name" allowed the newly minted French citizens to be recognized as French while serving the double purpose of preventing them from publicly claiming relations to their fathers and coding them as both mixed-race and illegitimate children. To Henri, this was a point of shame. In 1945, an embittered Henri became a citizen of the DRV, forfeiting his and his children's French citizenship. Henri André became Nguyễn Văn Kinh, and his children likewise assumed Vietnamese names.[23]

TRANSFER OF SOVEREIGNTY TO THE VIETNAMESE
AND THE "SACRIFICE" OF THE *MÉTIS*

As the DRV gained in influence and France gradually ceded power to Vietnam, *métis* faced the difficult question of whether to stay in their homeland or migrate to the *métropole*. Many Eurasians from Southeast Asian colonies chose to immigrate to Europe—a safer option, but one that presented the challenges of integrating into metropolitan society and making a living in the metropolitan economy. Other Eurasians chose to remain in Southeast Asia so as to be close to their maternal families. Yet staying there entailed not just serious safety risks but also potential cultural and political disenfranchisement. Leaders of the Eurasian community worried that Eurasians would lose the political and social standing they had once enjoyed due to their European ancestry. Worse yet, *métis* in Vietnam feared that they would be targeted by Vietnamese rebels—a realistic fear given that rebels in Indonesia had killed an estimated twenty thousand Eurasians during the 1945–1949 revolution. On the other hand, *métis* found themselves increasingly shunned by the French, who suspected them of joining anticolonial forces, as Eurasians had done in Indonesia.[24]

For those Eurasians who decided to remain in Southeast Asia, their citizenship status and their role in the local government became a point of contention during the decolonization process. In Burma, the Eurasian community debated integration or separate citizenship status. In 1946, General Aung San promised to integrate Eurasians and include them in planning the postcolonial government. Eurasians, for their part, formed the Anglo-Burman Congress to lobby their cause as Eurasian Burmese within Burma. In Indonesia, the 1949 independence negotiations offered Eurasians a two-year window (1949–1951) to apply for Indonesian citizenship; those who failed to act were Dutch by default. Virginia Thompson estimates that 89 percent of Indonesia's Eurasians remained Dutch citizens. In 1952, there were still ninety-seven thousand Eurasians with Dutch citizenship in Indonesia.[25]

Eurasian groups throughout Southeast Asia considered creating separate Eurasian settlements. Burmese Eurasians discussed settlements in Brazil or the Shan state, in eastern Burma, but they abandoned the idea because they worried that a separate territory would further isolate them. Indonesian Eurasians revived a 1920s plan to create a homeland in New Guinea, following the model of the Jewish homeland in Israel. Eurasian leaders lobbied the Dutch government to retain its claim to New Guinea, as it had for Surinam.

By 1950, the Eurasian population of New Guinea grew from 1,000 to 8,516 and attracted some Eurasians from British Malaya.[26] Indochina's *métis* population mulled over similar questions.

Leaders in the *métis* community wanted to remain in Indochina but feared that France would succumb to decolonization and abandon them in the process. The plight of fatherless *métis* children became a powerful tool for appealing to French sympathies to maintain the colony in Indochina. More so than adults, children could evoke sympathies. Without the French, it was believed, Eurasian children would be neglected or, worse yet, victims of violence.

The *métis* leaders' fears were realized when France gradually transferred sovereignty to the Vietnamese in a series of diplomatic maneuvers. In October 1946, the constitution of the Fourth Republic replaced the French imperial system with the French Union system, modeled after the British Commonwealth. The creation of the French Union transformed the relationship between the *métropole* and its colonies. Former colonies and protectorates became "overseas departments" and "associated states." Local peoples directed their own governments. The new system begot the Indochina Federation, an associated state governed by a high commissioner, replacing the position of governor general.

France, however, retained control over major state issues, and the precise nature of the changes introduced under the French Union was ambiguous. As a result, France renegotiated its sovereignty in Indochina—a move opposed by the colony's *métis* leaders, who feared that France's decreasing sovereignty over Vietnam would threaten their social, political, and economic status in Indochina. In March 1946, Vietnam became a free state within the Indochinese federation—albeit still part of France. The fate of Cochinchina remained disputed, and the French military would remain in Tonkin through 1951. Yet as Hồ Chí Minh negotiated with the French in the first months of 1946, the DRV smuggled arms to southern revolutionaries. That fall, to stop the flow of weapons, the French bombed Hanoi and Hải Phòng. The French Indochina War had begun.

Up until this point, most *métis* leaders had aligned with the colony's racially inclusive political left; however, as colonialism lost support among the political left in France, the colony's *métis* leaders found themselves siding with conservatives who wanted to maintain the empire. To lobby the French state to remain in Vietnam, *métis* leaders formed La Mutuelle des Françaises d'Indochine, the successor to Les Français de l'Indochine.[27] La Mutuelle's members described themselves as a "new race . . . born of a union of the French conqueror and the Annamite 'conquise.' "[28] One member asserted his Vietnamese identity: "I have some Vietnamese blood in my veins; I spoke the language of this country before speaking French."[29] La Mutuelle des Françaises d'Indochine maintained a close relationship with the *métis* protection societies, raising money for orphanages and scholarships to study in France. La Mutuelle leaders William Bazé, Henri Bouchon, and journalist Henry Chavigny de la Chevrotière were also leading administrators in the protection societies. The group allied with *métis* in French India, French Africa, French Guyana, and the Antilles.[30] Members of La Mutuelle described themselves as belonging to part of an empire-wide "family" in which the Eurafricans of Africa and the Eurasians of Indochina were brothers.[31] The group's close relationship with L'Eurafricains, a Senegal-based organization of *métis,* was evidenced by the frequency with which L'Eurafricains published their articles.

The position of *métis* grew uncertain after 1948. Until that date, French moves to give Vietnam control of its domestic affairs had been largely ceremonial. Under the June 5, 1948, Hà Long Bay agreement, France recognized Vietnam as a unified state within the French Union and separate from the other countries of the Indochina Federation. The understanding was codified under the March 1949 Elysée Agreement, which recognized a semiautonomous, noncommunist associated state in the south, known as the State of Vietnam (Việt Nam Quốc Gia), led by Emperor Bảo Đại. Although France created the State of Vietnam as a means of maintaining colonial connections in a new way, *métis* leaders recognized that this transfer of sovereignty marked a new phase of decolonization—and threatened *métis* ambitions in Indochina. Bazé, de la Chevrotière, Henri Bonvicini, and Beziat formed a group called the Union de Défense des Oeuvres Français en Indochine, or UDOFI, to oppose French negotiations with the DRV.[32] Bazé himself was a bit of a hothead: in 1946, at the start of the Fontainebleau talks, he publicly threatened to shoot Hồ Chí Minh if he dared step foot in Saigon.[33] La Mutuelle members accused the French government of neglecting *métis* and French colonialists in their negotiations.[34] Bazé denounced the Elysée Agreement and directed French leaders to "examine [their] conscience" after having "thrown [*métis*] out on the road" during the Elysée negotiations. Eurasians, he wrote, were "massacred for their fidelity to France," but it was "this *mère-patrie* that coldly abandons them" and treats them like "the bastards of the French community."[35]

Under the September 1949 Pau Agreement, Vietnam created a national army and France transferred more domestic power to the State of Vietnam, yet maintained the right to participate in all of the Vietnamese government's decisions. The French public, including La Mutuelle des Français d'Indochine, interpreted the Pau Agreement as foreshadowing the end of French rule. Bazé accused France of ignoring the needs of *métis* and Français d'Indochine and failing to include *métis* representatives in the talks.[36] The *métis,* Bazé wrote, were "conscious of having been sacrificed for a politics of convenience."[37] He also sent what he described as a "moving" telegram to Albert Sarraut, the president of the conference of Pau, who, Bazé lamented, "did not even dignify [La Mutuelle] with a response." Bazé called on the French government to create a national commission to investigate this "particularly tragic" situation.[38] Jean Letourneau, the French overseas minister, assured the president of the Union of Overseas Frenchmen that the French high commissioner of Indochina would "do as much as is in his power . . . to protect the interests of Eurasians."[39] Bazé, however, remained unconvinced.

Major changes in Asia's political landscape changed the nature of the war. The 1949 communist victory in China gave the Việt Minh a strategic edge by ensuring a nonhostile northern border and a steady flow of equipment. The following year, the USSR detonated its first atomic bomb and, along with the new Communist People's Republic of China, recognized the DRV. Only months later, the United States and Great Britain officially recognized the State of Vietnam. In June 1950, North Korean communist forces invaded South Korea, raising the stakes of the Cold War. France used the crisis to appeal to the United States for aid in fighting communist forces, and only six months after the start of the Korean War, France, the United States, Cambodia, Laos, and the State of Vietnam signed a mutual defense accord for Indochina.

The members of La Mutuelle and its allies warned the French government that the fate of *métis* was symbolic of France's imperial future. Eurasians, they wrote, were "the last French island in Indochina,"[40] and they "assured the durability of the French presence" in the region.[41] Bazé declared: "The progressive and unavoidable assimilation of a group of Eurasians by the Vietnamese masses signifies nothing less than the definitive loss of all French influence on Asian soil."[42] He warned that the metropolitan government's treatment of Eurasians was not a problem for Indochina alone but would have consequences for other territories as well, such as French West Africa and Equatorial Africa, given the ubiquity of *métissage*.[43] Disillusioned, Bazé cautioned his Eurafrican colleagues to learn from the "lesson" in Indochina.[44]

As France slowly transferred sovereignty to the State of Vietnam, local tensions increased between supporters of the DRV and those who supported the State of Vietnam. The Việt Minh launched assassination campaigns that targeted journalists who criticized the DRV.[45] The *métis* community lost two important members in these attacks. In July 1950, assassins murdered Henri Bonvicini, a *métis* member of La Mutuelle des Français d'Indochine and editor of *Saigon Presse,* one of the biggest French-language newspapers in the city.[46] Less than six months later, Henri Chavigny de la Chevrotière was also assassinated, allegedly by the Việt Minh.[47] Political violence and what La Mutuelle interpreted as French abandonment created a sense of panic that led to increased calls to remove fatherless *métis* children from the Vietnamese milieu.

CHILD WELFARE IN A TIME OF WAR

During the war, the desire to attract loyal citizens led both the DRV and *métis* protection societies to offer expanded welfare services to mothers and children. Among the many social programs enacted in the early days of the DRV were child-care programs designed to rival those of the French. Beginning in fall 1945, the DRV opened child-care services modeled on American and Soviet programs in rural villages. Homes for Destitute Children (*Nhà nuôi con trẻ nghèo khổ*) provided child care for working women and educated mothers in child rearing and hygiene while teaching them about the revolution.[48] In January 1946, the DRV dissolved the Jules Brévié Foundation and the French-run League for the Protection of Annamite Children, among other French welfare programs in areas under its control.[49] These acts were largely ceremonial, as protection society members disregarded DRV law.

The DRV also published propaganda to prepare children for war. The state-published children's magazine *Thiếu Sinh* urged children to join the military, which needed their "little hands,"[50] and glorified children who sacrificed for the revolution. Articles recounted stories of children who risked their lives to bring rice to revolutionaries or who gave money to the cause. The magazine taught children to use weapons and prepared them for war through battle-themed games.[51]

Once they came of age, children could join DRV paramilitary youth programs. These programs served the dual purpose of indoctrinating participants to become loyal citizens and forming the corpus of a much-needed military. As Anne Raffin shows, DRV youth groups derived their organizational structure, tactics, and rhetoric from French paramilitary youth groups of the Vichy era. DRV military youth groups trained the next generation of soldiers, promoted nationalism, and disciplined young people, many of whom came from impoverished homes and benefited from the DRV's social programs.[52] The most notable groups were the Vệ Út Quyết Tử Thủ Đô (children's guard, literally meaning "defenders who are willing to die for the capital") and the Thanh Niên Xung Phong (youth assault team). The Vệ Út children's guard drew its membership from the population of orphans and children from families who could not afford to feed them.[53] During the August Revolution, they aided the Việt Minh by working as guides, scouts, or communication agents (liên lạc viên), and by gathering intelligence on the French. As Bác Đặng Văn Tích, a former Vệ Út member, recalled as an adult, his comrades were "determined to die in order for the Fatherland to live" (quyết tử để Tổ quốc quyết sinh). The Vệ Út assisted the famous Capital Brigade, which prevented the French from taking Hanoi until February 1947. Thanh Niên Xung Phong developed later in the war to mobilize, support, and help with battle logistics.[54] The programs, policies, and propaganda targeted at mothers and children fostered loyalty to the new DRV government—precisely what the French government and military wanted to prevent.

The French government, for its part, changed the nature and scope of the métis child protection program. From 1939 to 1945, métis care was centralized under the office of the governor general of Indochina and run by the Jules Brévié Foundation. Just as the DRV had closed the Jules Brévié Foundation and other colonial organizations in territories under its control, the colonial government likewise dissolved the foundation so as to eliminate any association with the organization's namesake, who had been part of the Vichy regime after returning to the métropole.[55] The French government reorganized the métis protection system as a civilian charitable organization supported by the state. The métis protection system changed its name several times before December 1950, when it settled on the Federation of Charities for French Children of Indochina (Fédération des Oeuvres de l'Enfance Française d'Indochine, or FOEFI).[56] FOEFI was directed by William Bazé, a former low-ranking Jules Brévié Foundation administrator and member of Bảo Đại's cabinet.[57]

FOEFI's primary objective was to provide institutional child care and an education for "abandoned" and "morally neglected" métis children, with the ultimate goal of forming loyal citizens and "steering them toward France."[58] By 1947, the rate of known métis births was almost on par with the European birth rate in the colony,[59] and given the influx of French and colonial troops during the French Indochina War, the actual métis birthrate was likely much higher. FOEFI sponsored paternity research and rescued "the little abandoned beings" from "malfunctioning parents,"[60] raising them in institutions or providing academic scholarships.[61] Female wards followed educational tracks for secretarial jobs. Male wards attended the colony's French schools or matriculated into the École des Enfants de Troupe; after graduation, they would presumably take prestigious positions as military officers, lawyers, doctors, or businessmen.

Consistent with the practices of previous iterations of protection societies, FOEFI authorities vilified mothers, claiming that children who remained with their mothers were subject to moral turpitude and suffered from poor health.[62] The mothers of *métis,* according to FOEFI, "[did] not know how to love, even for one second." FOEFI presented them as "scheming" women who incorrectly "[assumed] that the act of having a child with a French citizenship who passes through Indochina confers upon them the right . . . to French citizenship." FOEFI went on to accuse indigenous mothers of selling their Eurasian babies and exploiting their "developed [pubescent] girls . . . for ends that we can guess," insinuating that the mothers prostituted their own daughters. Beyond the moral issue, French administrators lamented about wards who had been educated in the protection system and then returned to the Vietnamese milieu: the "vexing negation of the years of efforts towards a human point that is not always easy to obtain"—this "human point" being, of course, the supposed pinnacle of French culture towards which the Eurasian wards had been painstakingly guided. Mothers who had managed to reclaim their *métis* children from FOEFI had, administrators claimed, "[pushed] their 'found' children to the point of rebellion" against the French.[63]

When separating children from their mothers, FOEFI worked closely with L'Assistance Sociale—a French governmental organization that provided assistance in the form of medical care and financial or in-kind aid to the poor and injured, irrespective of their race. L'Assistance Sociale connected single mothers of *métis* children with maternity hospitals; educated them in child care, hygiene, and nutrition; and put them in touch with FOEFI officials. Aware that colonial troops were having sex with local women, L'Assistance Sociale would return to military camps nine months to one year after the military had left a site and offer assistance to the impoverished mothers of the soldiers' young children. Given the aid that L'Assistance Sociale offered and the opportunities that FOEFI promised, it is not surprising that mothers cooperated. Unable to care for her children after her French paramour died, Tra took her two *métis* boys to FOEFI in order to get them a free education.[64]

Other mothers brought their *métis* children to the protection societies to escape wartime hostilities. With the revolution in full force, many *métis* had been rejected by their extended families, villages, and Vietnamese society. FOEFI orphanages protected fatherless *métis* from rebel soldiers. In her memoirs of growing up as a *métisse* in Vietnam, Kim Lefèvre recalls that after her extended family refused to care for her, her uncle, a Việt Minh soldier, forced her mother to send her to a *métis* orphanage, as "the future independent Vietnam will not need these bastard children." With tears in her eyes, Kim's mother handed over the six-year-old girl to an orphanage and bribed an orphanage worker—herself a *métisse*—to look after young Kim. Crying, her mother insisted that she did not want to separate from young Kim and assured her "only Buddha will protect you."[65]

Those mothers who cooperated with FOEFI received child-rearing advice for a few years, after which point their *métis* children entered child-care institutions.[66] FOEFI records note that most mothers "disregarded due process" and attempted to avoid complete separation by demanding their children be placed in institutions that were convenient to visit.[67] FOEFI allowed some women, like the mother of *métis* Lê Văn Bảo, to maintain custody of their children, provided that they fulfilled certain expectations, such as sending their child to French schools or maintaining a French cultural environment.[68]

To "protect" *métis* children from "the whims of the mothers," FOEFI required women who had solicited care to sign a contract that required, among other things, that they not "interfere" with their child's education, that they respect the designated visiting times, and that they not take back their children in the middle of the school year. Mothers who defied these rules were subject to severe penalties. Women who insisted on reclaiming their children were barred from re-enrolling them and forced to reimburse FOEFI for all the expenses incurred in their children's education[69]—though it is unclear whether these women were notified at the time of entrusting their children to FOEFI of just how high the cost would be to reclaim their child. Most of the mothers could not afford the penalties; indeed, many of them had placed their children with FOEFI because they lacked the money to care for them. By making mothers pay the state for room, board, and education in exchange for reclaiming their children, the state effectively put a price on the raising of children, yet never acknowledged the worth of the work these mothers had done to raise their *métis* children before the state took custody of them. The penalty effectively functioned as a form of bureaucratic red tape that denied mothers the ability to reclaim their children.

Authorities separated *métis* children from their mothers even while admitting that the children were "generally happy" living with their families.[70] A caseworker in Laos acknowledged that "the majority of these little ones, not recognized, were taken in and adopted by Lao who do not want to be separated from them," yet authorities removed them nonetheless.[71] In some cases, the directive to remove *métis* children from their mothers came from French fathers or their families in the *métropole*. In 1948, four-year-old Anne-Noelle Hollande's paternal grandmother demanded that the colonial government remove the young girl from her Lao mother and send her to France. Although the police commissioner who investigated the case conceded that the girl was "well taken care of" by her Lao mother and new French stepfather, he acquiesced to the French grandmother's demands.[72] In another case, a Monsieur Lefebvre, who had never recognized his daughter and had no intention of raising her himself, demanded that authorities remove her from her Lao mother and place her in an institution. He also directed authorities to remove the Eurasian daughter of his ex-lover's sister, a child to whom he had no biological relationship.[73]

The changing demographics resulting from the influx of colonial troops during the French Indochina War led FOEFI to open its doors to Afro-Asian and Indian-Asian *métis*.[74] The FOEFI took in children like Denis Clementine Demba, the legally recognized child of a Senegalese soldier named Mbaye and Lê Thị Cam, the latter of whom gave her son a French name "Clementine" that was a loose French translation of his mother's Vietnamese name "Cam."[75] While this change in policy to accept children of African, and Indian parents was likely designed to prevent Afro-Asian, and Indian-Asian *métis* from joining the ranks of rebels, it also reveals a shift in the way that some French officials and protection society authorities understood French identity. To them, French identity was no longer contingent on white French ancestry and French cultural heritage as it had been during the Vichy years. As France fought to keep its colony, French identity became linked to the empire. Afro-Asian, and Indian-Asian children were French on account of having fathers from territories within the French empire. For example, when writing about l'École des Enfants de Troupe, advocates of the *métis* protection program wrote that "since 1945, the 'Eurasian' problem has doubled into an 'AfroAsian' problem," implying that he considered Afro-Asian children to be Eurasian and thus "European."[76]

The contributing factors behind this shift in the understanding of French identity are manifold. Under the 1946 Lamine Gueye law that granted limited French citizenship to all colonized people of the French empire, Africans and Indians were among those considered French citizens. During the Vietnamese Revolution, the influx of African, and Indian troops resulted in a surge in interracial births that neither the French government, FOEFI, nor the French military could afford to ignore. Indeed, many North African soldiers defected to the communist Vietnamese side, married Vietnamese

women, and raised Afro-Asian children.[77] Much of the French openness towards Afro-Asian, and Indian-Asian fatherless *métis* children was fueled by
the desire to prevent the DRV from using them as propaganda symbols.
Moreover, in light of the global condemnation of Fascist racial politics and
the horrors of the Holocaust, French administrators became more self-
critical about their own discriminatory policies. Given that they viewed child
removals as a humanitarian endeavor, denying these services to Afro-Asian
children would be discriminatory.

The most important factor behind the decision to include Afro-Asian
children in the *métis* protection societies was the new leadership of FOEFI.
Before 1945, white French men from the *métropole* ran these societies. These
men, for the most part, lived in the colony only temporarily before returning
to the *métropole,* their true home. As evidenced by pre-1945 protection society rhetoric, they frequently linked French identity to white racial heritage.
FOEFI, however, consisted of members of La Mutuelle des Français
d'Indochine, which included *métis* of all backgrounds, including African, Indian, and Caribbean. They were, therefore, more likely to empathize with
the plight of Afro-Asian children.

However open FOEFI and l'École des Enfants de Troupe were to
children of African, and Indian racial ancestry, FOEFI's—and the French
government's—policies continued to privilege European ancestry over African, or Indian ancestry. Bazé dismissed Afro-Asians as "posing a problem of
a different order."[78] When l'Action Sociale searched the countryside for
fatherless *métis* children, it was Eurasian children it sought. For the most
part, Afro-Asian, and Indian-Asian children entered FOEFI when their
mothers solicited aid. Once in their custody, the protection societies directed
Afro-Asian, and Indian-Asian *métis* boys into l'École des Enfants de Troupe,
indicating that they were destined to become little more than cannon
fodder. In September 1954, after the Geneva Accords dictated the end of
French rule in Vietnam, FOEFI administrators were loath to send Afro-
Asian children to the *métropole* along with Eurasian children. The FOEFI
General Assembly voted instead to send them to Madagascar or other over-
seas territories.[79]

L'ÉCOLE DES ENFANTS DE TROUPE

The March 9, 1945, Japanese *coup de force* wreaked chaos on l'École des Enfants de Troupe Eurasiens, the military school for Eurasians in Dalat. After

the coup, Japanese troops took over the school's barracks and sent the *métis* cadets and school administrators to relocation camps, where French colonial administrators and civilians were imprisoned. The school moved multiple times until April 1946, when it returned to Dalat for good.[80]

In the context of the French Indochina War, the school promised a two-fold benefit for the colony. The students would, upon graduating, serve a mandatory five-year term of military service (in 1948, this term was reduced to two years); in turn, the French government gained "French officers from in-country who understood the language and were acclimated to the conditions of life and the climate," a necessity for fighting the revolutionary army.[81] Second, by providing an education and guaranteed employment to young *métis,* the school forestalled the growth of an impoverished, disgruntled *métis* class and prevented fatherless *métis* children from being assimilated into Vietnamese culture—an eventuality that, in FOEFI's eyes, would "signify the definitive loss of French influence on Asian land." Instead, as Frenchmen, the school's *métis* alumni would "maintain the French presence in Indochina."[82]

As the war continued and the DRV gained in political and military power, l'École des Enfants de Troupe Eurasiens gradually became more racially inclusive. By 1948, the school had abandoned the word "Eurasians" and officially become l'École des Enfants de Troupe, perhaps to reflect its racially open admissions policy, which included the children of African, and Indian soldiers.[83] The school also opened its ranks to Eurasian children who had never been abandoned and whose fathers petitioned their admittance into the school. Yet the Dalat school continued to reject children of two Asian parents. Instead, these children enrolled in one of two Écoles des Enfants de Troupes Indigènes, located in Phủ Lạng Thương and Cap San Jacques.

Many of the cadets came to the school through FOEFI or l'Action Sociale. Given that FOEFI served as a feeding track for *métis* to enter l'École des Enfants de Troupe, the French military clearly had a vested interest in having *métis* removed from their mothers. In April 1946, after l'École des Enfants de Troupe Eurasiens had been moved to Kampong Chhnang, Cambodia, General Leclerc notified FOEFI and local authorities of vacancies at the school and ordered them to search for fifty-seven eligible *métis* children to fill those vacancies. This directive suggests that low enrollment motivated at least some of the decisions by colonial administrators to remove *métis* children from their mothers.[84]

As in the past, French women recruited or forcibly removed children and placed them in the school. Madame Pierson and Mademoiselle Ancian searched the countryside to recruit cadets or alert authorities of children they felt should be removed from their mothers. Olivier Ortoli of Chợ Lớn and Pierre-Martin Roux of Hanoi were among those whom Pierson and Ancian placed at the school. Men who had been appointed as the guardians under governor general Decoux's 1941 interpretation of the 1928 citizenship law (mentioned in chapter 4) also submitted wards. The Lt. Chef Poste Militaire de Bến Lức submitted Herman Lotz and Jean Deneuve, though it is not clear whether their mothers even consented to guardianship or sending their children to Dalat.[85]

Some parents, motivated by the free education and temporary refuge from wartime bombings, willingly enrolled their children in l'École des Enfants de Troupe. The school even permitted those cadets to remain in contact with their families. Cadet Marcel de Lamennais paid regular visits to his mother, who had voluntarily enrolled him.[86] Frequently, parents enrolled several, if not all, of their sons. The school roster included multiple sets of siblings—including half siblings, some of whom met for the first time at the school. The Ferino boys—half brothers who lived with their mothers in Lạng Sơn and Hanoi—likely met for the first time after their mothers enrolled them in the school.[87]

Despite its reputation as a "cul-de-sac" for academics, the school was a "springboard" for a military career,[88] offering older students an education in military science and weapons technology. Promising students studied at the Lycée Yersin, a few kilometers away from the campus of l'École des Enfants de Troupe, while weaker students pursued apprenticeships. Students had the opportunity to earn professional certificates that would enable them to enter specialized fields of the military or, when they finished their service requirements, specialized civilian fields.

If archived school newspapers and present-day alumni blogs are to be trusted, the military school was a good experience for the cadets overall. Students attended school by day, played sports in their free time, and spent their evenings singing or talking about France—ironic given that few, if any, of the cadets had ever been there.[89] Nonetheless, they considered metropolitan France their homeland. Cadets described the school in terms of a family. After being injured at war, one alumnus assured his fellow cadets that he was grateful "to do [his] best for the honor of the grand family that is the school."[90]

Upon graduation, students from l'École des Enfants de Troupe matriculated into the army, serving in military radio, in combat platoons, or as interpreters. While at war, alumni frequently crossed paths, and many wrote letters back to the school newspaper to detail their encounters, trade gossip, or send greetings to their favorite teachers. Most were sent into battle, and one alumnus was awarded a Croix de la Legion d'Honneur.[91]

For all the happy memories at l'École des Enfants de Troupe, some children ran away from the school to return to their mothers and extended family. In 1949, Xavier Duchamp, a successful student, ran away from the school, and authorities never found him.[92] Likewise, Antoine Slovic left the school and returned to his mother. When the colonial police located the boy, his mother insisted on keeping him, telling authorities that he was upset because his grandmother had died. FOEFI authorities doubted her story about the grandmother and ordered her to reimburse the institution for the $4,840 piastres that had been spent on her son's care. Apparently she was unable to pay this debt, since the records indicate that Antoine went back to the institution.[93]

THE END OF THE EMPIRE AND EVACUATION PLANS

During the war, administrators of FOEFI and l'École des Enfants de Troupe were conflicted about how to ensure the wards' safety. For its part, l'École des Enfants de Troupe put off evacuating cadets. Army General Ely predicted that the French military would be in Indochina through 1963 and decided it was "desirable" to keep the *métis* cadets in Indochina "for as long as possible and not slow down [further] recruitment [into l'École des Enfants de Troupes]."[94] FOEFI, for its part, resolved to send its wards to France, even if only temporarily. FOEFI administrators felt that the wards would be better off in France because "[of all the people in the world], the French are the [ones] who [have] the least racial prejudices."[95] Yet FOEFI planned to send only "the best elements" to the *métropole;* "the deficient [wards] will remain in Indochina," where these "inept" wards would be trained "in a profession that will place them above the rest of the people."[96] At the orphanage where *métisse* Kim Lefèvre stayed as a child, the nuns, realizing that they could not send all the wards to France, allowed mothers to reclaim their children. Sadly, when Kim's mother came to the orphanage, Kim did not initially recognize her.[97]

Wartime violence left FOEFI orphanages vulnerable. In 1947, fighting forced FOEFI to evacuate many of its wards from Tonkin to Cochinchina. That same year, FOEFI shipped to France a group of malnourished male and female wards, their hair sheared short to prevent lice and dressed only in raggedy shorts held up by suspenders—neither boys nor girls wore shirts.[98] In 1950, Việt Minh soldiers occupied the Orphelinat Honoré Tissot in Hanoi and the Asile Saint Joseph in Haỉ Phòng.[99] While some of the occupying rebel soldiers were gruff with the orphans, others were tender. Juliette Varenne, the young ward at the Saint Joseph Orphanage whose story opened this book, recalled that the Việt Minh soldiers were fascinated by the young *métis* children. One soldier cried as he told Juliette that she and her little *métisses* friends reminded him of his Eurasian daughter, whom he had been forced to leave behind in France with their French mother after he returned to his home country.[100]

The 1950 and 1951 assassinations of *métis* leaders Henri Bonvicini and Henri Chavigny de la Chevrotière added to the chaos. FOEFI sent wards evacuated from the North to Nha Trang, Saigon, Laos, or l'École des Enfants de Troupe in Dalat. FOEFI considered sending wards from Tonkin to Laos, but it is not clear if that plan ever came to fruition.[101] In Laos, FOEFI fostered cultural enclaves for wards that FOEFI administrator Charles Leca nicknamed "Les Petits Canadas," referencing the former French colony of Quebec, where French culture thrived even in the midst of a dominant culture that was non-French.[102]

In 1951, FOEFI created a Paris delegation to transfer operations and wards to the *métropole*. Most of the children who were sent to France were placed in institutions specifically for FOEFI wards, while others grew up in orphanages throughout the country. When possible, FOEFI reunited wards with fathers previously believed to have disappeared or been killed in World War II.[103] Other children reunited with their extended paternal families. For example, after her father died in battle, a young Eurasian girl named Julia arrived at St. Vincent de Paul orphanage for Eurasians in a suburb of Paris, where she met her father's family for the first time. A witness described the awkward scene that transpired in the cold orphanage parlor when a nun brought Julia in to meet her relatives: "A graying man and two women in black stood up, all three stared at . . . this child who was pushed towards them. The young child stood straight, [her eyes] fixed intensively on the new faces." Unexpectedly, the oldest of the women fell to her knees. She broke down in tears and held the child's arms: "*Ma petite,* I am the mother of your poor father, I am your grandmother." Satisfied with the reunion, the mother superior blessed them: "With the grace of God, the miracle of love is produced. Julia now has a family: she will no longer be alone in life."[104]

FOEFI fought to keep children out of the state welfare system. For those fatherless *métis* children who could not be connected with their paternal families, FOEFI found French families to adopt them. Most families preferred babies and little girls; little boys and older fatherless *métis* children were harder to place. Those who were not adopted stayed in FOEFI or religious institutions. FOEFI also found jobs and marriage partners for older *métis* children. Administrators encouraged most boys to join the military or to become doctors or lawyers. For girls, FOEFI paid for the wedding dress, hope chest, and household start-up money. Some female wards went on to become successful teachers, secretaries, lawyers, or aides to national politicians.[105]

The program, however, was not without problems. Few children were fully fluent in French. FOEFI sent eight children back to Indochina for unstated reasons.[106] Some of the older girls, "tortured by nostalgia for their birth nation," sent distressed letters to their families and implored FOEFI administrators to let them return to Indochina. The administrators admonished the girls for complaining and for representing the organization in a negative light. They reminded the girls that the organization had paid for their trip to France and, to discourage them from returning to Indochina, required wards to buy their own tickets back home, knowing that the girls could never afford to do so.[107]

The year 1954 marked the official end of the French empire in Indochina. That spring, while France negotiated the fates of Indochina and Korea with the United States, the USSR, and Britain, DRV forces attacked the French military at Điện Biên Phủ. That April, in the midst of fighting, France declared the independence of Laos and the Associated State of Vietnam; Cambodia had been independent since the end of 1953. On May 7, 1954, within two weeks of the opening of the Geneva Conference, France surrendered. Among the French casualties of the battle of Điện Biên Phủ were former FOEFI wards who died, disappeared, or were taken hostage.[108]

The Geneva Accords declared Laos and Cambodia neutral states, prohibiting them from aligning with any foreign power, and banned foreign military bases on their soil. The accords mandated a provisional military demarcation along the seventeenth parallel, located in what had been Annam. Never intended to be either a permanent separation or a political boundary, the Geneva Accords appointed the Democratic Republic of Vietnam and the Republic of Vietnam as representatives of the northern and southern zones, respectively, of a single Vietnam and set a referendum for a new national government for 1956.

That September, France transferred powers to the government of Vietnam, and both the DRV and the State of Vietnam permitted citizens three hundred days of free movement between the North and the South before the partition went into effect. At least one million refugees moved between the North and the South.[109] That October, French forces evacuated Hanoi, and the DRV officially took over the capital.

FOEFI closed its offices in North Vietnam, evacuated most of its Lao offices, and sent its wards to Cochinchina with the intention of sending them on to France. The U.S. military and the CIA, anticipating a larger role in postcolonial Vietnam, recruited some of the school's older cadets to work with the U.S. military in Indochina or the United States. The United States valued the *métis* for their bilingual abilities and dual ethnic identity. Newly commissioned Eurasian officers trained in psychological warfare at Fort Bragg, North Carolina, and the armed forces staff college in Norfolk, Virginia. The CIA, for its part, offered to train 150 Eurasian candidates in the United States.[110]

With French forces soon to pull out of Indochina, FOEFI and l'École des Enfants de Troupe abandoned the World War II–era politics of using *métis* children to maintain a French presence in the colony, not to mention their concern about preventing a *métis* revolution. FOEFI's main goal now was to preserve the reputation of the French empire. FOEFI administrators saw *métis* wards as key to the historical memory of this empire—not only for French people but also for Vietnamese, Lao, and Cambodians. A secondary yet important goal was to enable wards to return to Indochina one day. One member wrote: "Our children are destined to return to Indochina and live there."[111] This quote reflects the belief that even after decolonization, *métis* could remain important members of Indochinese society, much like their counterparts had in other former Southeast Asian colonies.

For the time being, FOEFI administrators feared that Indochina was unsafe for *métis* in the immediate postwar era, and implored the French government to include FOEFI wards among its evacuees. Noting the symbolism of *métis*, Bazé warned that *métis* who remained in Vietnam after the French pullout would be an uncomfortable reminder of the failed French empire: "The local population will look at them and say 'Voilà, here's the work of the French.'" As for *métis* who joined the DRV, they would amount to "our worst enemies" as a "propaganda line" against France.[112]

FOEFI resumed its efforts to locate fatherless Eurasian, Afro-Asian, and Indian-Asian children to send to France. William Bazé directed the military to check all the villages where French troops had been stationed for "blonde children with blue eyes" who "run naked in the road and are frequently undernourished." It would be "unconscionable," FOEFI members agreed, to leave Afro-Asians, and Indian-Asians in the Vietnamese environment. Invoking the cliché that indigenous mothers negatively influenced their *métisse* daughters, FOEFI administrators implored the French government to "defend" young girls "against their fickle mothers who, taking them [from FOEFI institutions] . . . risk exposing them to degrading turpitudes." The mothers, administrators warned, would erase "the painstaking years of effort devoted towards the humane goal [of transforming them into French women], which [was] not easy to achieve."[113]

Many of these "beautiful subjects . . . with blonde or chestnut hair" were not eligible for French citizenship because they lacked proof of French paternity. Claiming a "moral duty," a FOEFI administrator explained: "We could not abandon the children, so we took them." Indeed, rumors abounded among the local population that FOEFI was abducting children. Because of the volume of wards migrating from Tonkin to Cochinchina, the orphanages in the South were "crowded to the point of exposing the young ones to dangerous promiscuities." Those wards whom FOEFI considered less desirable were not evacuated but were instead left in South Vietnam, Cambodia, and Laos, where FOEFI administrators maintained offices and orphanages.[114]

FOEFI also experienced a "surge" in mothers reclaiming their children. Suspecting that l'Action Sociale may have forcibly taken children from their mothers and wanting to avoid bad publicity, FOEFI suspended its collaboration with the organization. Nonetheless, FOEFI decided that it was "best not to return children who were admitted by error."[115] George Bazé, brother of FOEFI president William Bazé, remained in Saigon, searching for fatherless *métis* children even after France left.

L'École des Enfants de Troupes waited until the last French forces had left before evacuating its wards. In fall 1955, tensions among the school's older wards were, understandably, high. Cadets were nervous and insecure.[116] Some cadets ran away, only to be arrested by police and returned to the school; other cadets dropped out.[117] Others asked school administrators to permit them to remain in Vietnam with their mothers, despite the academic and professional opportunities that awaited them in France.[118] The French military commander directed the school not to force any children to go to France.[119] This directive, however, would fall on deaf ears.

Mothers attempted to reclaim their children. The decision to send her youngest son to France was very difficult for a Vietnamese widow named Madame Tenner from Thủ Đức. Just months before the final evacuation, she sent her older children, Olivia and Pascal, to France, only to immediately regret her decision. In June 1955, she received a letter from the protection society requesting her consent to "repatriate" her youngest son, Georges, a student at l'École des Enfants de Troupe, to France. She indignantly replied: "I refuse to repatriate my son and ask that he be returned to me." Within a week, the French returned Georges to his mother. Not realizing that Georges had only returned because the school had closed for an academic break, his mother assumed that the French military had complied with her request or had closed the school and evacuated all of the students. In the miscommunication that ensued, the school demanded that she repay the fees spent on Georges' education. Scared and unable to pay, she sent her son back to the school. Eventually, and for unknown reasons—possibly violent behavior on the part of Georges—the mother regained custody of her child and the school struck him from its list of children who were eligible to be evacuated.[120]

Another widow, Mme. Lê Thị Liên, initially agreed to let her only child, Laurent Patrice Bellin, a cadet at l'École des Enfants de Troupe, go to France to live with his paternal grandmother. Mme. Liên was motivated by a desire to respect the Vietnamese tradition of honoring one's mother-in-law. Young Laurent, however, did not share these sentiments. He cried to his mother that he "was not capable" of leaving her and hid from authorities at his maternal grandmother's house. He declared he could "never live far from [his mother] and would risk everything to stay near [her]."[121] Like Mme. Tenner, Mme. Liên regretted her decision to allow her son to be sent to France—a decision she had made out of "supreme sacrifice . . . for his future and for the love of [her] mother-in-law, because [she] also never wanted to separate from [her] son . . . who [was] for [her] the only reason to live." She begged authorities to allow her son to stay because "a separation . . . for me would be inconsolable, and, for my son, an infinite suffering." A mother's pain was evident in her letters: "I feel incapable of continuing the everyday struggle for our existence . . . if I live separate from my child." Her son Laurent Patrice Bellin was scheduled to be evacuated to the *métropole* on December 3, 1955, but two weeks before his scheduled departure date, he ran away from the school, and authorities never found him.[122]

Two other adolescents at the school in Dalat posed discipline problems for administrators. Significantly, both boys had witnessed traumatic custody disputes between their mothers and the French welfare system. The first child was Robert Charles Henri, whose story of twice being forcibly removed from his mother opened chapter 4. In the early 1940s, Robert had posed a particular problem for the Jules Brévié Foundation. His mother, Nguyễn Thị Khai, refused to surrender him to French authorities, but colonial police managed to seize him nonetheless. Khai searched the Tonkin countryside, found her son in a church-run orphanage, and used physical force to reclaim him. Authorities eventually seized the boy again and later claimed his mother never had interest in her children. After being raised in the Jules Brévié Foundation and FOEFI, Robert, like other wards, matriculated into l'École des Enfants de Troupe in September 1949. The following year, Robert's brother attempted to find him, but by this point FOEFI had changed his name from Robert Henri to Charles Robert, possibly to prevent his mother from finding him. (The military would continue to use the name Robert Henri.)[123] Robert was scheduled to depart for France in early December 1955, but like other cadets, he resisted the evacuation and denounced the French government. Robert's teachers at l'École des Enfants de Troupe described him as a very intelligent but "deplorable" student, with frequent disciplinary problems and a "bad spirit." Robert was vehemently anti-French to "the point of being dangerous. . . . [His] presence at the school [was] particularly deadly." The school resolved to discharge him, yet they did not demand a reimbursement given his "family situation"—an allusion to the fact that Robert had effectively been orphaned by the French welfare system.[124] Robert was nonetheless evacuated to France with FOEFI.

Like his classmate Robert Henri, Antoine Slovic, as we have seen, attempted to run away from l'École des Enfants de Troupe in 1949. When authorities found him with his mother, Hồ Thị Linh, they demanded that she reimburse the school for an extravagant sum. Because Ms. Linh could not reimburse the school, Antoine remained in French custody for another seven years. In December 1955, only weeks before Antoine was scheduled to be evacuated to France, he committed a "crime against honor," "violently attacking" school officials and screaming "anti-military and anti-French remarks."[125] According to officials, Antoine had been recruiting classmates to join his rebellion. Shortly before his scheduled departure for France, officials transferred Antoine to a French school in Saigon, where he again denounced the French and refused to leave for France. Because Antoine posed such a disciplinary problem, French officials struck him from the list of students scheduled to go to the *métropole,* and the commander in charge of l'École des Enfants de Troupe abandoned his efforts to make Ms. Linh reimburse the school for its services.[126] Antoine and his mother lost their battle nonetheless. The boy would later show up among the list of fatherless *métis* children whom FOEFI sent to France in the late 1950s.

Like FOEFI, the military continued recruiting Eurasian, Afro-Asian, and Indian-Asian children for l'École des Enfants de Troupe for the 1955–1956 school year, well after evacuation plans were set.[127] FOEFI evacuated most of its *métis* wards by air or by sea. For the most part, the evacuations went smoothly, although one baby died on a March 1956 flight.[128] Understandably, many wards were traumatized. Former FOEFI ward Jacques Maurice recalls that "everything changed in 1954." Nuns at Jacques' orphanage prepared wards for their departure: "They talked about France, a country where there was snow—it fascinated us." Jacques, himself, was initially excited by the idea of traveling to a new country but experienced anguish at the moment of departure. Almost sixty years later, he choked back tears when recalling the incident: "The mothers came to say goodbye to their children. . . . I was with my little brother, and . . . we were the only kids alone. The others were with their mothers. We looked for [our mother], but she never came."[129]

Former FOEFI ward Henri Gaston Moller was consumed by anger and feelings of betrayal for many years after being separated from his mother at a young age. He remembers, "The last image I have of my mother was at the airport. . . . I think neither she nor I cried. I think she forced herself not to cry in order to hide the fact that it was the last time." Years later, he is struck by his ignorance of the significance of the departure: "It didn't really affect me because I thought it was a trip like any other. I got on the plane; it was nice. That's all. I didn't really realize it would be a one-way trip." Upon arriving in France, "I felt something was a bit odd, but that's all. That's when I felt . . . that what she did wasn't right. She should have told me the truth." His sorrow was evident as he continued: "For years and years that idea stayed with me. I have a lot of regrets about it."[130]

Antoine, another former FOEFI ward, also became visibly upset when recalling being removed from his family and uprooted from Vietnam: "They put me in a taxi and informed me it was over. They handcuffed me to prevent me from escaping. . . . They put us in the airplane, just like mail in a postbox." Former FOEFI ward René Pairn recalls, "We weren't told a thing. We were put on a ship the next day, without being told why."[131] FOEFI ward Guy recalls the evacuation from his homeland, which was his first time on an airplane. His ears buzzed and his head ached. Guy sat by the window and gazed mournfully at the "beautiful passage of the Red River tracing a curving line. The houses were miniscule and the countryside resembled colored handkerchiefs." The children sitting around him cried as they left their homeland.[132]

Shortly after FOEFI evacuated its wards, the l'École des Enfants de Troupe also began the transfer process. During the summer of 1955, the French military sent students to Saigon. The military chose the summer vacation to avoid interrupting the students' studies. That fall, the military evacuated students to Béziers, France—the location of a new military school, specifically founded for children from Indochina.[133] On February 2, 1956, the last of the cadets from l'École des Enfants de Troupe in Dalat left Vietnam for France.

Three weeks later, their ship landed in Marseille.[134] Fatherless *métis* children, once pariahs of French colonial society, had by the end of the colonial era ascended to a special place in French politics and French historical memory. FOEFI and French military officials hoped that because of their dual ancestry, *métis* children from Indochina would eventually serve as "elements of reconciliation" between France and the former colonies that had once made up Indochina. Their hope was that given the *métis* wards' maternal ties to Vietnam, Cambodia, and Laos, France could re-create a situation in the former colony similar to that of French Canada, where descendants of Frenchmen maintained strong cultural ties to France.[135]

The context of the French Indochina War for sovereignty led three different actors—the DRV, the French state, and *métis* leaders—to effectively compete over Indochina's *métis* population as a potent symbol of their respective political struggles. For the DRV, *métis* who aligned with the revolutionary state—like Anne Ramolino, whose story opened this chapter—were potential propaganda tools. For the French state, the *métis* population was a symbol of the failures of colonial paternalism; it was for this reason that the French government attempted to correct mistakes and continued to institutionalize fatherless *métis* children and educate them to be loyal to the colonial state. As for FOEFI administrators and Saigon's *métis* leaders, they likewise regarded the *métis* population as emblematic of the empire but took a more tragic view, emphasizing the plight of fatherless *métis* children to symbolize France's abandonment of Indochina as the French ceded political power to Vietnamese officials. Motivated by concern that France would abandon the colony, during the French Indochina War, prominent *métis* adults who led *métis* protection societies continued to uproot fatherless *métis* children.

During this period, the definition of what it meant to be French became significantly more inclusive. As *métis* community leaders in Indochina developed alliances with *métis* groups in French West Africa, the *métis* of Indochina came to define "French" to include Afro-Asian and Indian-Asian children of colonial soldiers. After decolonization, Bazé would continue to evoke the specter of *métis* children left behind in Vietnam to criticize France's role in the Vietnam War and to justify sending children and grandchildren of Frenchmen to France, at times without the consent of their Vietnamese mothers.

6

Victims of Decolonization, 1957–1980

In November 1979, a crowd of Franco-Vietnamese *métis* adults gathered at the French consulate in Ho Chi Minh City, formerly Saigon, to demand that the consulate process paperwork enabling them to go to France. After North and South Vietnam were reunited under the communist Democratic Republic of Vietnam (DRV), Prime Minister Phạm Văn Đồng was rumored to have entered into a verbal agreement with the French government that would allow all Franco-Vietnamese *métis* to immigrate to France. Yet according to the *métis* crowd, although the DRV issued exit visas, it was the French consular officials who stalled the immigration process. Desperate and afraid of the fate that awaited descendants of French colonizers under communist rule, the crowd broke through consulate security and scaled consulate walls, demanding that French officials hear their cases. In the ensuing scuffle, French consulate police fired shots, "brutally hit those who climbed the wall and pushed them around like beasts," broke their bones, and fractured their ribs. As one participant observed drily: the French consulate "showed no philanthropic attitude" towards *métis*.[1]

The 1979 incident marked the culmination of the postcolonial struggle between the French government and FOEFI, in which FOEFI leaders insisted that *métis* children of Frenchmen needed to be saved from Vietnam, while the French government doubted their claim. From 1954 to 1975, FOEFI continued to search for *métis* children and invoked defunct colonial-era laws to justify separating them from their mothers and sending them to France—evidencing the increasingly blurry distinction between colonial and postcolonial eras in Franco-Vietnamese history. While the actions of FOEFI had undeniably helped some mothers protect their children during the war, the organization's policies towards uncooperative mothers raised doubts with the French diplomatic mission in Saigon. To bureaucrats in the French state, FOEFI, with its colonial roots and questionable policies towards mothers, threatened France's reputation with the Vietnamese public and its delicate diplomatic relationship with South Vietnam during the war. On multiple occasions, French bureaucrats attempted to delimit—or even shut down—FOEFI operations in Saigon.

For FOEFI administrators, fatherless *métis* children had long been a literal embodiment of the colonial project—a living proof of its virtues. During the postcolonial period, these same children became a tragic reminder of France's loss of empire. To FOEFI, the metaphor was stark: Paris was abandoning its *métis* children just as it was abandoning its former colony to the communists. FOEFI's ongoing mission to care for *métis* families in the postcolonial era was driven by a desire to protect this symbolically precious population while showcasing its own benevolence, thereby reasserting the legitimacy of the widely discredited colonial project. After the 1954 Geneva Accords ended French rule in Indochina, French colonists, naturalized Vietnamese, *métis* families, and FOEFI wards were "repatriated" to the *métropole* to connect them with French culture and, once the Vietnam War began, to protect them from wartime violence. From 1954 to 1975, FOEFI sent *métis* children, grandchildren, and great-grandchildren from war-torn Vietnam to France. A postcolonial crusade to save these left-behind *métis* children gave meaning to the postcolonial lives of repatriated colonists, FOEFI administrators, and the colonial project. Ironically, for many *métis,* repatriation felt like exile from the only home they knew. In France, *métis* adults were socially displaced and *déclassé*; no longer could they rely on their French heritage to claim a privileged place in society. The *métis* protection system had given meaning to their lives.

MAKING A PLACE FOR CHILDREN OF THE COLONIES IN A POSTCOLONIAL WORLD

The postcolonial history of abandoned *métis* children is tied up with the politics that played out as France's world empire crumbled. From the end of World War II through 1960, colonized people throughout Asia fought or negotiated for independence. The British, Dutch, Belgians, and French all saw their empires fall within the span of only two decades. Soldiers from France's colonial army, many of whom had fathered *métis* children, had returned to their homelands in the French empire disaffected about colonial rule and savvy about revolutionary strategy and theory—in short, ripe for protest against the French government. Anticolonial activists around the world supported—and even collaborated with—revolutionaries from other colonies in other empires. In 1954, just as Vietnam, Cambodia, and Laos became independent, France gave up holdings in Pondicherry and Karaikal, India, and war erupted in Algeria. Over the next two decades, France lost colonies in North Africa, West Africa, and Equatorial Africa.

Former colonies Martinique, Tahiti, New Caledonia, and Réunion remained part of the French Union. In the newly incorporated territories, the French government took on the hefty task of integrating isolated territories with weak local economies and widespread poverty—itself the result of colonialism—into the economy of the French Union. Child removals were one solution to this problem. One case that famously shocked the French public at the beginning of the twenty-first century was the story of orphans from Réunion. From 1963 to 1982, the social services division of the French government systematically transferred impoverished children—often without the consent of either mother or child—from Réunion to orphanages in continental France. The separation had devastating effects on the children, many of whom later suffered from depression or committed suicide.[2]

After the fall of the empire, former French colonists flooded the *métropole,* many of them accompanied by their *métis* families. Although labeled *les rapatriés,* most of the white French, indigenous, and *métis* migrants coming from former colonies had never been to France. Geographically, economically, socially, and psychologically displaced, many of these *rapatriés* struggled to adjust to life in their new home. No longer were they part of the colonial privileged class; they had to find new ways to earn a living in the metropolitan economy—and the French public often scorned them as low-class relics of an inhumane colonial system. A well-known case in French historical memory is that of colonists from Algeria, known by the pejorative moniker *pieds-noirs* (black feet). Given the widespread discrimination against them, the *pieds-noirs* faced difficulties integrating into the metropolitan economy and social sphere. This situation left many *pieds-noirs* resentful towards the French government, which had promised to support them but had instead, in their eyes, abandoned both them and the colony.[3]

Less well known in French historical memory is the case of the *rapatriés* from Indochina. While their return was not as famously difficult as that of the *pieds-noirs,* their numbers were substantial, with between ten thousand and thirty-five thousand migrating from Indochina to France in the late 1950s. The group included white French, Cambodians, Lao, and Vietnamese, but consisted mostly of *métis* families and individuals.[4] The French government provided modest housing in camps on former military bases as well as services to facilitate their integration into metropolitan society, culture, and economy.[5] Yet although they held French citizenship, these new inhabitants were treated more like refugees than migrants. Camp inhabitants, along with soldiers and other *rapatriés* from Indochina, resisted integration and showed symptoms of suffering from *le mal jaune* (literally "yellow sickness"), a longing for life in Indochina.[6]

FOEFI leaders who had migrated to France also expressed a sense of displacement, exile, and longing for the colony. FOEFI leader William Bazé distanced himself from his French heritage, asserting that Vietnam was his "birth country" and Vietnamese his maternal language.[7] He made frequent references to his Vietnamese background and *métis* identity "of four generations"[8]—things he had rarely mentioned while living in Indochina. Bazé speculated ruefully that if French colonialism had not ended so abruptly in 1954, a "vibrant Franco-Vietnamese society would have developed on the Indochinese peninsula." Indeed, during the French Indochina War, FOEFI's goal had been to use wards as the foundation for a creolized society.[9] Instead, as "victims of decolonization"—an expression that FOEFI members frequently used in their documents—they were abruptly uprooted and exiled from their own homeland.[10] The sense of displacement they experienced in France was linked to their *métis* identity. According to FOEFI members, postcolonial life was especially difficult for *métis*, given the racism they faced from the French state as well as from their fellow citizens.[11] Bazé likened the *métis* experience to that of the well-known case of displaced *pieds-noirs* from Algeria.[12] He and other FOEFI members assuaged their sense of alienation by focusing on the fatherless *métis* children who remained in Vietnam, Cambodia, and Laos. This "veritable crusade in favor of [his] underprivileged compatriots" helped FOEFI members—and Bazé in particular—combat the anomie that pervaded the postcolonial landscape.[13]

This sense of displacement and exile among *rapatriés* arriving in France from Indochina was exacerbated by a new—or at least newly visible—interloper in Vietnam, Cambodian, and Lao politics: the United States, which appeared to be taking France's place in the *rapatriés'* homeland. The United States had been involved in Indochina, however minimally, since World War II. During the French Indochina War, the French government had requested U.S. aid to fight the communists. Desperate to prevent Vietnam from falling to communism yet realizing that colonial rule could not be reinstated, the United States had by 1954 financed approximately 80 percent of the war for France and supported anticolonial militias to fight the Việt Minh. After the French surrendered and relinquished colonial claims to Vietnam, the United States supported the rise of the new president, Ngô Đình Diệm, and the Republic of Vietnam, which ruled from Saigon.

Diệm's government made room for *métis* in the new Republic of Vietnam (RVN). In August 1955, following the Geneva Accords, the French government and the Saigon government signed the Franco-Vietnamese Convention on Citizenship, which stipulated the terms of postcolonial nationality. Under the agreement, nonrecognized *métis* adults (over eighteen years old at the time of the convention) who could prove that they had either one French parent or two *métis* parents were automatically French citizens, yet had the option to petition for Vietnamese citizenship. Nonrecognized *métis* minors inherited the citizenship of their father, with the option to change upon reaching adulthood. Article 19 of the convention, however, required all citizenship applicants to consult the RVN, which had the power to delay requests by six months.[14] The implications of this article meant that the RVN held discretionary control over citizenship claims. When FOEFI requested that the Republic of Vietnam agree not to raise objections to nonrecognized *métis* applicants, the latter agreed only to *consider* this request, meaning the citizenship of nonrecognized *métis* was ultimately decided by the RVN.[15]

As in the colonial period, life was difficult for the fatherless *métis* children of Frenchmen who remained in Vietnam. A popular Vietnamese saying from the time reflects the image of *métis* as a perpetual outsider in Vietnamese society: "Eurasians eat sweet potatoes with the skin, dog meat with the fur, and persimmons with the seeds."[16] An operetta titled *Những Đứa Con Lai* (Mixed-Race Children), which debuted in Saigon in 1967, detailed the struggles of the *métisse* daughter of a French plantation owner and her Indian-Vietnamese associate, giving particular attention to the discrimination they faced in the Vietnamese community as a result of their respective skin colors.[17] Laby Camara, an Afro-Asian man who grew up in Laos, recalls Lao children throwing rocks at him and refusing to play with "the child of a black man."[18] Nguyễn Thị Mai, who was conceived out of rape by a white French soldier, had a similar experience: children mocked and ostracized her as the "personification of the enemy race." As an adult, she was rejected by her new husband's family, who attempted to break up the marriage.[19] Few *métis* finished high school, let alone college, and Vietnamese families often forbade their children from marrying them.[20] Some *métis* migrated to France out of a fear that they would be ostracized or targeted for violence. Others feared that the Diệm regime would punish them if they chose to maintain French citizenship.[21]

The popular historical memory of the postcolonial period and the Vietnam War is rife with stories about the sexual assault and forced prostitution of some of the *métisse* daughters of French colonial soldiers. As prostitution and sexual assault are still considered shameful and very personal subjects in both Vietnam and France, only a few *métisse* women have opened up about their experiences. In her memoir, former protection society ward Juliette Varenne recounted multiple experiences of sexual assault by Frenchmen living in South Vietnam who had targeted her for her vulnerability and (to them) exotic appearance.[22] Vietnamese newspapers in the early 1960s ran occasional stories about beautiful underage *métisses* seductresses, who lured men into sexual encounters or had themselves been lured into the sex industry.[23] In one particularly disturbing account, a Eurasian woman named Jeanne was raped and impregnated by a Vietnamese man. In a complicated turn of events, the rapist's parents took the baby from Jeanne. Distraught and vulnerable, she was tricked into prostitution in one of the many illegal brothels set up by the South Vietnamese government and American military to service American soldiers. Jeanne recalls, "I didn't understand what the girls were doing. . . . They forced me to sleep with American [soldiers.]" The violent rapes left her hemorrhaging, but the military doctor who treated her forced her to continue taking customers. Eventually, Jeanne escaped, but she was captured and forced into prostitution a second time. "That night," she recalls, "I knew my life was over."[24] While Jeanne's story—and that of Juliette Varenne—can hardly be used to generalize about the experience of *métisses* women in the postcolonial era, their common themes suggest the particular vulnerability of *métisses* women to sexual assault.

Citing the postcolonial hardships faced by *métis,* FOEFI leaders in France garnered support from key officials in the French administration to bring *métis* children to France in lieu of "leaving them to stagnate [*végéter*] without an education, without an upbringing, and without definite life goals in Vietnam, where there are no means for a future to be guaranteed."[25] Yet hardship was hardly the only factor motivating FOEFI to bring fatherless *métis* children to France. Notes from FOEFI meetings reveal a particular interest in the racial features of the "little innocents who had light complexion, hair, and eyes" and "morphological characteristics that accentuated the French race."[26] Referring to one "pitiful case if there ever was one," FOEFI administrators demanded the expedited removal and repatriation of a boy with "a physique that reveals a striking predominance of the French race."[27]

FOEFI continued to search the South Vietnamese countryside for fatherless *métis* children even after the French departure in 1956, through the end of the Vietnam War in 1975. Most of the children found by FOEFI agents or brought to the FOEFI office in Saigon were unrecognized minors who had not proven their French filiation and thus were ipso facto Vietnamese citizens. Although these children were ineligible for French citizenship until adulthood, per the 1955 convention on citizenship, FOEFI members admitted that they "[had] not stopped lobbying the court of France to . . . declare them French," in order to facilitate FOEFI endeavors to remove the children from their mothers and send them to France.[28] When a court ruling proved impossible, FOEFI justified separating *métis* children from their mothers and declaring itself their legal guardian by resorting to a defunct 1928 decree that offered a means of granting citizenship to individuals with one parent "presumably of the French race" and to the 1943 Eurasian *pupille de la nation* law.[29] The reckless use of colonial-era laws would cause legal problems for *métis* children once they had migrated to France.

MATERNAL CONSENT IN THE POSTCOLONIAL ERA

To convince women to relinquish custody of their children, FOEFI used many colonial-era tactics, including "a lot of tact, a lot of diplomacy, and a lot of efforts of persuasion."[30] Throughout the 1950s and 1960s, the organization continued to employ French women to search for fatherless *métis* children in the areas surrounding former French military camps—where the soldiers' paramours had likely given birth—and to make every effort to convince the mothers of these children to entrust them to FOEFI.[31] FOEFI promised not only to provide children with food, education, and a safe home environment, but also to ultimately give them better lives. Decades later, Tra, mother of FOEFI ward Maurice, recalled that she entrusted her son to FOEFI "to guarantee his future."[32] Given that war was imminent, many mothers welcomed FOEFI offers.

Although FOEFI leaders admonished its agents in the Cambodia office that "it is humanly impossible to obligate a mother to abandon her child . . . if [the child] is of a young age,"[33] rumors abounded that FOEFI was forcibly separating children from their mothers, just as it had during the colonial era.[34] Indeed, notes from FOEFI annual meetings of 1964 and 1965 refer to the removal of "morally abandoned" children, referencing the *métropolitan* 1889 law on the divestiture of parental power for those whose mothers had neither physically abandoned them nor consented to separation.[35] Mothers who refused to relinquish custody—many of whom voiced concerns to FOEFI that their children would be homesick, poorly nourished, or insufficiently cared for[36]—faced further pressure or legal manipulation by FOEFI officials. In an investigation into FOEFI practices, one French inspector found that the organization often used the mothers' ignorance of bureaucratic matters against them. For example, even when a mother had registered the birth of her child but neglected to effect legal parental recognition, FOEFI insisted that she could not claim her parental rights.[37] FOEFI representatives sometimes persuaded the children's paternal French grandparents to write letters to reluctant mothers pressuring them to bring their children to France. In some cases, this appeal to the Vietnamese sense of filial piety worked, but in other cases, mothers "did not even want to hear the paternal branch of the family spoken of."[38]

Once FOEFI had succeeded in obtaining custody of children, it placed them in orphanages in Saigon while waiting to ship them to France—ideally within a year of taking custody of them. At the Saigon orphanages, wards learned French language and culture. Through the education process, FOEFI weeded out undesirable children, including those who proved "too old to be assimilated" into French culture and language. FOEFI also readmitted students, such as Antoine Slovic and Robert Henri (both mentioned in chapter 5), who had either been previously expelled for bad behavior or run away.[39]

The orphanages served the additional purpose of enabling FOEFI authorities to sway indecisive mothers. FOEFI influenced the mothers' architecture of choice, a psychological maneuver to sway decisions by controlling the environment in which the mothers make that choice. FOEFI officials told mothers who could no longer care for their children but were reluctant to send them to France that the orphanages would provide temporary relief until the mother's situation improved. To other leery mothers, FOEFI presented the orphanages in Saigon as a way for them to test their ability to live apart from their children before committing to a full-fledged separation. There is no evidence, however, that FOEFI officials ever intended to return the children.

As part of its strategy, FOEFI required mothers of nonrecognized *métis* children to consent to relinquish future rights over their children at a moment when they and their children were receiving perks from FOEFI. Meanwhile, FOEFI permitted mothers to retain custody of their children and issued them a monthly monetary stipend.[40] These FOEFI-issued stipends had the secondary effect of preventing mothers from skipping town with their children by requiring them to pick up the monthly payments.[41]

To further influence the mothers' architecture of choice, FOEFI required mothers to enroll their children in its schools. The catch was that when the children reached a certain age, they were to be handed over to FOEFI and subsequently sent to France. The assumption was that mothers would develop trust in FOEFI and become so enamored with the French educational system that they would want their children to continue their studies at all costs—even if it meant sending them to France. The children, for their part, would presumably grow attached to their peers and want to travel to France with them. Manipulations aside, the FOEFI plan was not legal. Because such children rarely held French citizenship, even the mothers' consent was insufficient to permit FOEFI to take them to France. Nonetheless, FOEFI authorities used contacts in the French court system to grant children a French *état civil,* under which the children were recognized as French nationals.[42]

FOEFI efforts to coerce mothers to separate from their children were not always successful. The stipend program sometimes backfired on FOEFI, as it "incited mothers to guard [their children] close." FOEFI administrators lamented that *métis* children typically "took the side of their mothers, who are diametrically opposed to the goal of the FOEFI, which is to integrate the little Frenchmen into France and make them French."[43] Dismissing such children as failures (*fruits-secs*), FOEFI cut off all funding for them.[44] FOEFI's loss of interest in any child of whom it could not obtain full custody raises questions as to whether FOEFI's mission was to protect the well-being of children with French ancestry or simply to acquire them.

Mothers who relinquished custody of their *métis* children—whether out of free will or desperation or by coercion or force—were required by FOEFI to sign a contract formalizing the agreement (see appendix). Proclaimed by FOEFI to be a "mandate from mothers,"[45] the contract served as a legal shield with which to protect the organization from mothers who might attempt to reclaim their children and from outside accusations that FOEFI had forcibly removed children. FOEFI offered the contract in both French and Vietnamese, and the organization provided a native Vietnamese speaker to read the contract aloud to illiterate mothers.

Despite FOEFI's efforts to make the contract comprehensible to Vietnamese-speaking and illiterate or semiliterate mothers, the agreement itself remained problematic. For one thing, the multiple spelling mistakes and incorrect diacritics that riddled the Vietnamese version would have presented difficulties for those who were barely literate. Moreover, key parts of the contract were articulated using Chinese-origin words (Hàn Việt)—the equivalent of legalistic terms—that would have been unfamiliar to most anyone lacking higher education. There were also subtle differences between the Vietnamese- and the French-language versions of the agreement that rendered the terms of the French version more stringent. Most obviously, the French version included visual cues, in the form of capital letters, stressing that the contract nullified any future maternal rights, whereas the Vietnamese version did not. The French version also included the phrase "without any exception," left out of the Vietnamese version, thus giving mothers who depended on the Vietnamese version the sense that it might be possible to obtain permission to reclaim their children. Moreover, unlike the French version, the Vietnamese version did not make clear that mothers would have to reimburse FOEFI for its expenses *before* FOEFI returned their child. Finally, whereas the last line of the French contract included a stipulation concerning employment, this is left out of the Vietnamese translation, which ends with a stipulation about finishing school.[46] The omission of the reference to post-schooling employment may well have led mothers to assume that their children would be returned to them upon finishing school and reaching adulthood. In short, those who depended on the Vietnamese version of the contract—likely many mothers of *métis* children— would have understood the terms of the agreement to be much more lenient than they actually were.

Even the French-language version of the contract was problematic. Although designed to clarify and codify the mother-child relationship, the contract conspicuously included important ambiguities and omissions that benefited FOEFI. For example, it did not specify how much money mothers would have to pay to retrieve their children, nor did it explain the 1943 guardian law or acknowledge that it was a now defunct relic of the colonial era. It also failed to state whether families would reunite once wards reached adulthood—and, if so, how this would be achieved. Finally, the contract failed to specify who would be responsible for the cost of sending the wards back to Vietnam.

Even after signing the contract, some mothers refused to send their children to France.[47] FOEFI administrators admitted that "[the contract] notwithstanding, mothers always oppose their [child's] evacuation to France."[48] FOEFI further acknowledged that "these mothers find themselves torn between the consideration of the heart and that of reason—they often hesitate to admit their children [to FOEFI]. The distance that will separate the two will scare them."[49] Although FOEFI's official policy was to return children to mothers who had petitioned to reclaim them "if that is their desire,"[50] that was hardly the practice. In fact, the organization often blocked mothers' efforts to reclaim their children. A 1965 letter written from the FOEFI office in Saigon to the Paris office begged for a quick "repatriation" of "these children *who are our pupils*," in order to prevent their mothers from reclaiming them while they were held in Saigon waiting to be sent to France.[51]

The ethics of the contract did not go unquestioned. When put to the task of reviewing FOEFI in 1965, the French inspector general of public health, Nafissa Sid Cara, criticized the severity of the contract's terms. She doubted the necessity of requiring mothers to relinquish all rights over their children and denounced the "ransom," which "seems heavy for mothers" to reclaim their children.[52] Yet as it turned out, Sid Cara had little influence on the contract itself, and FOEFI continued to use it. Decades later, when reading over the contract that his mother had signed, former FOEFI ward Henri Gaston held back tears, musing, "This proves my mother didn't have a choice."[53]

Some mothers insisted on reclaiming their children despite the formidable bureaucratic obstacles.[54] In a remarkable display of legal acumen, the mother of Henriette Ferry filed to have young Henriette naturalized as Vietnamese, to block FOEFI from taking her child to France. *Métisse* child Sylvie Lemont herself requested Vietnamese citizenship for the same reason.[55] The fact that mothers and children resorted to an alternative legal process—official Vietnamese naturalization—itself evidences the extent to which FOEFI disregarded maternal rights. In a unique situation, the mother of Pierre-Michel Poisson managed to find money to repay FOEFI and have her son sent home to Saigon.[56] Yet Poisson's case seems to have been an anomaly, as FOEFI records do not include any other cases of mothers who were able to pay back the fee required to have their children returned to Saigon. While FOEFI administrators would cite the Poisson case as proof of their respect for maternal rights, it was the exception to the rule that the maternal rights of well-to-do mothers were privileged over those of impoverished mothers.

FOEFI WARDS IN FRANCE

With the end of the French empire in Asia, boatloads of soldiers, former French *colons* (many of whom had never set foot in the *métropole*), Vietnamese, and FOEFI's *métis* wards, among others, immigrated to France. The trip to France was long, sometimes lasting weeks. Storms tossed the boats around like toys, leaving former FOEFI ward Roger Maurice with vivid memories of seasickness. But as Roger's older brother, Jacques, recalled, most wards managed to adapt to life aboard the ship. Jacques, Roger, and the other wards grew attached to the French soldiers on board and constructed a new reality to cope with the trauma of being uprooted: "It all happened so naturally. . . .

Each of us chose a soldier and pretended he was our father since most of us had French soldiers as fathers," Jacques recalled. Speaking separately about the episode, his brother Roger grew teary eyed when he recalled the relationship he had formed with his respective French soldier "because I really needed a father." He was heartbroken when, after arriving in Marseille that cold November day in 1955, the passengers alighted from the ship and went their separate ways. Roger never saw his pretend father again.[57]

When the wards arrived in France, FOEFI connected children with their long-lost biological fathers or paternal families whenever possible. Indeed, more broadly, reuniting separated families had come to be seen as an essential way to reconstruct post–World War II society and ensure the survival of European civilization.[58] To many of the *métis* wards arriving from Indochina, however, their fathers and paternal families were strangers. "Bonjour Monsieur" were the cold first words that former FOEFI ward Yên Noelle uttered upon meeting the father she had never known. Her formality reduced her father to tears.[59] A few mothers who found ways to travel to France, like the mother of René Robert, managed to visit their children.[60] The mother of Clement Maupit even managed to finance her own vacation to Nantes to spend the 1957 Christmas vacation with her son.[61]

Wards who could not be reunited with their French families were, for the most part, sent to orphanages in France, though a handful were sent to orphanages in Switzerland, England, and Monaco. Some children of African soldiers were sent to Senegal, Cameroun, or Morocco.[62] Most of the orphanages in France were FOEFI-run institutions for *métis* children, although a few children ended up alongside white French children in orphanages run by the French state. Former FOEFI ward René Pairn remembers being so petrified of his new surroundings that he refused to be separated for even a moment from other *métis* children for fear of getting lost in this strange land.[63]

In France, FOEFI deliberately separated those siblings who could not be reunited with their paternal families. Recalling his arrival in France, former ward Jacques Maurice—who journeyed to France with his brother, Roger reflected on the trauma of separation: "I still hold a grudge against them. Up until then, I still had a tie to my family, my little brother." Fighting back tears while recalling the events of some sixty years ago, he continued: "And they tore him from me. It was really hard . . . we didn't understand. They really tore us apart. . . . We were holding on tightly. They pulled us apart without explaining why." FOEFI sent Jacques to an orphanage in northern France and Roger to the southwest of France. The separation pierced both boys' psyches. "I was in a black hole," Jacques recalled. As for Roger, he wrote simply: "That day, a little boy died." For years, Roger insisted to the nuns that he had a brother named "Jacky," but his requests to see Jacky fell on deaf ears. A decade later, the brothers met again as teenagers, but having been raised separately, they were strangers and could no longer relate to each other. Other wards had similarly traumatic experiences. Facing questions about missing siblings, orphanage administrators at times refused to disclose any information or even denied the siblings' existence altogether. Former FOEFI ward Yên Noelle was too young to remember the exact details of her life in Vietnam, but she recalled having a sister and remembered her name. When she asked FOEFI officials—and later her father—where her sister was taken, they "kept telling me I was crazy, that I never had a sister, but I kept pushing." Years later, she learned that her memory of a sister was accurate, but it was too late; her sister had been put up for adoption.[64]

For the most part, FOEFI permitted communication between children and mothers who cooperated with FOEFI policy. George Bazé and Huynh Van Quy—FOEFI's Saigon administrators—remained accessible to answer questions from concerned mothers.[65] William Bazé, George's brother and the director of FOEFI headquarters in Paris, claimed to personally respond in Vietnamese to all letters from mothers who inquired about their children.[66] FOEFI administrators in France regularly sent mothers photos of children playing, eating, or studying. These photos functioned not only to assuage mothers' fears about the well-being of their faraway children but also to help persuade other mothers who might be reluctant to send their own children abroad.[67] As many mothers were illiterate, they hired public writers to write letters to their children.[68] Lucky children received letters and gifts from their mothers. In 1960, the mother of Laurent Martin David even sent him 150,000 "old Francs."[69] Sadly, not all correspondences made it to the wards. Based on the experiences of former wards who did not receive letters despite their mothers' insistence that they had written regularly, or who discovered undelivered letters in later years, it appears that FOEFI may have withheld letters. In the case of one child, it was not until he was an adult and his mother had passed away that he learned that she had tried to make contact with him in France, sending letters and hand-sewn clothing that were never delivered.[70]

At the orphanages, state doctors performed medical exams and x-rayed the *métis* wards' bones to determine their age. Many children had health problems. They had arrived in France frail and weak; some were recovering from polio infections; and many suffered from malaria, bronchitis, and stomach problems. One ward even had leprosy, though he was declared noncontagious.[71]

In the early 1960s, FOEFI allowed anthropologists to study its *métis* wards. As an adult, former ward René Pairn fought back tears when recalling the anthropologists: "They met with us one by one. . . . They measured our noses, our ears, all they could." Pairn looked down as he continued quietly: "That really left a mark on us. We were truly humiliated. Frankly, we were treated like livestock—that's exactly the word for it. We were no longer treated like human beings."[72]

FOEFI pursued a multifaceted program to assimilate wards into French society. With few exceptions, FOEFI changed the wards' names from Vietnamese to French, or changed the order of their French names (for example, René Robert became Robert René, and Jacques Marie Jean Charles Alain's name appears in multiple combinations in the documents).[73] The motivations behind the name reversals were complicated and not entirely clear. In some cases, they may have been intended to prevent mothers from Asia from tracing the location of their *métis* child. In other cases, they may actually have been intended to correct reversals made in Vietnam, thereby facilitating efforts to reunite children with their paternal families. For example, in Vietnam during the colonial period, the *métis* child of a man named Henri François was registered as François Henri. When the boy was sent to France in 1957, FOEFI corrected the child's name to Henri François, possibly to reconnect him with his father.[74]

Under William Bazé's leadership, the postcolonial FOEFI in France made every effort to cultivate in its charges a *métis* identity that was sufficiently French to pass as metropolitan. Although FOEFI purported to "raise wards to have a double love for France and their country of origin,"[75] Vietnamese language and cultural practices were forbidden in orphanages. This policy was likely to ensure that wards graduated speaking flawless French, but for some wards, this was particularly traumatic, as it was through speaking Vietnamese that they accessed memories of their mothers. Former ward Jacques Maurice recalled, "We had been uprooted and needed to maintain our Vietnamese side," but "they tried to make us forget [it]." He explained, "We were French by culture, but we had all had an idealized Vietnamese mother whom we never knew or saw again, but whom we kept inside of us. The language allowed us to maintain our culture; otherwise you forget."[76] Many wards secretly spoke a Franco-Vietnamese pidgin that, as adults, they referred to as "FOEFI language," or "Foefien."[77] At the Vouvray orphanage, wards caught speaking Vietnamese were fined; though the amount was negligible, to the young children it seemed that "what little we had [the orphanage director] would take from us."[78] FOEFI did, however, maintain certain elements of Vietnamese culture, serving a Franco-Vietnamese diet that included fried fish and rice. The hybrid diet is noteworthy considering how essential French food was to the colonial population in Vietnam.[79]

FOEFI wards had many of the same experiences as middle-class French children—and sometimes more. Within months of their arrival in France, FOEFI facilitated their conversion to Catholicism, bringing them up to speed in a quick succession of sacraments. In 1962, soon after young Philippe Banar had arrived in France, he received three sacraments—baptism, communion, and confirmation—within a span of only three months.[80] Wards were well educated: both boys and girls attended prestigious grade schools and universities, including France's elite Écoles Superieurs, and a handful of wards would go on to become doctors and lawyers. Teenage wards who had arrived in France too late to be admitted to the French school system entered into apprentice positions.[81] Authorities placed wards on local sports teams and encouraged friendships with local French children. In the winter, the children went skiing—a privilege unknown to most children growing up in France during the 1960s and 1970s—and in the summer they went to summer camps (*colonies de vacances*) at French beaches or in the mountains of Switzerland, Germany, Spain, or Italy.[82] Many former wards have fond memories of their time in FOEFI orphanages and expressed a sense of gratitude for the opportunities they enjoyed as FOEFI wards.[83] As former ward Jacques Maurice explained, "It wouldn't be fair to say our childhoods were unhappy."[84]

That said, some locals, like those in the town of Rilly, were openly hostile to *métis* wards.[85] Some former wards recalled being treated as outcasts. "To be blunt," Henri Gaston Moller remembers, "they treated us like bastard children." Many of the *métis* refused to be intimidated. As one recalled defiantly, "We didn't want to mix with those who treated us like gooks."[86]

Marriage to French men and women was an important part of FOEFI's "policy of assimilation" and "integration into the French nation."[87] Indeed, sexual naturalization had been a key part of French strategies to assimilate immigrants since the early twentieth century.[88] While there were a handful of intra-FOEFI marriages, FOEFI encouraged "*beaux mariages,*" meaning those between FOEFI wards and metropolitan French,[89] and discouraged wards from marrying other *métis* wards, whom they likened to siblings.[90] Of course, considering that FOEFI had taken pains to separate blood relatives, fellow wards who did marry were not actually committing incest. Administrators kept a strict watch over female wards' sexuality, even monitoring their menstrual cycles.[91] The notes of FOEFI meetings reveal a certain concern about raising female wards to become good wives.[92] One man who had married a *métisse* woman thanked FOEFI for raising female wards to be such good wives: "I hope with all my heart that other men are also as happy as I am in their lives, thanks to your work preparing good mothers."[93]

To facilitate marriages, FOEFI leaders assumed the interpersonal duties customarily reserved for parents. Representatives of FOEFI contacted the parents of prospective spouses to calm any fears of interracial marriage and to provide details on the wards' backgrounds, including the context within which they had migrated to France. Such discussions sometimes proved to be pivotal; many French families broke off their child's engagement as soon as they had been informed about the background of the prospective *métis* spouse. In cases in which families decided to proceed with the wedding, FOEFI sent a representative to the ceremony and offered the new couple a monetary gift—in 1975, wards received 500 francs—to help them start their family.[94] Reflecting back on his work with *métis* wards, William Bazé boasted that he married off his wards to "the best families."[95]

Not all FOEFI wards had positive experiences integrating into French society, and some children expressed a desire to return to Vietnam. FOEFI, however, set up bureaucratic red tape to impede their efforts to return. Wards who wanted to return had to buy their own airplane tickets—surely an impossible task for a young child—and agree to terms prohibiting them from returning to France if they changed their minds, an implicit threat. Jacques Maurice, the boy who had been brutally separated from his brother, immediately began calculating ways to escape FOEFI. He and a group of boys ran away. Most of the boys in his group wanted to find a way back to Saigon, but Jacques wanted to go to Marseille, where the brother he missed so much had been sent. The boys never made it to Saigon, and Jacques would not see his brother for years.[96]

Boys who resisted FOEFI assimilation programs were sent to the French juvenile court system or the military,[97] and the most serious cases were shipped back to Saigon. In 1954, FOEFI repatriated seven boys almost immediately after their arrival in Marseille; one was subsequently institutionalized in a psychiatric hospital.[98] In 1957, wards at the Foyer de Semblançay orphanage rebelled against authorities. The uprising was serious enough for officials to call in the local gendarmerie to restore order. FOEFI leaders acknowledged that the wards were suffering from the psychological trauma of having been uprooted. FOEFI returned the boys to Saigon—not out of sympathy but because they were too much trouble to care for.[99] Given the rebellious nature of youth culture in France, it is remarkable that so few of the teenage wards joined France's 1968 student protest movements. Reflecting on this phenomenon,

William Bazé chalked up their obedience to FOEFI's continual insistence that wards show gratitude to the French state for taking them out of Vietnam and bringing them to France.[100]

The wards who did manage to adjust to life in France still faced problems of bureaucratic integration. Upon maturing out of FOEFI, many wards discovered that they had a substandard—or nonexistent—*état civil*, meaning they were not French citizens. The problem stemmed from FOEFI's practice of invoking colonial-era laws to remove children who were actually Vietnamese nationals.[101] Up until 1965, French courts cooperated with FOEFI to employ a liberal interpretation of the 1928 law allowing children with one parent "presumably of French race" to become French nationals.[102] In 1965, however, FOEFI's shortcut ended when the Bureau of Nationality and the Ministry of Work and Health "showed resistance," and the Ministry of Justice declared that the 1928 law had been rendered inapplicable by the 1955 convention on citizenship; all nationality cases that had invoked the 1928 law were henceforth null and void. French law therefore considered FOEFI applicants "foreign" and barred them from soliciting naturalization.[103] The ruling complicated the status of FOEFI wards who had been naturalized prior to the 1965 ruling. For example, Claude Lotz had been awarded French citizenship in 1960 through the 1928 ruling; just five years later, French courts rescinded his French nationality.[104] As a result of the change, many former FOEFI wards could not obtain French identity cards or passports.[105] William Bazé denounced the situation as "an unacceptable form of racism" and authorities' actions as "vexing and racist measures."[106] Some former FOEFI wards continued to face citizenship problems through 2013.[107]

THE VIETNAM WAR AND FOEFI UNDER SIEGE

The fate of FOEFI operations in Vietnam during the Vietnam War was entangled in the complex history of France's role in facilitating negotiations between the two Vietnams. Recently divested of its empire, France aimed to reestablish some of its prominence in Southeast Asia as well as stem American presence in the region. In hopes of limiting American influence over Lao politics, Paris played an integral part in the 1962 Geneva Accords, which declared Laos a neutral state, independent of outside influences. Under the accords, France was also required to pull its air base from Seno, Laos. FOEFI stepped in to evacuate the base's nearly two hundred *métis* children, who had been abandoned by their French military fathers.[108]

Meanwhile, the relationship between U.S. diplomats and President Ngô Đình Diệm of South Vietnam deteriorated. After a series of violent police crackdowns in 1963, Washington advised Diệm to pursue a softer policy towards Buddhist dissidents and loosen its grip on civilians. But Diệm refused to heed the warnings. Instead, Washington's domineering attitude only pushed him further from the American camp, and Diệm and his brother Ngô Đình Nhu were rumored to be considering negotiating with the DRV. Indeed, some of those rumors were spread by Ngô Đình Nhu himself.[109]

For its part, Hanoi's openness—however minimal—towards talks with Diệm was inspired by the potential for creating a neutralization pact in South Vietnam that would be based on the model used in Laos.[110] French ambassador Roger Lalouette was rumored to have facilitated Ngô Đình Nhu's spring and summer 1963 secret negotiations with the DRV.[111] On August 29, 1963, French president Charles de Gaulle publicly called for a unified, neutral Vietnam that would be independent of foreign powers, namely the United States, and called on the DRV and the RVN to negotiate unification. Diệm ultimately dismissed de Gaulle's call for neutralization, and the French-led negotiations fell through.[112] France's reputation suffered as a result of its apparent willingness to ally with the DRV, and Saigon's student population protested at the French embassy all through the fall.[113]

Even before the 1963 protests, Paris had been distancing itself from FOEFI. For one thing, French officials began to question whether French *métis* even remained in Vietnam. In 1959 and again in 1962, officials accused FOEFI of inflating the number of *métis* in Indochina, leading the French Ministry of Finances to limit *métis* repatriations.[114] In 1963, the French government defunded the FOEFI program to send South Vietnamese *métis* children to France.[115] That fall, Bazé called in a favor from the Vichy-era former governor general of Indochina, General Georges Catroux, to appeal to de Gaulle for financial support for FOEFI and to call for an investigation of the fatherless *métis* children remaining in South Vietnam.[116] Despite these efforts, it would be another five years before the French government resumed financial aid to FOEFI.

Given the turmoil erupting in Saigon that summer of 1963, Washington grew frustrated with its inability to control Diệm and anxious about the potential relationship with the National Liberation Front and the DRV that the French were rumored to be orchestrating. Although the U.S. government publicly supported the Diệm regime, by late August the State Department wanted Ngô Đình Nhu out and made its support for Diệm contingent upon Nhu's departure.[117] Kennedy encouraged Army of the Republic of Vietnam (ARVN) commanders to overthrow Diệm and promised to support a new regime. On November 2, 1963, both Ngô Đinh Diệm and his brother were assassinated by a group of generals. While Kennedy had encouraged a change of power, the United States exerted no operational control over the coup or the assassinations.

France's reputation in Saigon was so bad that during the post-coup struggle for power, accusations of working with the French cost South Vietnamese politicians their careers. Indeed, during fall 1963, General Nguyễn Khánh spread rumors that General Dường Văn Minh, who had taken power after the coup, was working with Paris to reach a deal with Hanoi to install a pro-communist government in the South. Adding to the paranoia, in January 1964 de Gaulle publicly called for the United States to withdraw from Vietnam.[118] Shortly thereafter, General Khánh and his military junta launched a coup against Minh. That summer, protests against France for supposedly supporting the DRV erupted again throughout Saigon, with crowds hanging effigies of both Hồ Chí Minh and President de Gaulle. At the end of July, protesters demonstrated at the French embassy in Saigon.[119]

Just a week later, on August 7, 1964, U.S. President Lyndon Johnson went before the Senate to announce that U.S. ships had been fired on in the Gulf of Tonkin. In giving overwhelming support for the Gulf of Tonkin Resolution, the U.S. Senate gave Johnson the political capital he needed to commit forces to Vietnam. In February 1965, U.S. troops flooded into South Vietnam, marking the beginning of the "Americanization" of the war.

As the French government could not afford any scandals, Paris slashed FOEFI operations in Vietnam. By fall 1964, FOEFI orphanages in Saigon had developed a backlog of more than 350 children, many of whom had been waiting nearly two years to migrate to France. FOEFI administrators in Saigon made emotional appeals to the French government to reinstate funds. *Métis* boys growing up in Vietnamese culture, FOEFI administrators claimed, were "snatched up by idleness and bad acquaintances," while girls would "fall prey to unhealthy temptations." FOEFI cited an example of a mother who reclaimed her two *métisses* daughters reportedly in order to sell them.[120]

In the spring of 1965, Franco-RVN relations grew even more tense. Saigon was tired of French calls for diplomatic solutions with the DRV.[121] And when France failed to send representatives to the Southeast Asia Treaty Organization meeting, Saigon interpreted this move as an insult to the Republic of Vietnam's sovereignty. On June 24, 1965, Saigon officially cut diplomatic relations with France.[122]

In 1965, as Franco–South Vietnamese diplomatic relations were coming to an end, FOEFI was dealt another blow. The French government enlisted

Inspector General of Public Health Nafissa Sid Cara and the French consul general in Saigon, Charles Lambroschini, to investigate the workings of the FOEFI administration and orphanages. The resulting report was damning. The authors denounced FOEFI as "an *oeuvre* of the past; it is a manifestation of an outdated colonialism that is struggling to survive." For both FOEFI and the inspectors, the act of removing fatherless *métis* children was a public reminder of French colonialism. However, whereas that reminder was a source of embarrassment for the French government, it was a point of pride for FOEFI, which saw it as evidence of colonial benevolence.

The report challenged FOEFI's claims of having only the wards' and mothers' best interests in mind and charged FOEFI with "intolerable paternalism" and actions that would "only increase the mothers'—and maybe children's—resentment [towards France]." They warned that the French consulate and the French government would be held responsible for FOEFI's actions and advised the Ministry of Public Health and Population to shut down the organization.[123] Among other things, the report cast doubt on FOEFI claims about fatherless French *métis* children being left behind— FOEFI's entire raison d'être. The authors suspected that the younger *métis* wards were not the children of Frenchmen, suggesting that their fathers were instead American soldiers. Moreover, as the report pointed out, FOEFI money was supporting wards well into their adulthood, with some as old as twenty-six at the time of the investigation.[124]

Consul General Lambroschini and Inspector General Sid Cara expressed concern about the way FOEFI obtained consent from mothers. First, they called into question FOEFI's use of the term "abandonment," which, they observed, was "used in the largest possible sense that it can encompass." They also criticized FOEFI for "using persuasion to obtain the mothers' sacrifice." The authors pointed out that mothers who signed the contract were likely unaware that the juridical texts "could play against them," given that few mothers had an education, much less a legal one. Moreover, they wrote, the ambiguities of the contract would lead mothers to incorrectly assume that once wards had completed their education under FOEFI, the organization would pay for their return to Vietnam.[125]

The investigators disputed the legality of FOEFI's use of the colonial-era 1943 *pupille de la nation* law, which—well after the fall of the French empire— remained the legal means by which FOEFI justified its guardianship of fatherless *métis* children. And finally, FOEFI's terms of separation, investigators pointed out, were unnecessarily stringent; the whole process amounted to holding *métis* children "ransom." When mothers wanted to reclaim their children before they turned eighteen years old, FOEFI "mercilessly refuses," Consul General Lambroschini and Inspector General Sid Cara reported. Indeed, FOEFI created bureaucratic hurdles to discourage mothers, forbidding them from taking wards during the course of their studies, and requiring mothers who insisted on reclaiming their children to reimburse FOEFI. Of course, as the investigators noted ruefully, it was doubtful that mothers understood the price when they signed the contract.[126]

The report was likewise highly critical of FOEFI operations in France. In her investigation of FOEFI orphanages in France, Inspector General Sid Cara questioned the reason for isolating the *métis* wards from the white French orphans, raising them in conditions that would be considered substandard for French children, and providing them with only "limited comforts." Unfamiliar with Vietnamese cuisine, she was horrified by the wards' diet of fried fish and rice. Sid Cara insisted that life in FOEFI institutions took a toll on wards. The children she met appeared "somber, gloomy, and poor"; she found them "demoralized from the impersonal environment." She was "struck [*frappé*] by the number of deaths" and "surprised by their brutality." She concluded that the deaths were "probably caused by problems of adaptation" and raised concerns about FOEFI's failure to provide documents of inquests.[127] Among the questionable deaths were children who died of blood poisoning, internal hemorrhaging, and carbon monoxide poisoning, as well as multiple confirmed cases of suicide.[128] One particularly sad case involved a boy who suffered from partial deafness. This boy had been raised in the orphanage that was closed in response to what authorities euphemistically described as the problem of older boys who "pushed their will on others." FOEFI officials would later remark that the boy had developed a "belligerent attitude" to "protect himself against [other wards'] taunting." The orphanage closed when the incident came to light, and the boy was institutionalized in a mental hospital. He was released after a presumed recovery, but in 1962, he committed suicide.[129] His body was laid to rest at the Cimetière de Bagneux in Paris, in a tomb designated for FOEFI wards who died in their new homeland.[130]

Considering the problematic ways in which FOEFI separated children from mothers and the effects that separation had on children, Consul General Lambroschini and Inspector General Sid Cara made the case that mothers and children were left with no objective third party to help them resolve their differences with the organization. "In cases of conflict between a *pupille* and the Federation, between mothers and the Federation, who decides [the solution]? The Federation. Who, in all objectivity, can . . . take care of the child? No one. To whom does [the child] turn [in times of conflict with the FOEFI]? He only finds the Federation." In her visits to FOEFI orphanages, Sid Cara noted that FOEFI wards suffered over the separation from their mothers but had no recourse. Her report told the story of "a frail and listless, sweet and demure" ward who, for unknown reasons, resided in an orphanage in Switzerland. The young girl was haunted by the "sad moments when mother and child were separated" and had frequent nightmares in which she relived the trauma of separation. Moreover, FOEFI had separated the girl from her brothers and ignored her requests to be reunited with them. The investigators questioned why FOEFI made it so difficult for wards to return to their mothers "if that is their wish." FOEFI authorities even admitted to investigators that the organization felt no responsibility to pay for return tickets, even for wards who had matured out of the FOEFI program. To anchor wards in France, FOEFI encouraged them to marry French men and women; as one FOEFI member candidly told Sid Cara: "The marriage of children in France straightens everything out" (*arrange tout*).[131]

Lambroschini and Sid Cara directed FOEFI to make its policies more humane for wards and their mothers. They ordered the organization to return children to their families and allow them to maintain their Vietnamese citizenship. FOEFI, they declared, should only take custody of children who had been physically abandoned by both parents, and let *métis* children remain with their mothers "at all costs." The organization, they wrote, should devote its resources to supporting children in Vietnam instead of sending them to France. They also instructed FOEFI to allow its current wards to travel to Vietnam to visit their mothers.[132]

Not surprisingly, the report enraged FOEFI president William Bazé. He rejected its findings as "falsehoods,"[133] part of a "campaign against the FOEFI,"[134] and accused Consul General Lambroschini of launching "attacks" against FOEFI motivated by a desire to seize FOEFI real estate in Saigon.[135] He claimed that Nafissa Sid Cara, as a native of Algeria, was not qualified to evaluate Eurasian children and was, moreover, "inspired by racism that one would have thought would have disappeared [by now]."[136]

A mostly one-sided war of words between Bazé and FOEFI on one side and the French consulate of Saigon and l'Assistance Publique (the French public welfare system) on the other played out over the next few years. Bazé repeatedly claimed that FOEFI was under siege and accused the French consulate of conspiring with l'Assistance Publique to take control of *métis* affairs. According to Bazé, in 1965 the French consulate spread rumors around Saigon that FOEFI was shutting down operations, thus dissuading mothers from agreeing to entrust FOEFI with the care of their children.[137] France's public welfare system and the minister of social affairs then denounced FOEFI's use of the 1943 *pupille de la nation* law to make decisions on behalf of its *métis* wards and sent children through l'Assistance Publique. Bazé accused the French government of exaggerating an economic crisis "deliberately provoked to make the FOEFI disappear" and of masterminding a "conspiracy of silence," as French officials refused to give him information about the *métis* whose cases had been taken over by l'Assistance Publique.[138]

In an interesting rhetorical move, Bazé accused the French welfare system of the very infractions against mothers for which Consul General Lambroschini and Inspector General Sid Cara had criticized FOEFI. L'Assistance Publique, according to Bazé, "tore" [*arracher*] children from their mothers.[139] The French consulate, he claimed, forced mothers who solicited aid to sign acts of official abandonment and offered no guarantee that they would be able to remain in contact with their children—something FOEFI did facilitate, at least for most mothers.[140] In 1964, the mother of the Roussel children requested of the French consulate that her children be sent to France, but Lambroschini demanded that she sign an act of abandonment and send her child through the French state welfare system. Understanding that the act of abandonment also meant she could not contact her children, the mother refused, withdrew her request, and kept her children in Vietnam. Eventually, Bazé reported, she took her case to FOEFI, which promised to maintain correspondence between mother and child.[141] Other women who lacked the foresight of the Roussel mother signed away their rights to the consulate and later appealed to FOEFI to help them contact their children.[142] Playing off French concerns about public image in South Vietnam, Bazé suggested, "One can imagine the anti-French campaign that these letters would feed in Vietnam." Reflecting on the situation, he wrote, "My only regret is the inability to give satisfaction to Vietnamese mothers whose children are with l'Assistance Publique.[143]

Bazé also excoriated the French welfare system for its inability to communicate with wards in languages other than French. Most of the newly arrived *métis* spoke little if any French, and administrators did not speak Vietnamese, and this situation, he said, had a deleterious effect on the children. Bazé argued that only FOEFI—himself in particular—was qualified to raise *métis* children from the former Indochina colony insofar as they were well acquainted with *métis'* "problems" and "psychology" and had bilingual members—including three *métis*—working in Saigon.[144] (Of course, Bazé was one of only a few FOEFI administrators who spoke Vietnamese;

indeed, FOEFI orphanage workers in France forbade wards from speaking anything but French.) Bazé warned that biracial children from Vietnam would become "victims" of discrimination by l'Assistance Publique employees.[145] Children, he wrote, could not hide their sorrow at being separated from their siblings "like . . . a litter of dogs."[146] (He neglected to acknowledge that FOEFI had also separated siblings.) Fatherless *métis* children, Bazé concluded, had become "victims of decolonization."[147]

FOEFI REPATRIATIONS AND THE END OF THE VIETNAM WAR

In the late 1960s, changes in the course of the Vietnam War yielded positive results for FOEFI's relationship with the French government. The January 1968 Tết offensive launched a series of simultaneous uprisings in both the cities and the countryside of South Vietnam. The images portrayed on American television shocked the American public and fueled the antiwar movement at home and around the world. In May 1968, after the political losses incurred through the Tết offensive, the United States entered into formal peace talks with the DRV. That same year, FOEFI's standing with French politicians seemed to change when Laurent Giovangrandi replaced Charles Lambroschini as French consul general in Saigon. In stark contrast to his critical predecessor, Giovangrandi supported FOEFI policies and facilitated the shipping of 120 wards to FOEFI institutions in France. Given that French civilians and military had left Vietnam more than a decade earlier, this most recent batch of wards were in their late teenage years, spoke limited French, and were behind in their studies.[148]

Richard Nixon took office as president of the United States in 1969 and announced a plan in June for the "Vietnamization" of the war: a withdrawal of 25,000 U.S. troops, which were to be replaced by Vietnamese troops. FOEFI implored the French government to speed up repatriations. Those left in South Vietnam, he predicted, would grow "embittered" and pose "political problems" for the French.[149] Worse yet, he predicted, a communist victory would result in a "miserable life" for the *métis*.[150]

By that time, U.S. troops had officially been on the ground in South Vietnam for almost four years, and many had established relationships with Vietnamese women. The result was that fatherless mixed-race children—the sons and daughters of American (or allied) troops—were appearing throughout the South Vietnamese countryside. As the Amerasian population grew,

American humanitarian groups, including the Pearl S. Buck Foundation for the children of U.S. troops in Asia, flocked to South Vietnam to come to their aid or adopt them. Recognizing the potential political problem posed by fatherless mixed-race children, the U.S. government solicited advice from FOEFI.[151] William Bazé, never one to miss an opportunity to promote FOEFI, exploited U.S.-French animosity to shame the French government into increasing support for the organization, asking rhetorically, "Should it be that our *Patrie* renounces this inestimable asset, at a time when . . . the Pearl Buck Foundation is organizing [programs to repatriate] the mixed-race Americans born of the war in Vietnam?"[152] In contrast to France's stringent standards for *métis* repatriation, Bazé observed the United States allowed children of American soldiers to migrate to America "without formalities."[153] The FOEFI strategy of using the Amerasian example to shame the French government backfired. In France, rumors spread that FOEFI wards who were waiting to repatriate to France were actually the children of American soldiers.[154] These concerns would continue to dog FOEFI through the end of the war.

Bazé's claims of *métis* children left behind in South Vietnam were corroborated in 1972 when the President of the Central African Republic Jean Bedel Bokassa contacted the French Ministry of Foreign Affairs asking for help finding the daughters he left in the former Cochinchina. Bokassa, who was only eighteen when he was drafted to fight in Indochina, had a *métisse* daughter Bixi with a Vietnamese woman named Ba Thân. Soon after that relationship ended, he met Nguyễn Thị Huệ, a water vendor in Bien Hoa. Because the two never married, the French military would not permit a pregnant Huệ to repatriate with Bokassa. Huệ was left to raise their Afro-Asian daughter Nguyễn Thị Martine by herself. Meanwhile, Bokassa had risen the ranks in the military and in 1968 he became president of the Central African Republic after leading a military coup. In 1972, he used his diplomatic connections to find his daughters who followed him back to the Central African Republic. The story of Afro-Asian *métis* left behind only to become political royalty was an overnight sensation in the Vietnamese press and functioned to highlight the existence of French *métis* who remained in Vietnam.[155]

With the war leaving increasing numbers of Vietnamese children parentless, international attention turned to South Vietnam's crowded orphanages. The RVN's Ministry of Society declared that the country's sizable orphan population—estimated to be 12,645 in 1970—was one of the country's biggest problems, and stories of mistreatment abounded.[156] Young couples from all over Europe traveled to Vietnam to adopt children; international adoption agencies expatriated groups of children en masse.[157] Some RVN authorities disapproved of international adoptions, no matter what the conditions, warning that orphans would "lose their roots [*mất gốc*]" and their culture. They deemed orphan expatriation to be "contrary to the fundamental self-strength [*tự cường*] and self-reliance of the race [*dân tộc*]."[158] Officials warned that exporting orphans would be "unfavorable [*bất lợi*]" for the RVN,[159] which needed to preserve what it saw as an "effective source of manpower" for building up the new postwar society.[160] Other officials opposed foreign adoption on the grounds that foreign orphanages mistreated Vietnamese children—a possible allusion to FOEFI. They suggested imposing a waiting period on foreign adoptions to give living birth parents the opportunity to change their minds or reclaim their children.[161] Only after the state had exhausted prospects of finding a suitable Vietnamese home for them would officials consider sending orphans abroad.[162] While RVN officials preferred to keep orphans in Vietnam, in the end they reluctantly permitted international adoptions with the stipulation that these agencies assume responsibility for raising, educating, and teaching the orphans to speak Vietnamese. The RVN also required that adoptees maintain their Vietnamese citizenship status and insisted that they be repatriated to Vietnam at the RVN government's request[163]—although it is doubtful that all of these conditions were fulfilled.

Similar rhetoric appeared in discussions about the issue of *métis* relinquishing their Vietnamese citizenship in exchange for French citizenship. One RVN official suggested limiting such citizenship changes, as "[renunciations] decrease national prestige [*uy tín quốc gia*] and ethnic honor [*danh dự dân tộc*]."[164] Vietnamese police conducted long inquests into wards' background to verify their French ancestry and ensure that wards—most of whom were in their late teenage years and early twenties—were not evading the draft.[165] The RVN government stalled *métis* Trần Văn Ngọc Anh Michel Vinh and his sister's citizenship case for many years, accusing Michel of evading the draft. In the end, the RVN rejected their request to renounce their Vietnamese citizenship in favor of French citizenship.[166]

Bazé's anxieties grew as the war progressed. In 1970, Cambodian prime minister Lon Nol's U.S.-backed government deposed King Sihanouk, resulting in civil war. At least forty-eight fatherless Franco-Cambodian *métis* children flooded the French embassy in Phnom Penh.[167] By the end of 1972, with most of the *métis* descendants of Frenchmen having reached adulthood, it became apparent to the French government that FOEFI's services would no longer be needed. That year, the French government pressured FOEFI into agreeing to end its activities in Southeast Asia and to shut down all operations by December 31, 1976. Bazé grudgingly complied.[168]

As American troops were leaving South Vietnam, the RVN government restricted FOEFI's activities.[169] Moreover, the 1973 cease-fire under the Paris Peace Accords and the withdrawal of U.S. troops led some mothers to reclaim children who had been wards of FOEFI. The mother of the Maunin children refused to expatriate her children to France and demanded that they be returned to her.[170] *Métisse* ward Jeanne-Marie Coulin announced her desire to remain in Vietnam.[171] The French government, for its part, also restricted *métis* immigration to France and refused to repatriate wards until they learned French. Those who failed to attend French language classes—like Nguyễn Văn Hiêu, Ngô Ân, and Nguyễn Thị Quỳnh—were punished with delays to their repatriation.[172] Because most FOEFI charges were maturing out of the system at a rate of 150 wards per year, the French government halted repatriations in 1973.[173]

REUNIFICATION

As it turned out, the Paris Peace Accords yielded only a tenuous peace between the two Vietnams. After a series of small skirmishes over the years, in January 1975, northern troops attacked South Vietnam from the Cambodian border and through the central highlands. When it became apparent that the United States would not return to Vietnam, People's Army of Vietnam (PAVN) troops continued the attack. President Gerald Ford requested aid for South Vietnam, but Congress refused. Amid the chaos that spring, aid organizations rushed to evacuate children—especially mixed-race children of American soldiers—from Vietnam. On April 3, 1975, Ford allocated $2 million to evacuate Vietnamese and Amerasian orphans from Saigon. The very next day, flights full of children left for San Francisco. In one of the notorious tragedies of the Vietnam War era, a plane carrying orphans for Operation Baby Lift crashed as it left Saigon, killing almost all the children on board. It was later discovered that many of the children who had perished, as well as their fellow wards who had made it safely to San Francisco, had not actually been orphans but had instead been separated from their mothers against the mothers' will.[174] In the following weeks, as the PAVN army closed in on Saigon, the French embassy and the French Red Cross rushed to evacuate Vietnamese and *métis* orphans from Saigon.[175]

On April 30, 1975, the Republic of Vietnam finally surrendered to the communists of the North; only two weeks earlier the notoriously brutal Khmer Rouge had declared victory in Cambodia. As the Saigon government came crumbling down, mothers flooded FOEFI's Saigon office and the French consulate, begging to send their *métis* children to France.[176] The French government processed only requests from a few dozen FOEFI wards, who had been waiting to go to France since before 1975, but the provisional Vietnamese government initially refused to let new applicants leave the country.[177] As two decades had passed since the end of French colonialism, most wards, such as the Heindhart and Bellevue families, were the grandchildren or even great-grandchildren of Frenchmen.[178] Bazé fought as hard for such cases as he did for the others: "Regardless of generation, they are still part French. It is unthinkable that this quality would disqualify [their bid to immigrate] in the current crisis."[179]

Life after the war was trying for all southerners, *métis* included. Initially, the DRV set up a provisional government in Saigon before integrating the South into the administrative and economic structure of the North. The transition was less than smooth, with economic crises and food shortages. Exacerbating the economic suffering south of the seventeenth parallel, the newly unified Vietnamese regime was particularly brutal to southerners. The state sent hundreds of thousands of men and women to "reeducation camps" as punishment for having worked in the Saigon government or serving in the ARVN military, however low-level their position. Lê Văn Bảo, a Franco-Vietnamese *métis* adult, was told he would be interned for only a few days, but it turned out to be more than nine months—and he considers himself lucky.[180] Meanwhile, the state shipped mothers of Amerasian and Franco-Vietnamese children off to reeducation camps on the suspicion that they had been prostitutes. The combination of internment camps, economic privations, and an imminent war with Cambodia led hundreds of thousands of families to escape the country by boat. The number of people willing to risk their lives on such treacherous voyages stunned the international community. In 1979, the Geneva Conference on Refugees expanded the United Nations' Orderly Departure Program, hastening the placement of legal migrants and imposing requirements that countries accept at least a quota of refugees.[181] From the end of the war through 1980, France received some sixty-five thousand refugees.[182]

After the fall of Saigon, many French *métis* who had chosen to stay in Vietnam after decolonization searched for a way to immigrate to France. Although FOEFI had officially closed in 1976, it continued to use diplomatic and political connections to aid *métis* who remained in Vietnam, specifically those who wished to immigrate, through at least 1979.[183] Yet migrations stalled due to power struggles between FOEFI and various agencies in the French government. Bazé once again charged the French welfare system with misrepresenting statistics on *métis* refugees and refusing to give him access to those *métis* who had been repatriated to France by other means. L'Assistance Publique demanded that all FOEFI *métis* wards be transferred to the Ministry of Health, out of FOEFI influence. In the process, l'Assistance Publique workers discovered that the wards' *état civil* files were incomplete and that many had migrated to France illegally. FOEFI launched a counterattack, accusing the French government—among other things—of racism for blocking the migration of Afro-Asian *métis* to France. Meanwhile, René Lenoir, head of l'Action Sociale, dismissed the need for FOEFI: "France left Indochina a long time ago and there is no reason why France should have any particular interest in the sperm of American soldiers in Indochina."[184]

In 1977, rumors abounded on the streets of Ho Chi Minh City that Vietnamese Prime Minister Phạm Văn Đồng had entered into a verbal agreement with the French government to allow all Franco-Vietnamese *métis* born between 1945 and 1956 to immigrate to France. *Métis* rushed to the city's immigration office to request exit visas for themselves and their immediate family. This process was not without fraud: in some cases, families deceitfully claimed to be related to *métis* children so as to obtain an exit visa; in other cases, children of two Vietnamese parents falsely claimed to be *métis*. After being released from the reeducation camp, French-educated *métis* Lê Văn Bảo translated petitions and bureaucratic forms for those *métis* who lacked French writing skills. Bảo's renown as a translator made him well known among *métis* in Vietnam and would eventually make him an object of police attention.[185]

In 1977, Lê Văn Bảo applied for French citizenship and passage to France with his wife and two children. This would be the third time that Bảo changed his citizenship: unrecognized by his French father, he was born a colonial subject, meaning Vietnamese. In 1946, he received French citizenship and was given a French name. After the 1954 Geneva Accords declared Vietnam free of French rule, Bảo chose to stay in Vietnam, relinquish his French citizenship and name, take South Vietnamese citizenship, and reclaim his Vietnamese name. In theory, Bảo's 1977 case should have been easy given that his French heritage had already been established in 1946. Yet because Bảo was born three years before the birth date stipulated in the recent verbal agreement between Phạm Văn Đồng and the French government, he was not eligible for French citizenship and repatriation.[186] FOEFI estimated that tens of thousands of Vietnam's *métis* were left in a similar position.[187] While it is likely that FOEFI overestimated its statistics, in 2003 this author met a few Franco-Vietnamese *métis* in Vietnam whose repatriation requests had been rejected by the French government because they were born before 1946.

From 1979 to 1982, the French government rejected *métis* applications for repatriation in cases in which applicants could not prove their French filiation. As some *métis* themselves pointed out, establishing filiation was virtually impossible insofar as they had been abandoned by their French fathers and thus had no French relatives to claim them.[188] FOEFI demanded the French government reinvoke the 1928 colonial law allowing children of an unknown parent presumably of the French race to access French citizenship. The French government refused, and FOEFI denounced the new requirements as "draconian."[189]

Bảo, the *métis* translator—along with other *métis*—turned to the FOEFI Saigon office for assistance. William Bazé's brother George remained in Saigon to lead FOEFI. George—a tall, slender man who resembled his French ancestors—used his flawless Vietnamese and French language skills to negotiate with both French and Vietnamese authorities on behalf of the *métis*. Such efforts notwithstanding, Bảo and many other *métis* would have to wait for at least three years before receiving permission to repatriate to France. Multiple sources estimate that the French government allowed fewer than ten *métis* per week to repatriate with their families,[190] and rumor had it that French authorities stalled applications from Afro-Asians more frequently than those of Eurasians.[191] From the documents available, it appears that both the French and the Vietnamese governments were to blame for the stalled repatriations: the Vietnamese government refused to permit *métis* Vietnamese citizens to leave the country, and the French government slowly processed entry-visa paperwork. After 1979, Vietnamese officials changed course and encouraged the departure of all citizens and subjects whom it considered "difficult to assimilate";[192] it was the French government that continued to delay immigrations. Some *métis* denounced the French government's actions as "both cruel and unjust."[193]

In 1977, a small group of *métis* from Ho Chi Minh City issued a collective demand to the French government to permit them to immigrate. Since 1975, they claimed, the Welfare Committee for Refugees from Indochina had allowed thirty thousand Vietnamese, Cambodian, Lao, and Chinese to take refuge in France but had failed to extend the same welcome to the few thousand "compatriots who are still in Indochina."[194] The situation reached a crescendo with the November 1979 protest at the French consulate in Ho Chi Minh City, the story of which opened this chapter. While it made the French national news, stories chronicling the brutality of consulate guards towards the handful of *métis* who scaled the consulate walls were overshadowed by stories on the war in Cambodia. In September 1980, *Le Monde* published a petition signed by eleven *métis* demanding permission to immigrate to France.[195] Back in Ho Chi Minh City, *métis* sent "heartfelt" letters to FOEFI, begging for help. FOEFI expressed its "disappointment" with the French chancellery and lamented the "racial injustice" on the part of the French government.[196]

Some French *métis* escaped Vietnam through American programs for children of U.S. soldiers. The United States, also dealing with the problem of soldiers' children being left behind, followed the French model of expatriating mixed-race children. In 1982, Congress passed the Amerasian Act, to allow children of American soldiers to immigrate to the United States; however, because the United States and Vietnam had yet to normalize diplomatic relations, the congressional act proved impotent. Amerasians found an alternative way out of Vietnam through the Orderly Departure Program. Created in 1979 as a joint effort by the United States and Vietnamese governments to mitigate the crisis that came to be known as the "boat people," it was administered by the Office of the United Nations High Commissioner for Refugees. The 1988 Amerasian Homecoming Act reduced legal barriers that had impeded immigration for children of U.S. soldiers born between 1962 and 1976. In his oral history of Amerasians, Steven DeBonis interviewed Vu, the *métis* son of a French African soldier, who admitted that he claimed to be the child of an American soldier in order to benefit from the Amerasian Homecoming Act.[197]

The end of the Vietnam War had devastating effects on FOEFI wards in France, who, according to FOEFI, "had their eyes fixed on their compatriots in Indochina" as the events of 1975 unraveled.[198] A few lucky *métis* found ways to bring their mothers to France, but others, still resentful of their mothers for having abandoned them, were not so eager for a reunion.[199] After the fall of Saigon, the mother who had abandoned former FOEFI ward Jacques Maurice wrote to him, imploring him to use his FOEFI ties to help her migrate to France. He confessed, "After years of silence, her letter hurt me.... I was unhappy.... I wasn't ready to do it. As a result, I lost contact with her and I later learned that she ... had died. I didn't cry."[200]

After the communist takeover of South Vietnam, FOEFI changed its rhetoric about the unwed mothers of *métis* children. For the first time in a century, FOEFI no longer presented Vietnamese, Cambodian, and Lao mothers of *métis* children as manipulative women with loose morals. Instead, it presented them as victims of history. In 1983, Madame Marguerite Graffeuil, a FOEFI administrator and wife of Maurice Graffeuil, former resident superior of Annam, wrote a heartfelt letter to former FOEFI wards, portraying mothers as loving women who were unable to take care of their children.[201] This change of tune likely stemmed not only from genuine empathy but also from the arrival of a new and much more threatening enemy in the eyes of FOEFI administrators: the communist government of a unified Vietnam.

To FOEFI and Bazé in particular, the *métis* protection system represented everything that was right about French colonialism—close relations between France and Indochina, social welfare, and the uplifting power of French culture—at a time when France had lost its colony to the United States and the communists. Yet to many within the French government, the *métis* protection system was a source of embarrassment that would remind South Vietnam of the sexual violence, paternalism, and racial domination associated with French colonial rule—just as France was attempting to reinvent itself as an ally. As a result, FOEFI activities in the years after decolonization were marred by conflicts with the French government. FOEFI accused the French government of abandoning its children as it had abandoned its empire. Recognizing the blurry distinction between colonial and postcolonial practices of FOEFI, French bureaucrats attempted on multiple occasions to end FOEFI activities in Saigon. In 1980, William Bazé had a series of heart problems that impaired his ability to lead FOEFI. He died in 1984, after fifty-eight years of working in the *métis* protection system.

Epilogue

Jean Battin took a deep breath as he faced the studio audience for the television program *As Though Never Separated* [*Như chưa hề có cuộc chia ly*] in Ho Chi Minh City in 2012. Slowly, he began speaking in Vietnamese, his voice shaking as he shared with the audience his reasons for traveling from France to participate in this nationally broadcast, wildly popular show. He paused a few times to apologize for his poor Vietnamese, explaining that he had had few opportunities to speak his mother's language over the past fifty years. His listening comprehension, it should be noted, remained stellar nonetheless.[1]

Battin, whose birth name was Nguyễn Văn Trọng, was born in 1943 to a Vietnamese mother and an unknown French soldier. When he was four years old, his mother died, and he went to live with his uncle. Unable to afford another mouth to feed, his uncle placed him in a FOEFI orphanage, where he was renamed Jean Battin. The television show includes a home video taken in 2012 of Battin and another former ward, Jean Weber, in France. The men in the video converse in Vietnamese, Weber helping Battin when he forgets certain words. Battin motions at his body as he tells the camera: "I want to say that Vietnam is inside of me."[2]

French-sounding music accompanied Battin's recollections to the audience that his uncle paid him regular visits during his time in the orphanage in Vietnam, but in September 1955, when Battin was twelve years old, FOEFI sent him to an orphanage in Semblançay, France, and his life changed forever. There, he was forbidden to speak Vietnamese, though he and the other wards spoke and sang in Vietnamese on the sly. The Vietnamese language stayed with him not only in his mind but "in [his] heart." Reflecting on his experience at the orphanage, he tells the audience: "I thank France [for raising me], but my heart was always in Vietnam."[3]

In the late 1990s, Battin returned to Vietnam to look for his uncle. He said that stepping out of the airplane to the familiar smells of his homeland made him "feel alive again," even if his quest for his uncle proved to be unsuccessful. More than a decade later, he contacted the producers of the new show *As Though Never Separated* to solicit help in finding any surviving family members. Though it turned out that his grandparents and uncle had passed away, Thu Uyên, the host, introduced him on the air to cousins he had never met.[4]

Jean Battin's story is just one of the more than four thousand stories I tracked in seven archives spanning three countries. What began in the 1890s as a small movement composed of a handful of concerned French *colons* and their contacts in the colonial administration quickly became a systematic process of uprooting fatherless *métis* children from the native milieu—a process that continued well beyond decolonization, until 1975. Throughout this period, protection society authorities urged, or forced mothers to relinquish custody of their children. Although fatherless *métis* were a small and marginalized group, they were politically symbolic nonetheless. Protection society administrators feared that as the children of French men and colonial soldiers, this population might embarrass or even threaten the stability of the colonial state if its members were to engage in prostitution, become white paupers, or rebel against France. Yet officials soon came to regard fatherless *métis* children not just as a potential threat but also as a potential asset. These children came to symbolize not only colonial benevolence but also the potentially harmonious relationship between the colonizers and colonized that the French *mission civilisatrice* purported to cultivate. Indeed, these children represented the very future of France in Southeast Asia—or so officials believed.

Removals and reclassifications were made possible by a few factors. First, colonial society marginalized and subjugated indigenous mothers, especially those who had had extramarital sexual relations with French men, other European men, or colonial soldiers from Africa and India—even though it was these very mothers who were giving birth to the French nation in Indochina. From 1890 all the way through 1975, protection society rhetoric maligning the mothers of *métis* remained uncannily the same, like a broken record denouncing mothers as loose women eager to profit off their *métis* children. It was only after the Vietnam War had ended, the communist government had taken over, and wards had been sent to France with no foreseeable chance to return to Vietnam that protection society administrators finally expressed sympathy for the mothers of *métis* children.

Second, the removal program, in all of its iterations, targeted young children whose racial identity was believed to be mutable. The state then replaced the parental influence, reared these children to become proper French men and women, and repeatedly reconceived their racial formations. Until World War I, the French colonial population classified such children as indigenous and treated them as outcasts; from 1914 to 1945, state authorities and orphanage administrators reconstituted them as white "little Frenchmen" who could be useful in fulfilling colonial demographic initiatives; and from 1945 to 1975, *métis* protection society authorities reenvisioned all *métis*—including those of African and Indian fathers—as part of a broad *métis* identity group that would play a key role in maintaining the former colony's ties to the motherland. The colonial *métis* protection system was an effective project in that it mitigated the chances of a *métis* rebellion and safeguarded colonial prestige in Indochina. But the program failed on two counts: it did not produce a sufficient number of "Frenchmen" to maintain an enduring presence in Indochina, and it did not help the *métis* of the postcolonial era become the link between France and the former colonies.

Aside from the shocking revelation that *métis* children were systematically being removed from their mothers, one of the most surprising parts of this research was the discovery that the program lasted beyond the colonial period. Twenty-six years after the French government and French military had pulled out of Indochina, FOEFI and other aid organizations remained in South Vietnam and used defunct colonial-era laws to justify removing children from their mothers. These practices resulted in numerous legal problems for former wards, which lasted through at least 2014. As Indochina remained a soft spot in the French historical memory, Bazé and his FOEFI managed to continue raising funds—albeit not unchallenged—among influential members of the French government to maintain their operations. FOEFI went on encouraging mothers to relinquish custody of their *métis* children, trapping them with ambiguous contracts, and forcibly removing some women's children. Colonial practices, in short, did not die with the 1954 Geneva Accords.

Sadly, this story of child removals that persisted into the late twentieth century is far from unique. As in Indochina, the Australian, Canadian, and American governments used child removals to manage indigenous populations throughout most of the twentieth century. The forcible removal of Australian aboriginal children continued through the 1970s. Stories came to light in the early 1980s, prompting a national inquiry in 1995; and in 2008, the Australian government formally apologized. In Canada, the last Indian residential school closed in 1996. The assembly of First Nations was able to negotiate the Indian Residential School Settlement Agreement in 2006 with the Canadian government after more than eighty thousand residential school survivors filed individual or class action lawsuits against churches and the federal government. The agreement compensated survivors, required an official apology (delivered in 2008), and set up a Truth and Reconciliation Commission between 2009 and 2014. In the United States, Native American children experienced removal to federal Indian boarding schools through 1975, when the Indian Self-Determination and Education Assistance Act placed tribes in control of education among other things. Meanwhile, after World War II, adoptions and foster care were introduced as a new mode of removing and assimilating indigenous children. The 1978 Indian Child Welfare Act placed adoptions and fostering decisions in the hands of tribal governments, although the act remains controversial and under threat from a 2013 Supreme Court decision (the so-called Baby Veronica case).[5]

States used child removals not only to manage demographic issues but also to address broader economic and political problems. In Réunion, child removals were used to foster the economic integration of the former colony into the metropolitan French nation-state and national economy. During the 1960s and 1970s, to alleviate the widespread poverty in the former colony, l'Assistance Sociale removed impoverished children from their families and sent them to orphanages on the mainland. The story became public only in the last decade, after a striking number of former wards committed suicide.[6] In Spain and Argentina, child removals served as a means of punishing political dissidents. During the Spanish Civil War through the end of the Franco dictatorship in 1975, more than thirty thousand Spanish children were taken from their dissident parents.[7] After Portugal abandoned its claim to East Timor in 1974, the Indonesian military invaded and occupied the country from 1975–1999. As part of a larger neocolonial plan to integrate East Timor into the Indonesian nation-state, the Indonesian government removed roughly 4,000 East Timorese children and sent them to Java. There, some children were used as forced labor, while others were educated in Bahasa Indonesian, the national language, and raised in Indonesian culture. The goal of the program was to raise a generation of East Timorese who were sympathetic to Indonesian rule and would facilitate integration into the Indonesian nation-state.[8]

While these other cases of child removals in Australia, Canada, the United States, Réunion, Argentina, Spain, and East Timor have already come to light, the history of child removals in Indochina has barely been explored. The story of the systematic uprooting of fatherless *métis* children in colonial and postcolonial Indochina is not part of the Vietnamese, Cambodian, Lao, or French historical memory. Nonetheless, over the last ten years, some fatherless *métis* have made their stories public. FOEFI itself has a Facebook page, a web page, and multiple electronic newsletters. Former ward Joseph Christian Aubry maintains a website that is both a personal history and a tribute to the mother with whom he reconnected. Others, such as René Pairn, Henri Gaston Moller, and Jacques and Roger Maurice, have told their stories in documentary films. Laby Camara published an account of his journey to find his father in Cameroun and his mother in Laos, only to find that both had passed away. Juliette Varenne, whose story opened this book, made sense of her past by publishing her memoirs; and three others (for whom I use pseudonyms) are currently writing their own memoirs.

The Vietnamese historical memory is also coming to terms with the past. The *métis* children of the colonial and postcolonial eras had long been ignored in accounts of Vietnamese history, not only because mixed-race people have historically been excluded from the Vietnamese nation but also because these children were an uncomfortable reminder of the women who slept with the enemy (*me tây*). Recently, however, things have begun to change. Stories of *métis* left behind in Vietnam have begun appearing in the news.[9] Major Vietnamese newspapers have covered stories of *métis* returning to Vietnam.[10] As mentioned in the beginning of this epilogue, *As Though Never Separated* has aired episodes chronicling the return of former FOEFI wards to Vietnam to find their maternal families. This show has played a significant role not just in framing the history of *métis* removals within the broader context of Vietnamese history but also in including *métis* people within the Vietnamese nation.

The child removal program was unquestionably life changing for those mothers and children who were uprooted and separated from one another. Young fatherless *métis* children and their Vietnamese, Cambodian, and Lao mothers found themselves at the mercy of colonial authorities and protection society administrators, who determined their fate by recategorizing their racial identity. During the 1970s and early 1980s, with waves of refugees arriving in France, FOEFI director William Bazé received numerous letters from families looking for their *métis* loved ones. With the Vietnam War over, Bazé genuinely tried to help wards like Julienne Augustine find her siblings, who were sent to France but lost contact with their family in 1968. In a letter to Bazé, Julienne expressed concern that her brother, who had been close to their mother, would not have been able to cope emotionally with the separation.[11] It is not clear from Bazé's records if the family was ever reunited.

More recently, decades after leaving Vietnam, the last generation of former protection society wards have begun searching for answers about their past. Jean Battin is one of many former *métis* wards who returned to Vietnam to search for their mothers. Thu Uyên, the producer of *As Though Never Separated,* estimates that more than seventy *métis* have contacted her to request help in finding loved ones. Marie Claire André, who was only eighteen months old when she was sent to France, placed an ad in a Vietnamese newspaper asking for information about her mother.[12]

As it turns out, some *métis* former wards have managed to reconnect with their families. Photographs from the FOEFI archives show proud Vietnamese mothers dressed in *áo dài,* the Vietnamese traditional dress, at their adult children's weddings in France.[13] Former FOEFI ward Maurice recalled the precise moment he reunited with his mother after forty years of separation: "My brother saw a little lady coming our way. I was expecting a tall one, like a French woman. I couldn't imagine her being so tiny.... I felt a little petrified. I don't know if it was joy or sadness, words can't describe it.... We cried. My brother and I held our mother tightly. We were so happy to see her."[14] Former FOEFI ward Jacques Marie Jean Charles Alain, for his part, was grateful simply to be able to take care of his mother on her deathbed.[15] Posting on a FOEFI webpage message board, former ward François Beroult wrote, "I was lucky to see my mother just once after 47 years of separation. The year after, she departed to rejoin the angels. That's the life of a Eurasian, it's very difficult but you deal with it and move on."[16]

Other wards, however, had no interest in contacting their families. Former FOEFI ward René Pairn, for example, was initially uninterested in finding the African father he thought had abandoned him. FOEFI's misuse of the defunct 1928 citizenship ruling in the post colonial period left him in legal limbo concerning his citizenship, thus forcing him to consult FOEFI files in Aix-en-Provence. It was only then that he found documentation that his father had financially supported him all along. Pairn became visibly emotional as he thought back: "I blame myself.... Without that file, I had no idea he had always kept track of me. I greatly regret not looking for him sooner."[17]

Many wards who never connected with their families nonetheless made pilgrimages to Vietnam to see their country of origin, experience their maternal culture, and visit former orphanages and schools. The artist Mihagui, a former *métis* ward also known as Robert Bouchin, frequently returns to Vietnam and, in 2006, displayed his work at a gallery in Ho Chi Minh City.[18] Although Jacques Maurice, whose story was recounted in chapter 6, refused to sponsor his mother's immigration to France, he later brought his daughter with him to Vietnam to meet his many half siblings and to make incense offerings at his mother's grave.[19]

Because of their unique life journey, the last generation of former protection society wards have constructed complicated identities for themselves that run the spectrum from French to Vietnamese. Lê Văn Bảo—the *métis* translator who helped other *métis* fill out immigration documents after the Vietnam War—sees himself as fundamentally Vietnamese. René Pairn frequently asks himself, "I was born in Vietnam. What am I doing in France?" and former FOEFI ward Antoin asserts: "I am French, but my heart is Vietnamese, from my birthplace."[20] Yet other former FOEFI wards with whom I spoke saw themselves as having a hybrid identity, one that was *métis* unique to the FOEFI experience. Some even went so far as to call themselves "Foefien."[21] As Yên Noelle explains, "We're neither French nor Vietnamese. We're FOEFI—it's another identity."[22] She expresses her Vietnamese identity through food choices, home decoration, and jewelry. As an adult, she tried to relearn Vietnamese but failed. She attributes her difficulty with the language to a mental block caused by her mother's absence.[23] Robert Bouchin, the artist also known as Mihagui, quips: "In my blood do I have . . . nước mắm [Vietnamese fish sauce]?" He tears up when using a popular Vietnamese saying to describe his past in poetic terms: "My mother was a chicken incubating a duck egg. The little duck swam across the river, the chicken mother watched from the riverbank, but she could not do anything."[24]

As earlier generations of *métis* protection society wards have passed away, most of those I got to know through conversations or emails, or learned about from documentaries, books, television, or newspapers, were of the last generation raised under FOEFI or l'Assistance Sociale and sent to France. Almost all are grateful to FOEFI for taking them from what they believe was a dangerous environment due to the war and public anger towards children of the former colonizers. As Yên Noelle explains, "I am grateful that my mother left me to the FOEFI. I have a better life. What would I have become there?" She continues, "Maybe I'd be dead because they would have killed me. Or maybe I would have become a prostitute or a slave."[25] Etienne Tesson wrote to me, "I sincerely recognize that the FOEFI . . . brought me a lot of protection and for that reason, today I am more than 77 years old." He mused, "A lot of mistakes were made, but we were not in a simple situation."[26]

Attesting to their positive memories of growing up in FOEFI, former wards kept in close contact with FOEFI administrator Madame Graffeuil. After being released from FOEFI care, wards sent Graffeuil letters detailing milestones of their lives, invited her to their weddings, and hosted her at their homes for Christmas. As evidenced by the effort that Madame Graffeuil put into compiling a photo album of former wards, she clearly cared about her FOEFI charges. The album includes photo progressions, depicting smiling, toothless young wards when they first arrived in France; older, school-age youth; and then young adults sporting miniskirts and French cravats. Penciled in Graffeuil's handwriting are notes detailing wards' lives, including their academic achievements, love stories, and heartbreaks. Photographs also shed light on her involvement in their lives. Dressed to the nines with her pearls and a red beret tipped to one side, a white-haired Graffeuil escorts fashionable young FOEFI women down the street, proudly attends wards' weddings, and bounces their babies on her knee. Still intrigued by their racial ambiguity, Madame Graffeuil never missed a chance to note her pleasure in the margins that wards gave birth to light-haired or blue-eyed children.[27]

Few of those former wards from the last generation with whom I spoke or whose memoirs I read were aware that the *métis* protection societies sometimes forcibly removed children from their mothers. Nor were they aware of the ways in which *métis* children figured in the large-scale demographic agendas of the French colonial government or FOEFI. Many of those who became wards of the French state may have been too young to remember their mothers' protests; in other cases, their mothers may have actually asked for FOEFI assistance in raising their children. The former wards with whom I spoke have varied understandings of how and why they became wards of the French state.

Nonetheless, some wards do harbor anger towards FOEFI. Even though he does not recall any of the details, Robert Vaeza sensed that the French had taken him from his mother and uprooted him from his culture.[28] Former wards who were interviewed for the documentary *Inconnu, Présumé Français* recall overly strict—even borderline abusive—orphanage rules, and some expressed outrage that FOEFI withheld information about their families. Said René Pairn: "If we had parents who were still alive, then [FOEFI should have said], 'We have documentation if you would like to find your parents.'" He grew visibly emotional when recalling that instead of introducing wards to their families, FOEFI had "released [them] into the wilderness."[29]

My biggest regret in writing this book was never finding Robert Henri, whose story opened chapter 4 and was discussed in chapters 5 and 6. Documents from four archives in Vietnam and France tell a complicated story of a boy whose family tried desperately to keep him. In 1942, after taking his brother and sister, Madame Aumont and the Jules Brévié Foundation forcibly removed Robert from his mother. His mother then tracked him down in an orphanage, seized him back, and went into hiding. Authorities managed to track down the mother and son and forcibly removed young Robert a second time. Eventually Robert was sent to France—his name having been changed multiple times along the way. His brother, also a FOEFI ward, sought to reconnect with Robert, but not knowing about the name changes, he never managed to track him down. Robert would have had no way of knowing any of this, as those files were left scattered in archives in Vietnam. None of the information about his mother's or brother's efforts is included in his official file that FOEFI prepared for him in the French colonial archives in Aix-en-Provence (where former FOEFI wards are directed to learn about their pasts). The official documents instead claim that his mother was never interested in her son. Over the decade I spent working on this book, I searched for Robert in hopes of showing him all the documents I collected that reveal that his mother had fought hard to keep him and that his brother had tried to track him down. It was only in the last month of revising the book for publication that I learned from another former FOEFI ward that Robert had died long ago, never knowing how much his family had wanted him.

Sadly, many former wards of Indochina's *métis* protection societies, like Robert, have passed away without ever finding their families, telling their stories, or learning about the political agendas behind their uprooting. In 2014, I traveled to Paris to pay my respects and follow the Vietnamese, Cambodian, and Lao custom of lighting incense at the grave of *métis* wards who had been laid to rest in the FOEFI tomb in the Bagneux Cemetery, just south of the city. When I arrived at the cemetery, the caretakers looked up the location of the tomb and informed me that it had been destroyed. Because no one had renewed the plot's forty-year lease, in the late 1990s the bodies of these uprooted fatherless *métis* children had been disinterred and their remains moved to the Père Lachaise Cemetery, where they were left to be forgotten in the unmarked common pauper grave.

APPENDIX

FEDERATION DES OEUVRES DE L'ENFANCE
FRANÇAISE D'INDOCHINE
(Reconnue d'Utilité Publique)
100 Rue Hông-Thâp-Tu à Saigon
CERTIFICAT DE DECHARGE

FRENCH VERSION OF CONTRACT

Je soussigné,........ déclare vouloir confier mon enfant....... né le.........
à............. à la FEDERATION DES OEUVRES DE L'ENFANCE
FRANÇAISE D'INDOCHINE qui se chargera entièrement et jusqu'à ma-
jorité de son instruction et de son éducation.

Dans ce but, je donne tous pouvoirs snas exception aucune à la FOEFI.
Celle-ci a le droit SANS ACCORD ULTERIEUR DE MA PART, d'envoyer
mon enfant en France ou dans n'importe quel pays de l'Union Française, pour
y poursuivre ses études ou acquérir une formation professionnelle.

Je déclare en outre avoir pris connaissance de l'Article 14 du Décret 2.986
du 24 Novembre 1943 pourtant institution des pupille eurasiens d'Indochine
qui subordonne le retrait de on enfant à l'obligation par moi de rembourser
intégralement les dépenses faites pour son entretien.

Je m'engage, enfin, à reprendre mon enfant au cas où il se rentrait indé-
sirable, tant par sa mauvaise conduite que par son refus de travailler./.

ENGLISH TRANSLATION OF FRENCH
VERSION OF CONTRACT

"I, the undersigned,....... ..... declare my willingness to entrust my child......
born on...... to the FEDERATION DES OUEVRES DE L'ENFANCE
FRANÇAISE d'INDOCHINE, which takes total care to raise and educate
[the child] until the child reaches adulthood.

To this end, I give all powers without exception to the FOEFI. [FOEFI] has the power, without later consent on my part, to send my child to France or any country within the French Union, to study there or acquire a professional skill.

I declare as well my understanding of Article 14 of the Decree of 1886 [promulgated on] 24 November 1943 relative to the institution of Eurasian *pupilles* from Indochina that makes the withdrawal of my child contingent on the decision of the Federation and my obligation to fully reimburse the expenses accrued in raising [my child].

Finally, I commit to taking my child back in the event that [my child] is undesirable, either for [his or her] conduct or because [the child] refuses to work."[1]

VIETNAMESE VERSION OF CONTRACT

Tôi tên là . . . . bang lòng giao con tôi tên là . . . . sanh ngày . . . . tai . . . . cho Hôi Mô Côi nuôi duong và cho an hoc dên ngày con tôi truong thành.

Tôi giao tron quyên cho Hôi dinh doat sô phân con tôi và Hôi khoi cân do hoi y kiên tôi truoc, nêu Hôi muôn goi con tôi sang Phap hoac môt xu nào trong Liên Hiêp Phap dang ăn hoc thêm, hoac trao dôi môt nghê nghiêp chuyên môn nào khac.

Tôi khai rang tôi duoc biêt ro Nghi dinh sô 14 cua Dao Luât 2,986 dê ngày 24 Novembre 1943 noi vê cách giao phó nhung tre Lai-Phap o toàn coi Dông Duong cho Hôi Mô Côi coi soc, và theo Dao Luât ây thi lanh con tôi vê nhà là khi nào co su ung thuân cua Hôi; còn nêu tôi mang phép đem con tôi vê ngan, thi tôi phai bôi thuong cac so phi mà Hôi da tôn kém dang nuôi duong con tôi tu bây lâu nay.

Sau rôt, tôi bằng lòng lanh con tôi vê, nêu con tôi không tuân ky-luât nhà truong hoác gi hanh kiêm xâu hay là không chiu châm lo vê việc học hành./.

ENGLISH TRANSLATION OF VIETNAMESE VERSION OF CONTRACT

"I [name] . . . . agree to entrust my child named . . . . . . , born . . . . . . in . . . . . to the Orphan Society to rear and educate until my child reaches maturity.

I entrust my full power to the Society to determine the fate of my child and the Orphan Society does not need to ask my consent ahead of time, if the Society wants to send my child to France or another place in the French Union in the process of educating or instead give [my child] some other occupation or profession.

I declare that the Decree no. 14 of the Bill/Act 2.986 from Nov. 24, 1943 regarding the way(s) of entrusting the care of metis French youngsters in entire Indochina to the Society for Orphans has been made clear to me; and [it is also clear to me that] according to that Decree my child can return home only with approval from the Society; and if I have permission to withdraw my child early, then I must recompense the society for all the fees that it paid to raise my child up to that point.

Last, I agree that my child will return home, if my child does not obey school discipline, or behaves badly or does not manage to improve his/her studies."

NOTES

INTRODUCTION

1. Juliette Varenne, *Juliette du Tonkin*, 11–13.
2. I will follow Françoise Lionnet's lead in not translating the term *métis* into English, as there is no English equivalent that is free of negative connotations. See Françoise Lionnet, *Autobiographical Voices: Race, Gender, Self-Portraiture*.
3. As of June 2015, the database currently tracks 4,337 fatherless *métis* children who passed through the protection society system.
4. Protection societies never compiled centralized statistics, and because societies moved children around multiple orphanages in any given year, it is impossible to get a real number on wards. No comprehensive statistics exist for the colony's entire population of *métis*—recognized and unrecognized— as the colonial census recorded *métis* according to their citizenship and rarely by their ethnicity. For an excellent critique of the colonial census, see Marie Paule Ha, *French Women and the Empire: The Case of Indochina*, 122. Other authors have also expressed frustration with colonial statistics on the *métis* population. See Emmanuelle Saada, *Empire's Children: Race, Filiation, and Citizenship in the French Colonies*, 38; Nathalie Huynh Chau Nguyen, "Eurasian/Amerasian Perspectives: Kim Lefèvre's *Métisse blanche* (White Métisse) and Kien Nguyen's "The Unwanted," *Asian Studies Review* 29 (June 2005): 114.
5. Colonists in French West Africa and French Equatorial Africa also created protection societies for Eurafrican *métis* children. Owen White, *Children of the French Empire: Miscegenation and Colonial Society in French West Africa, 1895–1960*.
6. Article 1, page 3, states that the law applied to Cochinchina. "Décret portant application aux colonies de la loi du 24 juillet 1889 sur la protection de l'enfance," Secretary of State of the Colonies to Governor General of Indochina [hereafter GGI], May 7, 1890; Cambodian National Archives [hereafter CNA], files of the Resident Superior of Cambodia [hereafter RSC] 5995.
7. During the colonial period, the French government divided Vietnam into three administrative units: Tonkin, Annam, and Cochinchina. When referring to an ethnographic, cultural, or linguistic unit, I will use the term "Vietnam."
8. "Note 2440," by Paul Chauvet, Director of Political Affairs, November 17, 1942, Vietnam National Archives [hereafter VNNA] 1, GGI 89.

9. For the article series, see Vũ Trọng Phụng, "Kỹ nghệ lấy tây," in *Kỹ nghệ lấy tây & cơm thầy cơm cô.*"

10. Kim Lefèvre, *Métisse blanche;* Philippe Franchini, *Continental Saigon;* Juliette Varenne, *Juliette du Tonkin;* Nadine Bari and Laby Camara, *L'enfant de Seno.* Three other former protection society wards are in the process of publishing their memoirs.

11. Srilata Ravi, "Métis, Métisse and Métissage: Representations and Self-Representations"; Srilata Ravi, "Métisse Stories and the Ambivalent Desire for Cultural Belonging," 15–26; Isabelle Thuy Pelaud, "Métisse blanche: Kim Lefèvre and Transnational Space"; Jack Yeager, "Kim Lefèvre's Retour à la saison des pluies: Rediscovering the Landscapes of Childhood"; Lionnet, *Autobiographical Voices;* Nathalie Huynh Chau Nguyen, "Eurasian/Amerasian Perspectives"; Karl Ashoka Britto, *Disorientation: France, Vietnam, and the Ambivalence of Interculturality.*

12. Britto, *Disorientation,* 3–4.

13. Saada, *Empire's Children.*

14. Ann Laura Stoler, *Race and the Education of Desire: Foucault's History of Sexuality and the Colonial Order of Things;* Ann Laura Stoler, *Carnal Knowledge and Imperial Power: Race and the Intimate in Colonial Rule;* Gilles de Gantès, "Les métis franco-indochinois à l'époque coloniale. À l'interface des dominants et des dominés ou à leur marge?"; Pierre Guillaume, "Les métis en Indochine," *Annales de Demographie Historique* (1995): 185–195; David M. Pomfret, "Raising Eurasia: Race, Class, and Age in French and British Colonies"; Yves Denéchère, "Les 'rapatriements' en France des enfants eurasiens de l'ex-Indochine: Pratiques, débats, mémoires."

15. After slavery was banned in the French empire, slaves and colonized peoples of the "anciennes colonies" were given French citizenship. *Métis* children in these colonies technically had the same rights as white French men and women, giving them little reason to rebel and little need for the colonial state to fear them. Saada, *Empire's Children.*

16. White, *Children of the French Empire.*

17. Ivan Jablonka, *Enfants en exil: Transfert de pupilles réunionnais en métropole (1963–1982).*

18. Satoshi Mizutani, *The Meaning of White: Race, Class, and the 'Domiciled Community' in British India, 1858–1930,* 111–114; Sarah Heynssens, "Practices of Displacement: Forced Migration of Mixed-Race Children from Colonial Ruanda-Urundi to Belgium."

19. Françoise Vergès, *Monsters and Revolutionaries: Colonial Family Romance and Métissage,* 6.

20. Mizutani, *The Meaning of White.*

21. Marie-Paule Ha, *French Women in the Empire: The Case of Indochina,* 122.

22. Since 1848, French legal code required all laws to be decided "without distinction of race."

23. Elisa Camiscioli, *Reproducing the French Race: Immigration, Intimacy, and Embodiment in the Early Twentieth Century.*

24. Nira Yuval-Davis and Floya Anthias, introduction to *Woman, Nation, State.*

25. Saada, *Empire's Children,* 20, 76.

26. For more information on Vietnamese women who had sex with French men, see Nguyen Xuan Tue, "Congai: Une race des femmes annamites, produit de la colonization," in Bernard Hue, *Indochine: Reflets littéraires,* 69–77.

27. Vũ, "Kỹ nghệ lấy tây."

28. Saada, *Empire's Children,* 35.

29. Centre des Archives d'Outre Mer [hereafter CAOM], 90APC79.

30. "Concerning the non-recognized métis, it is impossible to evaluate the number, even to approximate, for their birth is declared by their Annamite mothers to the officers of the Annamite *état civil* under Annamite names. We can, however, say that they are generally very young and the majority of them live *à l'annamite* with their mothers in the villages or on the interior of the province; only a few live in urban areas," "Enquête n4 sur le problem des métis," by P. Berthault, Résident de France [hereafter RF] in Hà Tỉnh, May 14, 1938, CAOM, FM Guernut 97; "Number of statistics of non-recognized in reality are much higher than indicated. It's higher even than the numbers of recognized métis, but it is extremely difficult to obtain precise results on this subject.... The majority of Eurasians live, in effect, in the indigene milieu. Only the physical characteristic could distinguish them (from annamites) in the eyes of the enquêteur." "Le problème Eurasien au Tonkin," undated, 1938, FM Guernut 97. As Emmanuelle Saada notes, the population of fatherless *métis* children was viewed as a threat not because of its size but because of its symbolic importance. Saada, *Empire's Children,* 41.

31. Emmanuelle Saada, *Les enfants de la colonie.*

32. Patrick Wolfe, "Land, Labor, and Difference: Elementary Structures of Race," *American Historical Review* 106, no. 3 (2001).

33. For example, compare the files Letter, Madame Aumont to M. Resident Mayor of Haĩ Phòng, October 28, 1942, VNNA 1, GGI 495; "Note de Madame Aumont, charge de l'oeuvre des enfants eurasiens à Hai Phong," CAOM, 90APC62.

34. "Fédération des Oeuvres de l'Enfance Française d'Indochine, Exercice 1966, Assemblée Générale Ordinaire Du 9 Octobre 1967."

35. Philippe Rostan, *Inconnu, présumé français.*

36. Britto, *Disorientation,* 41.

37. "Fédération des Oeuvres de l'Enfance Française d'Indochine, Délégation Métropolitaine, Exercice 1957, Assemblée Générale Ordinaire des 28 et 29 Juillet 1958."

38. Letter, GAK to Chánh Toà Sơ Thẩm, September 23, 1945, CAOM, Fonds Gouvernment du Fait [hereafter GF] 9; "Nghị Định 1–11–1945" (Decree November 1, 1945) CAOM, Fonds GF 9.
39. White, *Children of the French Empire*, 83.
40. "Note de service," General Martin, August 21, 1939, VNNA 1, Fonds Resident Superior of Tonkin [hereafter RST] 71908.
41. Service Historique d'Armée de Terre [hereafter SHAT] 10H1110.
42. Adult unrecognized *métis* had a similar experience. Lt. Cornel Louret, August 7, 1939, CAOM, RST NF 3903; Ann Laura Stoler, "Sexual Affronts and Racial Frontiers: European Identities and the Cultural Politics of Exclusions in Colonial Southeast Asia," in *Tensions of Empire: Colonial Cultures in a Bourgeois World*.
43. White, *Children of the French Empire*, 83.
44. CAOM, 90APC62.
45. "Fédération des Oeuvres de l'Enfance Française d'Indochine, Exercice 1982, Rapport du Conseil d'Administration, Assemblée Générale Ordinaire Du Mardi 22 Mars 1983."
46. "Fédération des Oeuvres de l'Enfance Française d'Indochine, Exercice 1980, Rapport du Conseil d'Administration, Assemblée Générale Ordinaire Du Samedi 6 Décembre 1980."
47. Rostan, *Inconnu, Présume Francais*.

CHAPTER 1: FOUNDING OF THE *MÉTIS* PROTECTION SOCIETIES

1. It is not clear what year authorities took custody of the child. "Note," April 30, 1912, VNNA, Center 1 [hereafter VNNA 1], Files of the RST 5495.
2. *Tableau de population, de culture, de commerce et de navigation, formant pour l'année 1872*, 204.
3. Gregor Muller, *Colonial Cambodia's "Bad Frenchmen": The Rise of French Rule and the Life of Thomas Caraman, 1840–87*, 130–149.
4. Charles Meyer, *La Vie Quotidienne des Français en Indochine 1860–1910*, 165, 173.
5. There were 356 men and 73 women in Hanoi, and 411 men and 99 women in Hải Phòng. Ibid., 198.
6. Marie-Paule Ha, *French Women and the Empire*, 30.
7. Comte D'Haussonville and Joseph Chailley-Bert, *L'émigration des femmes aux colonies*, 21–22; Ha, 20–30; Muller, 135; Emmanuelle Saada, *Empire's Children: Race, Filiation, and Citizenship in the French Colonies*, 15.
8. Ha, 30–45, 129.
9. Meyer, 198, 218.
10. *Oeuvre de la Sainte Enfance ou Association des Enfants Chrétiens pour le rachat des enfants infidèles en Chine et dans les autres pays idolâtres*, 12.

11. Van Nguyen-Marshall, *In Search of Moral Authority: The Discourse on Poverty, Poor Relief, and Charity in French Colonial Indochina*, 26–30; Ngô Vinh Long, *Before the Revolution: The Vietnamese Peasants Under the French*, 92–97.

12. Laurence Monnais-Rousselot, *Médecine et Colonisation: L'adventure Indochinoise, 1860–1939*, 22.

13. Similarly, in Senegal, Catholic nuns were in charge of orphanages for *métis*. Hilary Jones, *The Métis of Senegal: Urban Life and Politics in French West Africa*, 99.

14. Charles Keith, *Catholic Vietnam: A Church from Empire to Nation*, 36.

15. Chanoine Jean Vaudon, *Les filles de Saint-Paul en Indo-Chine*, 1–16.

16. Keith, *Catholic Vietnam*, 60.

17. Vaudon, 202, 345.

18. Keith, *Catholic Vietnam*, 60.

19. Ibid., 38.

20. Vaudon, 72; Churches frequently relied on parishioners' labor to maintain costs of churches, orphanages, and hospitals. Keith, *Catholic Vietnam*, 34.

21. Vaudon, 73–74.

22. In 1906, there were 5,943 known *métis*. "Tableau récapitulatif de la population de l'indochine française en 1906," in Ministère des colonies office colonial, *Statistiques de la population dans les colonies françaises pour l'année 1906*, 276–277.

23. "Statistique par professions dans la population europeéne," in ibid., 290–297, 346–349; "Tableau récapitulatif de la migration française et étrangèrs dans la population europeéne en 1906," in ibid., 389; "Statistique par professions dans la population europeéne," in ibid., 424–431.

24. "Tableau récapitulatif des mariages dans la population européen en 1906," in ibid., 288.

25. "Société de Protection et d'Education des Jeunes Métis Français du Cambodge, Procèss Verbal des Séances du 26 Octobre et de 21 Fevrier 1904," CNA, files of the RSC 5424; Rebecca Hartkopf Schloss, *Sweet Liberty: The Final Days of Slavery in Martinique*.

26. According to the 1895 census, of the 63,000 Europeans in the archipelago, "very few could claim to have two European parents." The majority were Eurasian. "Consulat de France à M. Le Gouveneur Général," December 12, 1901, VNNA 1, GGI 3823; Jean Gelman Taylor, *The Social World of Batavia: European and Eurasian in Dutch Asia;* Ann Laura Stoler, "Making Empire Respectable: The Politics of Race and Sexual Morality in 20th-Century Colonial Cultures," *American Ethnologist* 16, no. 4 (1989): 634–660.

27. Letter, signed G.C.C., December 10, 1903, VNNA 1, GGI 3823; "Rapport sur le paupérisme à Java," October 3, 1903, French National Archives, Centre des Archives d'Outre Mer [hereafter CAOM], GGI 54225.

28. Dutch law considered recognized Eurasians to be "legally European, physically heterogeneous." Letter, signed G.C.C., December 10, 1903, VNNA 1, GGI 3823.

29. Taylor, *The Social World of Batavia*, 148.

30. Letter, signed G.C.C., January 10, 1903, VNNA 1, GGI 3823.

31. Albert de Pouvourville, "L'Indochine et ses métis," *La Depêche Coloniale*, September 16, 1911.

32. Charles Gravelle, "Les métis et l'oeuvre de la protection de l'enfance au Cambodge," *Revue Indochinois* 16 no. 1 (January 1913): 37.

33. Owen White, *Children of the French Empire: Miscegenation and Colonial Society in French West Africa, 1895–1960*, 46.

34. Keith, *Catholic Vietnam*, 71.

35. Patrick J. N. Tuck, *French Catholic Missionaries and the Politics of Imperialism in Vietnam, 1857–1914: A Documentary Survey*, 275.

36. M. Montagne à M. Paris, November 10, 1903, CAOM, GGI 7701; J. P. Daughton, *An Empire Divided: Religion, Republicanism, and the Making of French Colonialism, 1880–1914*.

37. See articles 41 and 43 of the "Comité local de protection des enfants métis abandonnés, Annam, statuts 1900," VNNA, Center 4 [hereafter VNNA], fonds of the Resident Superior of Annam [hereafter RSA] 215.

38. RF à Bắc Giang à RST, May 11, 1904, CAOM, GGI 7701.

39. Pierre Albertini, *L'école en France XIXe–XX siècle: De la maternelle à l'université*, 75.

40. White, *Children of the French Empire*.

41. In 1906, Cochinchina had the highest population of Europeans, yet there were rarely more than thirty European children in any of the provinces. With 156 European children registered in Chau Doc, it is the exception; however, it is not clear if those children were born of two French parents or were *métis*. "Tableau récapitulatif de la population européen en 1906," in Ministère des colonies office colonial, *Statistiques de la population*, 282–285.

42. "Thời sự tổng thuật," *Đông Dương Tạp Chí*, July 3, 1913.

43. Sylvia Schafer, "Between Paternal Right and the Dangerous Mother: Reading Parental Responsibility in Nineteenth-Century French Civil Justice," *Journal of Family History* 23, no. 2 (1998): 173–189.

44. Sylvia Schafer, *Children in Moral Danger and the Problem of Government in Third Republic France*, 4–5.

45. Article 1, page 3, states that the law applied to Cochinchina. "Décret portant application aux colonies de la loi du 24 juillet 1889 sur la protection de l'enfance," May 7, 1890, CNA, RSC 5995.

46. Saada, *Empire's Children*, 91.

47. Camille Paris to GGI, February 29, 1904, CAOM, GGI 7701.

48. Procureur général to GGI, March 30, 1904, CAOM, GGI 7701.

49. RF Bắc Giang to RST, May 11, 1904, CAOM, GGI 7701.

50. Muller, *Colonial Cambodia's "Bad Frenchmen,"* 137.

51. Jane Jenson, "Representations of Gender: Policies to 'Protect' Women Workers and Infants in France and the United States before 1914," in *Women, the State and Welfare,* ed. Linda Gordon, 152–177.

52. Charles Gravelle, "Enquête sur la Question des Métis," *Revue Indochinois,* no. 10 (January 1913): 32.

53. Note, April 21, 1906, CAOM, GGI 7701.

54. "Société de protection des enfants métis abandonnés du Tonkin, Statuts revisés à l'assemblee générale, 18 mars 1904," VNNA 1, RST 5545.

55. Untitled document, presumably 1903, CAOM, GGI 21654.

56. "Note," February 29, 1904, CAOM, GGI 7701.

57. Sambuc, "Notes et Documents: Enquête sur la Question des Métis," 208–209.

58. Letter to GGI, September 24, 1898, CAOM, GGI 7701.

59. Camille Paris to GGI, February 29, 1904, CAOM, GGI 7701.

60. M. Montagne to M. Paris, November 10, 1903, CAOM, GGI 7701.

61. M. Montagne to M. Paris, January 29, 1904, CAOM, GGI 7701.

62. George Chevallier to Public Prosecutor in Saigon, February 6, 1904, CAOM, GGI 7701.

63. Letter to GGI, September 24, 1898, CAOM, GGI 7701.

64. "Société de protection et d'education des jeunes métis français du Cambodge, process verbal des séances du 26 octobre et de 21 fevrier 1904," CNA, RSC 5424.

65. "Note," February 29, 1904, CAOM, GGI 7701; "Société de protection des enfants métis abandonnés du Tonkin, Statuts revisés à l'assemblée générale du 18 Mars 1904," VNNA 1, RST 5545; "Rapport de la chamber de commerce de Hanoi regardant la Proposition de loi relative à l'abrogation de l'article 340 du code civil (Reconnaîssance Legale de la Paternité Naturelle)," December 26, 1910, VNNA 1, RST 41624; Stoler, "Making Empire Respectable," 361.

66. "Note," February 29, 1904, CAOM, GGI 7701.

67. Camille Paris to GGI, February 29, 1904, CAOM, GGI 7701.

68. Letter to RSA, April 8, 1910, VNNA 4, Dalat RSA 215.

69. Françoise Vergès, *Monsters and Revolutionaries: Colonial Family Romance and Métissage,* 6; "La question des enfants métis," September 24, 1898, CAOM, GGI 7701.

70. Gail Paradise Kelly, *French Colonial Education,* 4–5; Gail Paradise Kelly, *Franco-Vietnamese Schools, 1918–1938: regional development and implications for national integration,* 98–99.

71. "Séance de 17 Septembre 1901," VNNA 1, RST 8459.

72. Director of Public Education to Mayor of Hanoi, January 4, 1904, CAOM, GGI 7701.

73. "Séance," February 29, 1904," CAOM, GGI 7701.

74. RSC to M. Fontain, November 28, 1907, CNA, RSC 2458; Letter to Inspector of Education in Cambodia, November 24, 1907, CNA, RSC 2458.

75. Opened in 1848, the first agricultural schools were part of a plan to develop specialized schools, including economic schools, agricultural schools, and business schools. Authorities developed agricultural schools as part of a mid-nineteenth-century campaign to protect the country's environmental heritage. Antoine Prost, *L'Enseignement en France, 1800–1967*. For an excellent study of colonial mental institutions, see Claire Ellen Edington, "Beyond the Asylum: Colonial Psychiatry in French Indochina, 1880–1940."

76. Michel Foucault, *Discipline and Punish: The Birth of the Prison*, 294.

77. Ceri Crossley, "Using and Transforming the French Countryside: The 'Colonies Agricole' (1820–1850)," *French Studies* 45, no. 1 (1991).

78. In the mid-nineteenth century, the Dutch colonial government established several agriculture schools in the Netherlands Indies. The schools failed because the Dutch government could not fulfill its promise for high-level agricultural jobs. Ann Laura Stoler, *Along the Archival Grain*, 114–118.

79. Note, undated, 1910, VNNA 1, Service d'Enseignement du Tonkin [hereafter SET] 215.

80. Crossley, "Using and Transforming the French Countryside."

81. Judith Surkis, *Sexing the Citizen: Morality and Masculinity in France, 1870–1920*, 49–50.

82. Note to Administrator in Hưng Hóa, January 8, 1910, VNNA 1, SET 215.

83. Ibid.

84. "Minute," undated 1910, VNNA 1, SET 216; Head of the Service of Education to RST, September 13, 1910, VNNA 1, SET 216.

85. Surkis, *Sexing the Citizen*, 74; Margaret D. Jacobs, *White Mother to a Dark Race: Settler Colonialism, Maternalism, and the Removal of Indigenous Children in the American West and Australia, 1880–1940*.

86. Head of the Service of Education to RST, January 27, 1910, VNNA 1, SET 215.

87. Director of the School to RST, undated 1910, VNNA 1, SET 213.

88. RST to GGI, October 11, 1907, VNNA I, SET 213.

89. Surkis, *Sexing the Citizen*, 41.

90. Ibid.

91. RST to GGI, October 11, 1907, VNNA 1, RST 12836.

92. Ibid.

93. Director to RST, undated 1910, VNNA 1, SET 213.

94. [Illegible signatures] to RF à Phú Thọ, January 18, 1910, VNNA 1, SET 215.

95. "Note sur le Collège Agricole de Hưng Hóa," undated, 1910, VNNA 1, SET 215.

96. "Extrait de la lettre n. 53," January 8, 1910, VNNA 1, SET 215.

97. Ibid.

98. On the relationship between race and food consumption in colonial Indochina, see Erica J. Peters, "Culinary Crossings and Disruptive Identities: Contesting Colonial Categories in Everyday Life," in *Of Vietnam: Identities in Dialogue*, ed. Jane Winston; Erica J. Peters, *Appetites and Aspirations in Vietnam: Food and Drink in the Long Nineteenth Century*.

99. [Illegible signatures] to RF à Phú Thọ, January 18, 1910, VNNA 1, SET 215.

100. Ibid.

101. Ibid.; Delegate à Hưng Hóa à RF Hưng Hóa, January 20, 1910, VNNA 1, SET 215.

102. "Minute n.9032," April 16, 1910, VNNA 1, SET 215.

103. "Réglement Intérieur du Collège Agricole de Hưng-Hóa," September 5, 1908, VNNA 1, RST 8457; "Minute," April 18, 1910, VNNA 1, SET 213.

104. Head of the Service of Education to RST, January 19, 1910, VNNA 1, SET 215.

105. Head of the Service of Education to RST, January 27, 1910, VNNA 1, SET 215.

106. Head of the Service of Education to RST, January 19, 1910, VNNA 1, SET 215.

107. Ibid.

108. "Minute n.9032," April 16, 1910, VNNA 1, SET 215.

109. Similarly, in metropolitan French engineering education in the mid-nineteenth century, "disdain for manual labor shaped the technical curricula," and students were separated by class. The curricula managed the students so that those of higher classes never used their hands and would thus be managers of those who did engage in manual labor, the lower class. French students even wrote about their shame, rooted in performing manual labor. Eda Kranakis, *Constructing a Bridge: An Exploration of Engineering Culture, Design, and Nineteenth-Century France and America*, 215–232.

110. Head of the Service of Education to RST, January 27, 1910, VNNA 1, SET 215.

111. Head of the Service of Education to RST, January 17, 1910, VNNA 1, SET 215.

CHAPTER 2: FRENCHMEN'S CHILDREN

1. "Note sur la Société d'Assistance aux enfants Abandonées Franco-Indochinois," undated, probably 1929, VNNA 1, RST 73758; Letter, June 10, 1932, VNNA 1, RST 48400.

2. Ibid.

3. Letter, June 10, 1932, VNNA 1, RST 48400.

4. Kristen Stromberg Childers, *Fathers, Families, and the State in France, 1914–1945*, 27.

5. Elisa Camiscioli, *Reproducing the French Race: Immigration, Intimacy, and Embodiment in the Early Twentieth Century*, 17.

6. Margaret Cook Andersen, "Creating French Settlements Overseas: Pronatalism and Colonial Medicine in Madagascar," *French Historical Studies* 33,

no. 3 (2010); Anderson, "A Colonial Fountain of Youth: Imperialism and France's Crisis of Depopulation, 1870–1940"; Ha, *French Women and the Empire*, 31–33.

7. "Ligue des Pères et Mères de Familles Nombreuses," *Courrier d'Haiphong*, April 4, 1922; "Chronique de Hai Phong," *L'Avenir du Tonkin*, undated, VNNA 1, GGI 5041.

8. "Ligue Populare des Pères et Mères de Familles Nombreuses de France," by Henri Perot, July 20, 1916, VNNA 4, RSA 1170; "Ligue Populare des Pères et Mères de Familles Nombreuses de France, section Indochine," by Henri Perot, no date, VNNA 4, RSA 702 (formerly 699).

9. Table 5.7, "European Population with Gender and Age Breakdown in Indochina (1921–1937)," in Ha, *French Women and Empire*, 124, 130.

10. Memorandum, undated World War I, probably 1916, VNNA 2, RSA 867.

11. During World War I, colonial officials worried that with the mobilization of French colonists and dwindling French population, the numerically dominant Vietnamese population would gain economic and political power, thereby threatening the authority of the French administration. Administrator of the Province of Cần Thơ to Goucoch, February 12, 1916, VNNA 2, Goucoch IB25/109 (4); Champanht to the Minister of War in Paris, January 8, 1917, VNNA 2, Goucoch IA.6/051; Administrator of the Province of Rạch Giá to the Goucoch, February 2, 1917, VNNA 2, Goucoch IA.6/052.

12. Rachel Ginnis Fuchs, *Contested Paternity: Constructing Families in Modern France*.

13. "Mẹ con nói chuyện cách trí," *Nữ Giới Chúng*, February 1, 1918; "Cách trí: Mẹ con nói chuyện," *Nữ Giới Chúng*, March 22, 1918; "Phép nuôi con: Dưỡng thai," *Nữ Giới Chúng*, April 5, 1918.

14. Đam Phương, as quoted in David G. Marr, *Vietnamese Tradition on Trial, 1920–1945*, 210.

15. Đặng, *Vấn Đề Phụ Nữ Trên Báo Chí Tiếng Việt Trước Năm 1945*, 53.

16. Mayor of Saigon to Goucoch, March 3, 1916, VNNA 2 Goucoch IA6/015.

17. RSA to GGI, July 29, 1921, CAOM, GGI 15298.

18. "Quan Báo Trích lục: Luật Nhận Cha Con," *Đông Dương Tạp Chí*, July 3, 1913.

19. Letter to GGI, October 28, 1923. CAOM, GGI 65316; Jean Elisabeth Pedersen, " 'Special Customs': Paternity Suits and Citizenship in France and the Colonies, 1870–1912," in *Domesticating the Empire: Race, Gender, and Family Life in French and Dutch Colonialism*, ed. Julia Ann Clancy-Smith and Frances Gouda.

20. GGI to Goucoch, Residents of Huế, Phnom Penh and Vientiane, May 5, 1915, VNNA 2, GCC 1B24/0718.

21. From Administrator of Cần Thơ, January 28, 1928, VNNA 2, GCC 1B35/n32(3).

22. Emmanuelle Saada, *Les Enfants de la Colonie*, 140, 51.

23. "Quan Báo Lược Lục," *Đông Dương Tạp Chí,* July 24, 1913.
24. GGI to Minister of Colonies, April 12, [year unclear, presumably 1919], CAOM, Service de Liason avec les Originaires des Territoiers Francais d'Outre Mer [hereafter SLOTFOM] XII 1.
25. "Société de Protection de l'Enfance au Cambodge," March 31, 1915, CNA, RSC 2455.
26. CAOM, GGI 42656.
27. "Société de Protection de l'Enfance, Process Verbal de la Réunion du 9 Mai 1922," CNA, RSC 2455.
28. Letter to Lieutenant Commander, October 28, 1928, CAOM, GGI 42658.
29. Minister of War to Minister of Colonies, June 16, 1917, CAOM, GGI 26921. Indeed, the metropolitan government tried to discourage relationships between any of the colonial soldiers and white French women. See Tyler Stovall, "Love, Labor, and Race: Colonial Men and White Women in France during the Great War," in *French Civilization and Its Discontents: Nationalism, Colonialism, Race,* ed. Tyler Edward Stovall and Georges Van den Abbeele.
30. From RS, January 4, 1924, CAOM, GGI 16776.
31. Révérony to GGI, December 7, 1923, CAOM, GGI 16776; GGI to Minister of Colonies, December 20, 1923, CAOM, GGI 16776.
32. From RS, January 4, 1924, CAOM, GGI 16776.
33. "Arrête, n 1481," May 8, 1919, CAOM, SLOTFOM XII 1.
34. The results were not reported. "Memorandum," undated, before October 1916, VNNA 2, RSA 867.
35. No precise number was given, and the accuracy of this is, of course, impossible to access. "Société de protection des enfants métis abandonnés, Assemblée générale du 20 Janvier 1917." VNNA 1, RST 5545.
36. Childers, *Fathers, Families, and the State in France,* 28.
37. Saada, *Les Enfants de la Colonie,* 229.
38. "Petit Guide pour l'Application de Loi du 27 Juillet 1917 Institutant les Pupilles de la Nation," CNA, RSC 37339.
39. Minister of War to Minister of Colonies, June 16, 1917, CAOM, GGI 26921.
40. Saada, *Les Enfants de la Colonie,* 1–5.
41. Arthur Girault, "La condition juridique des métis dans les colonies français."
42. In 1941, the colonial government would interpret the 1928 law to justify the forcible removal of Eurasian children from their mothers. Découx to President of Jules Brévié Foundation, August 12, 1941, VNNA 1, RST 71816.
43. Saada, *Les Enfants de la Colonie,* 1–5.
44. Minister of the Interior to GGI, October 8, 1928, CAOM, GGI 42714.
45. Micheline Lessard, "Tradition for Rebellion: Vietnamese Students and Teachers and Anticolonial Resistance, 1888–1931," 244.
46. Gravelle to GGI, May 25, 1920, CAOM, GGI 15297.

47. Justus M. Van Der Kroef, "The Indonesian Eurasian and His Culture," 459.
48. RSC to GGI, July 24, 1921, CAOM, GGI 15298.
49. After a few run-ins with the law during World War I, de la Chevrotière went on to become the editor of *Trung Lập Báo* and its French counterpart, *L'Impartial*. He also served on the colonial council. De la Chevrotière portrayed himself as the champion of public virtue and morality, criticizing the colonial government for taking a soft stance towards rebels and even threatening to set up his own police force to defend French colonists against rebels. Walter Langlois, *André Malraux: The Indochina Adventure*, 42, 46, 86–88, 174; "Henri De Lachevrotier," *L'Eurafricain*, 1951; Philippe M. F. Peycam, *The Birth of Vietnamese Political Journalism: Saigon, 1916–1930*, 135; Virginia Thompson, *French Indo-China*, 310; Jacques de la Chevrotière, *Les chavigny de la Chevrotière: En nouvelle-France à la Martinique*, 41.
50. As quoted in Langlois, *André Malraux*, 59.
51. Trần Huy Liệu, *Đảng Thanh Niên 1926–1927: Tập tài liệu và hồi ký;* Hue Tam Ho Tai, *Radicalism and the Origins of the Vietnamese Revolution*, 126; Peycam, *The Birth of Vietnamese Political Journalism*, 131.
52. Gravelle to GGI, May 25, 1920, CAOM, GGI 15297.
53. Donnat to Lt. Col., August 7, 1916, CNA, RSC 2452.
54. President of the Society for the Protection of Childhood to Goucoch, August 25, 1921, CAOM GGI 15298.
55. Reverony to RST, May 15, 1924, VNNA I, RST 5488.
56. Tissot to RST, undated, February 1925, VNNA I, RST 5488.
57. The British had abandoned the term "Eurasian" in 1911 for its racialist undertones and, instead, took the term "Anglo-Indian." Satoshi Mizutani, *The Meaning of White: Race, Class, and the "Domiciled Community" in British India, 1858–1930.*
58. Saada, *Les Enfants de la Colonie.*
59. RSA to GGI, August 3, 1928, VNNA 4, RSA 1313.
60. Reprint of an extract of a 1928 note, Tissot to Mayor of Hanoi, November 1937, CAOM, FM Guernut 25.
61. RSA to President of the Society for Métis in Huế, October 9, 1916, VNNA 4, RSA 2862.
62. Ibid.
63. RSA to President of the Society of Métis in Hue, October 9, 1916, VNNA 4, RSA 2862.
64. RSA to GGI, August 3, 1928, VNNA 4, RSA 1313.
65. "Bulletin de la Société de Protection de l'Enfance en Annam," VNNA 4, RSA 2862.
66. Galuski to RSA, May 15, 1917, VNNA 4, RSA 2862; President of the Society for the Protection of Childhood in Annam to RSA, May 30, 1917, VNNA 4, RSA 2862; Signed Galuski, June 12, 1917, VNNA 4, RSA 2862.

67. Graffeuil, to President of Red Cross, September 12, 1922, VNNA I, RST 74095.

68. Letter to GGI, May 22, 1929, VNNA I, RST 48857.

69. CAOM, GGI 18213.

70. "Note sur la société de protection des enfants métis abandonnés," no date, after 1914, VNNA I, Maire Ville de Hanoi [hereafter MHN] 5899.

71. Minister of War to Minister of Colonies, June 14, 1920, CAOM, SLOT-FOM XII 1.

72. GGI to RSA, July 4, 1919, VNNA 2, RSA 867.

73. Letter to Mayor of Hanoi, January 17, 1928, VNNA 1, MHN, 5899.

74. "Société d'assistance aux enfants franco-indochinois, assemblée générale annuelle ordinaire du 4 april 1939," VNNA I, GGI 505.

75. Minister of War to Minister of Colonies, June 16, 1917, CAOM, GGI 26921.

76. Commander Revenroy to MHN, January 1922, VNNA 1, MHN 5899.

77. Marquette to RST, March 14, 1916, CAOM, RSTNF 1099.

78. "Société de Protection de l'Enfance au Cambodge," March 31, 1915, CNA, RSC 2455.

79. Head of Batallion Edon to RST, June 16, 1920, VNNA I, RST 48379.

80. RST to President of the Society, November 4, 1916, VNNA I, RST 23931.

81. Christina Firpo, "Shades of Whiteness: Petits-Blancs and the Politics of Military Allocations Distribution in World War I Colonial Cochinchina."

82. VNNA 2, RSA 1015.

83. Letter to RF of Fai Fo, December 22, 1917, VNNA 2, RSA 1015.

84. President of the Society for the Protection of Métis Children to MHN, May 22, 1920, VNNA I, MHN 5899.

85. CAOM, GGI 16775.

86. Ha, *French Women and the Empire,* 161.

87. RSC to GGI, August 13, 1915, CNA, RSC 2452.

88. Ibid.

89. "Procès Verbal de la Réunion du 9 Mars 1922," CNA, RSC 2455

90. In India, the British colonial government educated Eurasians in skills that would lead to jobs in sectors created specifically for them to ensure that they could compete with "home born" British or Indian workers. Mizutani, *The Meaning of White,* 92–93; "Société de Protection de l'Enfance au Cambodge," March 31, 1915, CNA, RSC 2455.

91. RSC to GGI, August 13, 1915, CNA, RSC 2452.

92. Mizutani, *The Meaning of White,* 111–114.

93. Robert C. Bone, *The Dynamics of the Western New Guinea Problem,* 32; Jan Van Eechoud, "Nota Inzakekolonisatie van Indo-Europeanen in Nieuw-Guinea," 1949, Special Collections of the KITLV, University of Leiden, the Netherlands.

94. Margaret Sarkissian, "Cultural Chameleons: Portuguese Eurasian Strategies for Survival in Post-colonial Malaysia." *Journal of Southeast Asian Studies* 28, no. 2 (1997): 249–262.

95. Inspector General of Public Instruction to GGI, July 17, 1919, CAOM, GGI 2711.
96. RSC to GGI, August 13, 1915, CNA, RSC 2452.
97. Eric Thomas Jennings, "Đà Lạt, Capital of Indochina: Remolding Frameworks and Spaces in the Late Colonial Era."
98. Mizutani, *The Meaning of White*, 138–146.
99. Lan to RSA, October 7, 1916, VNNA 2, RSA 867.
100. RSC to GGI, August 13, 1915, CNA, RSC 2452.
101. "Note sur la société de protection des enfants métis abandonnés," undated, presumably 1920, VNNA I, MHN 5899.
102. "Note," January 20, 1917, CAOM, GGI 16772.
103. Andersen, "A Colonial Fountain of Youth."
104. "Conseil Général de la Seine, 1921, Proposition tendant à assurer aux enfants assistés de la Siene elevés sur les exploitations agricoles l'accès propriété," VNNA I, GGI 7807.
105. Long to Godin, February 1, 1922, CAOM, GGI 15299.
106. For information on the immigration debates, see Camiscioli, *Reproducing the French Race.*
107. Minister of Colonies to GGI, October 18, 1926, VNNA 1, RST 48972.
108. Lan to RSA, October 7, 1916, VNNA 2, RSA 867.
109. RSA to Lan, October 9, 1916, VNNA 4, RSA 2862.
110. "Note sur les oeuvres de protection de l'enfance," undated, presumably between 1933 and 1937, VNNA 1, RST 73758.
111. Tissot to RST, undated, February 1925, VNNA 1, RST 5488.
112. Director of Health to the Mayor of Coutance, October 1, 1925, CAOM, SLOTFOM XII 1.
113. "Note, Pour M. le Conseil d'Etat directeur des affaires politiques," August 3, 1926, VNNA 1, RST 48972.
114. Letter to Governor de colony, May 16, 1924.
115. Minister of Colonies to Galuski, February 1, 1925. CAOM, SLOTFOM XII 1.
116. Letter, June 10, 1932, VNNA 1, RST 48400.
117. Galuski to Minister of Colonies, July 1, 1925, CAOM, SLOTFOM XII 1.

CHAPTER 3: THE GREAT DEPRESSION AND CENTRALIZATION

1. Letter to RST, August 29, 1938, VNNA 1, MHN 5900.
2. Pierre Brocheux, "The State and the 1930s Depression in French Indochina," 251; Đình Tân Phạm, *Chủ Nghĩa Đế Quốc Pháp và Tình Hình Công Nghiệp ở Việt-Nam dưới Thời Thuộc Pháp*, 63–64.

3. Van Nguyen-Marshall, *In Search of Moral Authority: The Discourse on Poverty, Poor Relief, and Charity in French Colonial Indochina*, 1.

4. Ibid., 6, 57.

5. The article uses the term yêu nước, which also means "to be patriotic." "Tình Mẹ Con," *Phụ Nữ Tân Văn*, February 13, 1930; "Tình Mẹ Con Của Loài Vật," *Phụ Nữ Tân Văn*, December 1, 1932; "Con Phải Săn Sóc Cho Cha Mẹ," *Phụ Nữ Tân Văn*, April 3, 1930"; "Công Đức Cha Mẹ," *Phụ Nữ Tân Văn*, May 9, 1929; "Yêu Nước thì Phải Học," *Phụ Nữ Tân Văn*, May 2, 1929; "Con Chim Con, Con Cá Con," *Phụ Nữ Tân Văn*, June 19, 1930.

6. Although the government had begun centralizing social services in 1929, the Great Depression provided the impetus for a large-scale government takeover of social programs. In 1929, the Social Assistance Service was created. The decrees of February 21, 1933, and July 1, 1935, gave the colonial state regulatory powers over private and public charities. Edouard Marquis, *L'Oeuvre humaine de la France en Cochinchine*, 4–6.

7. "Khuyên Ấy vào Hội Dục Anh," *Phụ Nữ Tân Văn*, March 3, 1932.

8. Today, hộ sinh means "midwife." Hoàng Trọng Phu Tong Do SE, "Les Oeuvres de Protection de la Maternité et de l'Enfance de la Province de Hadong" (paper presented at the Congrès International pour la Protection de l'Enfance, 1933), 499.

9. "Dục Anh Viện! Dục Anh Viện!," *Phụ Nữ Tân Văn*, January 14, 1932.

10. Thiện, *Phụ-Nữ Tân-Văn: Phấn Son Tô Điểm Sơn Hà*, 62–66; "Khuyến Ấy vào Hội Dục Anh," *Phụ Nữ Tân Văn*, March 3, 1932.

11. "Một đứa nhỏ ba tháng bị cha mẹ bỏ ở viện dục anh," *Phụ Nữ Tân Văn*, May 11, 1933.

12. The most famous was Nhất Linh, *Đoạn tuyệt*; Martina Thucnhi Nguyen, "The Self-Reliant Literary Group (Tự Lực Văn Đoàn): Colonial Modernism in Vietnam, 1932–1941"; Neil L. Jamieson, *Understanding Vietnam*, 106; Cao Thi Nhu Quynh and John Schaefer, "Ho Bieu Chanh and the Early Development of the Vietnamese Novel," 100–111; Harriet M. Phinney, "Objets of Affection: Vietnamese Discourses on Love and Emancipation," 329–358.

13. Quang Anh Richard Tran, "From Red Lights to Red Flags: A History of Gender in Colonial to Contemporary Vietnam," 1–3.

14. Jamieson, *Understanding Vietnam*, 101.

15. Philippe M. F. Peycam, *The Birth of Vietnamese Political Journalism: Saigon, 1916–1930*, 173–174.

16. "Một ý kiến về vấn đề hôn nhân của người Pháp và người Nam," *Đông pháp*, January 24, 1937.

17. "Vì một thiếu phụ mà xảy ra cuộc ẩu đả giữa một người Âu và một người Nam," *Đông Pháp*, July 20, 1938; "Anh kéo xe cho em," *Báo Loa*, July 16 or 18, 1935.

18. Vũ Trọng Phụng, *The Industry of Marrying Europeans*, trans. Thúy Tranviet, 37.

19. "Note de Service," June 1, 1931, CAOM, RSTNF 3987.

20. "Note de Service," February 19, 1936, CAOM, RSTNF 3987.

21. Unsigned letter (authors referred to themselves as *vợ lính tây,* meaning "wives of western soldiers") to resident superior, March 1926, CAOM, RSTNF 3987.

22. Gendarmerie Rey to RF Quang Yen, March 11, 1936, CAOM, RSTNF 3987; Philippot to RST, March 26, 1936, CAOM, RSTNF 3987.

23. Head of Battalion Pinault to General Commandant of the Subdivision, March 10, 1936, CAOM RSTNF 3987.

24. "Chống lừa đảo! Bạn chống lừa đảo! Tiền mất, chống cũng mất nốt," *Việt báo,* August 6, 1937, 5.

25. "Một cô gái 17 tuổi, bỏ nhà đi lấy lính da đen," *Ngọ báo,* August 18, 1935; "Có phải cô Ninh bỏ nhà theo 1 người lính Tây, mẹ đến tìm còn hành hung?" *Đông Pháp,* March 4, 1937, 2.

26. "Người bếp Tây-đen Samba bắt vợ để lõa lồ thân thể dẫn đi rong phố đã bị kết án ba tháng tù," *Việt Báo,* September 19, 1936.

27. "Ghen với ông chồng da đen, một cô gái Thổ định từ giã cõi đời," *Đông Pháp,* July 4, 1937; "Người chồng 'da đen' ấy phụ bạc khiến vợ thắt cổ tự vẫn không chết," *Việt Báo,* July 4, 1937.

28. "Một ý kiến về vấn đề hôn nhân của người Pháp và người Nam," *Đông pháp,* January 24, 1937.

29. Vũ, *The Industry of Marrying Europeans,* 43.

30. Ibid., 48.

31. Marie-Paule Ha, *French Women in the Empire,* 137; Table 5.7, "European Population with Gender and Age Breakdown in Indochina (1921–1937)," in Ha, *French Women in the Empire,* 131.

32. "Les rendifications des francais d'indochine II," *L'Alerte,* January 6, 1937; "Compte Rendu sur la Situation Morale et Financière de la Société de Protection de l'Enfance au Cambodge pendant l'Année 1936," VNNA I, GGI 10329.

33. See notes crossed out of the first draft of the letter. "Note sur la Société d'assistance aux enfants franco-indochinois de Tonkin," signed Tissot, April 25, 1937, VNNA 1, RST 73758.

34. Hue Tam Ho Tai, *Radicalism and the Origins of the Vietnamese Revolution,* 206.

35. "Xã hội là gì?" *Phụ Nữ Tân Văn,* November 10, 1932; "Nuôi con để cấy về sau," *Phụ Nữ Tân Văn,* January 14, 1932.

36. Nghệ An: Hội liên hiệp phụ nữ tỉnh Vĩnh Phú Nghệ An, *Lịch Sử Phong Trào Phụ Nữ Nghệ An (1930–1975),* 49; Trần Huy Liệu et al., eds., *Cách Mạng Cận Đại Việt-Nam,* vol. 6, 30; *Lịch Sử Truyền Thống Cách Mạng Phụ Nữ Hà Tây; Lịch Sử Truyền Thống Phụ Nữ Nam Hà (1930–1995).*

37. Tai, *Radicalism and the Origins of the Vietnamese Revolution,* 244; Sophie Quinn-Judge, "Women in the Early Vietnamese Communist Movement: Sex, Lies, and Liberation," *South East Asia Research* 9, no. 3 (2001): 245–269.

38. "Note sur la Société d'assistance aux enfants franco-indochinois de Tonkin," signed Tissot, April 25, 1937, VNNA 1, RST 73758.

39. "Le problème Eurasien au Tonkin," undated, 1938, CAOM, FM Guernut 97.

40. Esquivillon to Sister Rosalie Bonvin, March 17, 1938, VNNA 2, Goucoch VIA.8/282(13).

41. See Laura Lee Downs, *Childhood in the Promised Land: Working-Class Movements and the Colonies de Vacances in France, 1880–1960.*

42. See Elizabeth Ezra, "Colonialism Exposed: Miss France D'Outre-Mer, 1937."

43. "Renseignments sur la Société de protection de l'enfance au Cambodge 1938–1939," VNNA 1, GGI 10329.

44. VNNA 1, RST 48426.

45. Letter to Mayor of Hanoi, July 30, 1935, VNNA 1, MHN 5900.

46. "Notice sur le Société d'assistance aux enfants franco-indochinois du Tonkin," April 25, 1937, VNNA 1, RST 73758.

47. Letter to Colonel Commandant, November 28, 1932, VNNA 1, RST 48405.

48. Vũ, "Kỹ nghệ lấy tây," 68.

49. "Note sur la Société d'assistance aux enfants franco-indochinois de Tonkin," signed Tissot, April 25, 1937, VNNA 1, RST 73758.

50. Esquivillon to Sister Rosalie Bonvin, March 17, 1938, VNNA 2, Goucoch VIA.8/282(13).

51. The *traite des jaunes,* "trade of yellow women," was a human trafficking scheme that traded Asian women. "Notice sur le Société d'assistance aux enfants Franco-Indochinois du Tonkin," April 25, 1937, VNNA 1, RST 73758.

52. Letter to Gallois Montbrun, December 24, 1931, VNNA 1, RST 48427.

53. Head of Police and *Sûreté* to Mayor of Hanoi, April 24, 1933, VNNA 1, MHN 5899.

54. Vũ, "Kỹ nghệ lấy tây," 55.

55. As Marie-Paule Ha shows, the term *Français d'Indochine* had no fixed meaning in popular discussion. Ha found evidence of the term referring to metropolitan French living in the colony and, in another case, all those with French citizenship, including naturalized indigenous. This political group defines *Les Français d'Indochine* as colony-born French; naturalized Vietnamese, Cambodian, and Lao; French citizens from *anciens colonies;* and both recognized and nonrecognized *métis.* Ha, *French Women and the Empire,* 119.

56. Justus M. Van Der Kroef, "The Indonesian Eurasian and His Culture," *Phylon* 16, no. 4 (1955).

57. Henri Bonvincini, *Enfants de la Colonie,* 44; Virginia Thompson and Richard Adolff, *Minority Problems in Southeast Asia,* 149.

58. Paul Ballous, preface to *Enfants de la Colonie,* by Henri Bonvicini, V.

59. Henri Bonvicini, *Enfants de la Colonie,* 44.

60. Ibid., 44–46.

61. "Revendication des francais d'indochine," *L'Alerte,* December 30, 1936.

62. "Français d'indochine," "fils des francais," "les français né dans la pays," "français du pays," "la progeniture es francais," "enfant de la colony," "ces francais," and "nos enfants." His unwillingness to call attention to the mixed heritage of fatherless *métis* children, however, only applied to the case of Indochina, as he consistently referred to mixed-race people of the Dutch Netherlands Indies as "*eurasiens*." "Les rendifications des Français d'Indochine III, Les employs privé dans la plantation et la riziere," *L'Alerte*, January 8, 1937; "Les rendifications des Français d'Indochine IV-V," *L'Alerte*, January 13–14, 1937; "Les rendifications des Français d'Indochine final," *L'Alerte*, January 18–19, 1937.

63. Bonvicini, *Enfants de la Colonie*, 15–16.

64. Ibid., 17.

65. Ibid., 16, 24–26.

66. "Revendications des Français d'Indochine (suite en fin): Un element regulative indispensable," *L'Alerte*, January 18–19, 1937.

67. "Les rendifications des français d'Indochine IV-V," *L'Alerte*, January 13–14, 1937.

68. "Revendication des Français d'Indochine," *L'Alerte*, December 30, 1936.

69. "Tribune des Lectures: Hommes Heureux Pensez aux Petits *Métis*," *Blanc et Jaune*, September 27, 1937.

70. "Memoire sur la question des Français d'Indochine," undated, presumably 1937. CAOM, FM Guernut 25; Bonvicini, *Enfants de la Colonie*, 24–26.

71. "Les rendifications des Français d'Indochine III," *L'Alerte*, January 8, 1937; "Les rendifications des Français d'Indochine IV-V," *L'Alerte*, January 13–14, 1937; "Les rendifications des Français d'Indochine final," *L'Alerte*, January 18–19, 1937; Jan Van Eechoud, "Nota Inzakekolonisatie van Indo-Europeanen in Nieuw-Guinea," 1949, Special Collections of the KITLV, University of Leiden, the Netherlands.

72. "Les rendifications des Français d'Indochine III," *L'Alerte*, January 8, 1937. This plan was repeated in Vidal to Goucoch, November 14, 1937, CAOM, FM Guernut 25.

73. "Revendication des Français d'Indochine," *L'Alerte*, December 30, 1936; "Les rendifications des Français d'Indochine III," *L'Alerte*, January 8, 1937.

74. Ibid.

75. Martina Nguyen, "The Self-Reliant Literary Group (Tự Lực Văn Đoàn): Colonial Modernism in Vietnam, 1932–1941," 197, 206.

76. Charles Fourniau, "Les Années 1930 et l'Impasse Coloniale en Indochine," 20.

77. Tony Chafer and Amanda Sackur, *French Colonial Empire and the Popular Front: Hope and Disillusion*, 3.

78. " Một bức thư của ông Justin Godard," *Trung hoà báo*, March 18, 1937.

79. "Le problème Eurasien au Tonkin," 1938, CAOM, FM Guernut 97.

80. "Enquête n4: Sur la situation des eurasiens d'Indochine," by Le Bon, 1938, CAOM, FM Guernut 97.

81. "Enquête n4: Sur le problème des *métis*," from the province of Kampong Chhang, June 11, 1938, CAOM FM Guernut 97.
82. Table 5.7, "European Population with Gender and Age Breakdown in Indochina (1921–1937)," in Ha, *French Women and the Empire*, 131.
83. "Le problème Eurasien au Tonkin," 1938, CAOM, FM Guernut 97.
84. Ibid.
85. Ibid.
86. Ibid.; Table 5.7, "European Population with Gender and Age Breakdown in Indochina (1921–1937)," in Ha, *French Women and the Empire*, 131.
87. "Le problème Eurasien au Tonkin," 1938, CAOM, FM Guernut 97.
88. Responses from Vĩnh Long, Trà Vinh, Tân An, Sa Đéc, Biên Hòa, Bà Rịa, Bạc Liêu, and Bến Tre, CAOM, FM Guernut 97.
89. "Enquête n4: Sur la situation des eurasiens d'Indochine," response from the province of Bạc Liêu, 1938, CAOM, FM Guernut 97.
90. "Le problème Eurasien au Tonkin," 1938, CAOM, FM Guernut 97.
91. Stoler, "Making Empire Respectable"; Ha, *French Women and the Empire*, 137.
92. "Enquête n4: Sur la situation des eurasiens d'Indochine," response from province of Bà Rịa, 20 April 1938, CAOM, FM Guernut 97.
93. "Enquête n4: Sur la situation des eurasiens d'Indochine," response from province of Bạc Liêu, 1938, CAOM, FM Guernut 97.
94. "Enquête n4: Sur le problème des *métis*," response from province of Vĩnh Long, 20 April 1938, CAOM, FM Guernut 97.
95. "Enquête n4: Sur la situation des eurasiens d'Indochine," response from Bến Tre, 1938, CAOM, FM Guernut 97.
96. See files on Les Français de l'Indochine in CAOM, FM Guernut 97, 25.
97. François Bilange, Charles Fourniau, and Alain Ruscio, *Rapport de Mission en Indochine 1 January—14 Mars 1937*, 159.
98. "Note sur la situation des eurasiens d'Indochina au point de vue social et politique," by Marinette, 1938, CAOM, FM Guernut 97.
99. "Enquête sur les *métis*," response from Bạc Liêu, 1937, CAOM, FM Guernut 97.
100. "Enquête sur les *métis*," response from RST, 1937, CAOM, FM Guernut 97.
101. William H. Schneider, *Quality and Quantity: The Quest for Biological Regeneration in Twentieth-Century France*, 208–229.
102. "Le problème Eurasien au Tonkin," 1938, CAOM, FM Guernut 97.
103. RSA to GGI, July 24, 1938, CAOM, FM Guernut 97.
104. "Le problème Eurasien au Tonkin," 1938, CAOM, FM Guernut 97.
105. Ibid.
106. Responses from Gia Định, Bạc Liêu, and Qui Nhơn, CAOM, FM Guernut 97. For an excellent analysis of French colonizers adjusting to the environment, see Eric T. Jennings, *Curing the Colonizers: Hydrotherapy, Climatology, and French Colonial Spas*.

107. *Métis* protection society officials in French West Africa also believed that mixed-race people were better acclimated to the local climate than were monoracial whites. "Enquête n4: Sur le problème des *métis*," response from RF Qui Nhơn, May 14, 1938, CAOM, FM Guernut 97; White, *Children of the French Empire*.

108. "Le problème Eurasien au Tonkin," 1938, CAOM, FM Guernut 97.

109. "Enquête n4: Sur le problem des *métis*," from Hà Tĩnh, May 14, 1938, CAOM, FM Guernut 97.

110. "Le problème Eurasien au Tonkin," 1938, CAOM, FM Guernut 97.

111. "Ibid.

112. "Enquête n4: Sur le problème des *métis*," response from Kompongcham, June 11, 1938. CAOM, FM Guernut 97.

113. "Voeux de l'Association des legionnaires en Indochine," 1937, CAOM, FM Guernut 25.

114. RSA to GGI, June 24, 1938, CAOM, FM Guernut 97.

115. Plante to RSC, May 5, 1938, CAOM, FM Guernut 97.

116. "Enquête sur les *métis*," response from Bạc Liêu, 1937, CAOM, FM Guernut 97.

117. "Le problème Eurasien au Tonkin," 1938, CAOM, FM Guernut 97.

118. Ibid.

119. Ibid.

120. Ibid.

121. "Favor enfants 1—voeux deposé en faveur des enfants eurasiens abandonnés," by Tissot, 1937, CAOM, FM Guernut 25.

122. "Enquête n4: Sur la situation des eurasiens d'Indochine," by Le Bon, 1938, CAOM, FM Guernut 97.

123. "Le problème Eurasien au Tonkin," 1938, CAOM, FM Guernut 97.

124. Report by Tran Van Don, 1937, CAOM, FM Guernut 25.

125. RSA to GGI, June 24, 1938, CAOM, FM Guernut 97.

126. Response from Saigon, 14 November 1937, CAOM, FM Guernut 97.

127. "Enquête n4: Sur la situation des eurasiens d'Indochine," response from Gia Định, April 20, 1938, CAOM, FM Guernut 97.

128. "Enquête sur les *métis*," 1938, VNNA 1, RST 71816.

129. RSA to GGI, June 24, 1938, CAOM, FM Guernut 97.

130. Bilange, Fourniau, and Ruscio, eds., *Rapport de Mission en Indochine*, 157–160.

131. For an excellent study on colonial psychiatric institutions, see Claire Ellen Edington, "Beyond the Asylum: Colonial Psychiatry in French Indochina, 1880–1940."

132. "Note sur la société d'assistance aux enfants franco-indochinois de Tonkin," signed Tissot, April 25, 1937, VNNA 1, RST 73758.

133. "Note pour M. le Chef de Troisieme Bureau," August 24, 1938, CAOM, RSTNF 3915.

134. Tissot to RST, May 31, 1938, CAOM, RST NF 3915.

135. Ibid.; RST to Tissot, August 1938, CAOM, RSTNF 3915. The child was eventually sent to l'École des Enfants de Troupe. Tissot to RST, May 22, 1939, VNNA 1, RST 71819.

136. RSC to GGI, August 13, 1915, CNA, RSC 2452.

137. Martin to GGI, June 23, 1938, VNNA 4, RSA 3864.

138. Martin to GGI, September 20, 1938, VNNA 4, RSA 3864.

139. "Très Urgent" from GGI, September 15, 1938, VNNA 4, RSA 3864.

140. Arrêté by GGI Jules Brévié, October 10, 1938, VNNA 4, RSA 3864.

141. "Très Urgent," from GGI, September 15, 1938, VNNA 4, RSA 3864.

142. CAOM, RSTNF 3890.

143. RSA to RF of Thua Thien and Mayor of Tourane, September 19, 1938, VNNA 4, RSA 3864.

144. From Martin, March 28, 1939, VNNA 1, GGI 10330.

145. Mayor to RST, May 20, 1939, VNNA 1, RST 71819.

146. "Instruction général n 83," July 27, 1939, SHAT, 10H327.

147. "Ligue de droites de l'homme," April 30, 1938, VNNA 2, Goucoch VIA.8/282(13).

148. Elisa Camiscioli, *Reproducing the French Race: Immigration, Intimacy, and Embodiment in the Early Twentieth Century*; "Rapport à Monsieur Mandel, Minister des Colonies," signed Corsil, December 16, 1938, included in letter to GGI, January 26, 1939, VNNA 1, GGI 10332.

149. "Rapport à Monsieur Mandel, Minister des Colonies," signed Corsil, December 16, 1938, included in letter to GGI, January 26, 1939, VNNA 1, GGI 10332.

150. For an important study on policies towards Eurasian *métis* in the AOF, see White, *Children of the French Empire*.

151. Brévié to Minister of Colonies, July 14, 1938, VNNA 2, Goucoch VIA.8/282(13).

152. Goucoch to GGI, September 19, 1938, VNNA 2, Goucoch VIA.8/282(13).

153. Brévié to Minister of Colonies, July 14, 1938, VNNA 2, Goucoch VIA.8/282(13).

154. Goucoch to GGI, September 19, 1938, VNNA 2, Goucoch VIA.8/282(13).

155. Goucoch to President of Human Rights League, September 9, 1938, VNNA 2, Goucoch VIA.8/282(13).

156. Sister Rosalie Bonvin to President of AMAS, March 6, 1939, VNNA 2, Goucoch VIA.8/282(13).

157. GGI to Goucoch, October 3, 1938, VNNA 2, Goucoch VIA.8/282(13).

158. RSA to GGI, March 9, 1939, VNNA 1, GGI 76.

159. Goucoch to GGI, January 12, 1939, VNNA 1, GGI 4810; Esquivillon to Goucoch, August 26, 1938, VNNA 2, Goucoch VIA.8/282(13).

160. RST to M.M. les Residents of Provinces, Commanders of Military, Mayors of Hanoi and Haiphong, March 18, 1939, VNNA 1, MH 5917.

161. "Ville de Hanoi, police municipal, liste des enfants eurasiens abandonnés . . ." April 6, 1939, VNNA 1, MH 5917.

162. RST to GGI, April 13, 1939, CAOM, RSTNF 3901; RF Son Tay to RST, March 1, 1938, CAOM, RSTNF 3901.

163. "Arrêté 2 August 1939," VNNA 1, GGI 72.

CHAPTER 4: WAR, POLITICAL LOYALTY, AND RACIAL DEMOGRAPHY

1. Aumont to Mayor of Haỉ Phòng, October 28, 1942, VNNA 1, GGI 495; CAOM 90APC62.

2. Aumont to Mayor of Haỉ Phòng, October 28, 1942, VNNA 1, GGI 495.

3. "Note de Madame Aumont, charge de l'oeuvre des enfants eurasiens à Hai Phong," CAOM, 90APC62.

4. Letter to Mayor of Hanoi, June 29, 1940, VNNA 1, MHN 5900.

5. Virginia Thompson and Richard Adolff, *Minority Problems in Southeast Asia*.

6. Felicia Yap, "Eurasians in British Asia during the Second World War," *Journal of the Royal Asiatic Society* 21, no. 4 (2011): 485–505.

7. Elly Touwen-Bouwsma, "Japanese Minority Policy: The Eurasians in Java and the Dilemma of Ethnic Loyalty," *Bijdragen tot de Taal-, Land- en Volkenkunde, Japan, Indonesia and the War Myths and Realities* 152 no. 4 (1996); Justus M. van der Kroef, "The Eurasian Minority in Indonesia," *American Sociological Review* 18 (1953): 484–493.

8. Rebecca Kenneison, *Playing for Malaya: A Eurasian Family in the Pacific War*, 72, 150, 182; Yap, "Eurasians in British Asia during the Second World War."

9. Eric Jennings, *Vichy in the Tropics: Pétain's National Revolution in Madagascar, Guadeloupe, and Indochina, 1940–1944*.

10. Bernard Fall, however, cautions against considering Hòa Hảo leader Huỳnh Phú Sổ a Japanese collaborator, given that he predicted a Japanese failure. Fall, "The Political-Religious Sects of Viet-Nam," 243–249.

11. Anne Raffin, *Youth Mobilization in Vichy Indochina and Its Legacies, 1940 to 1970*, 13, 64, 77.

12. Anne Raffin, "Easternization Meets Westernization: Patriotic Youth Organizations in French Indochina during World War II," *French Politics, Culture, and Society* 20, no. 2 (2002): 20.

13. In February 1944, *Thể Thao Đông Dương* changed its name to *Thanh Niên Đông Pháp*, emphasizing closer ties to France. This paper lasted through March 8, 1945. "Vệ sinh thường thức," *Thanh Niên Đông Pháp*, January 25, 1945; "Trong vườn khoa học, sanh tố K là gì?," *Thanh Niên Đông Pháp*, March 7, 1944; "Cho được sống lâu, vô bịnh, loài vật cũng cần tập thể thao như người," *Thanh Niên Đông Pháp*, February 10, 1944.

14. Raffin, *Youth mobilization in Vichy Indochina and Its legacies, 1940 to 1970:* 1–13, 143, 95; Nguyễn Khánh Toàn, *Lịch Sử Việt Nam tập II, 1858–1945.*

15. William H. Schneider, *Quality and Quantity: The Quest for Biological Regeneration in Twentieth-Century France,* 208–229.

16. P. Huard and Do Xuan Hop, "Recherches sur l'importance numérique des européens et des eurasiens," *Bulletin de l'Institut Indochinois pour l'Etude de l'Homme* 1942 (1943).

17. "Tableau III, Movement de Certaines Catégories de la Population 1937 à 1948," in Direction de la Statistique Générale, *Annuaire Statistique Abrégé, 1943–1949,* 321.

18. VNNA 1, GGI 89.

19. Jennings, *Vichy in the Tropics,* 163–178.

20. See reference to Coedès' suggestions in letter to the Inspector General of Labor and Social Provisions, December 10, 1942, VNNA I, GGI 89; "Note," December 24, 1942, VNNA I, GGI 89.

21. Putting what they thought were the interests of the wards over the interests of the colony, some members of the Jules Brévié Foundation [hereafter JBF] considered sending fatherless *métis* children to the *métropole,* where they would be "drowned [*noyés*] in French society," and young *métisse* girls would be assured an "honorable future." Wartime hostilities, however, delayed this plan, and the organization focused on demographic plans in the colony. "Rapport Annuel sur la Situation et le Fonctionnement de la Société de Protection des Métis d'Annam," November 3, 1940, VNNA 1, GGI 78; Durand to Lambert, January 26, 1941, VNNA 1, GGI 76; Durand to Bazé, December 28, 1943, VNNA 1, GGI 76; Letter from President of JBF, November 10, 1942, VNNA 1, GGI 89; "Rapport sur l'Activité de la Fondation Brévié Pendant l'Année 1943," VNNA 1, GGI 482.

22. "Notes a/s du Problèm des Eurasiens," undated, most likely 1942, VNNA 1, GGI 89; Goucoch to GGI, December 14, 1943, VNNA I, GGI 10349.

23. "Rapport sur l'activité de la Fondation Jules Brévié pendant l'année 1943," 1944, VNNA I, GGI 482.

24. "Rapport sur le Fonctionnement de la Société d'Assistance aux Enfants Franco-Indochinois du Cambodge," June 29, 1944, VNNA 1, GGI 90; "Rapport Annuel sur la Situation et le Fonctionnement de la Société de Protection des Métis d'Annam," November 3, 1940, VNNA 1, GGI 78.

25. "Notes a/s du Problème des Eurasiens," undated, presumably 1942, VNNA 1, GGI 89. A Japanese military officer who inspected the French *sûreté* files told David Marr that *métis* men were the most effective *sûreté* agents during World War II. David G. Marr, *Vietnam 1945: The Quest for Power,* 72.

26. "Rapport sur le Fonctionnement de la Société d'Assistance aux Enfants Franco-Indochinois du Cambodge," June 29, 1944, VNNA 1, GGI 90.

27. "Notes a/s du Problème des Eurasiens," undated, presumably 1942, VNNA 1, GGI 89.

28. Pierre Gourou, *Les paysans du delta tonkinois;* Andrew Hardy, *Red Hills: Migrants and the State in the Highlands of Vietnam,* 74–78; AJP, "Colonisation familiale," *Indochine Hebdomadaire Illustré,* February 10, 1944; Gregoire Khérian, "Le problème démographique en Indochine," (Hanoi: Imprimerie d'Extrême-Orient, 1937). See reports by Gourou and Eckert for the Guernut commission, CAOM, Guernut 23; René Robin, "L'effort français en Indochine," *Indochine Hebdomadaire Illustré,* July 30, 1942.

29. Jean Paillard, *L'Empire Francais de Demain,* 40.

30. Jennings, *Vichy in the Tropics,* 166.

31. "De son côté, M William Bazé nous écrit," Private archive of the Fédération des Oeuvres de l'Enfance Française d'Indochine [hereafter FOEFI], France; Letter from Sister Françoise Régis, October 11, 1951, SHAT 10H327.

32. Goucoch to GGI, November 3, 1941, VNNA I, GGI 4806.

33. "Fondation Jules Brévié, Réunion Annuelle de 1943 du Conseil d'Administration, Procèss Verbal de la Séance de 20 Décembre 1943," VNNA 1, GGI 482.

34. "Note," October 10, 1942, VNNA I, GGI 89; Letter to Coedès, November 26, 1942, VNNA I, GGI 472; Inspecter General of Labor and Social Provisions to George Coedès, November 16, 1942, VNNA 1, GGI 89.

35. Note to Director of Economic Services, October 10, 1942, VNNA I, GGI 89.

36. Note from treasurer of JBF, March 11, 1943, VNNA 1, GGI 95; Head of Veterinary Services to Inspector General of Agriculture, May 26, 1944, VNNA 1, GGI 95; Inspector General of Agriculture to Director of Administrative Affaires, December 14, 1944, VNNA 1, GGI 95.

37. André Baudrit, "La Naissance de Dalat," *Indochine Hebdomadaire Illustré,* February 10, 1944.

38. Claude Perrens, "Lettre de Dalat," *Indochine Hebdomadaire Illustré,* July 8, 1943.

39. Ibid.

40. Baudrit, "La Naissance de Dalat."

41. Eric T. Jennings, *Imperial Heights: Dalat and the Making and Undoing of French Indochina;* L. G. Pigneau, "Dalat—Capital Administratif de l'Indochine?," *La Revue Indochinoise Juridique et Economique* 2 (1937).

42. For the relationship between orientalists, colonial administrators, and welfare institutions, see Emmanuelle Saada, *Les Enfants de la Colonie,* 112–126; Pierre Singaravélou, *L'Ecole française d'extrême-orient ou l'institution des marges (1898–1956): Essai d'histoire sociale et politique de la science coloniale,* 142.

43. Lan to RSA, October 7, 1917, VNNA 2, RSA 867.

44. Graffeuil to Lambert, October 19, 1940, VNNA I, GGI 76; "Note de Bureau de Affaires Politiques pour le Secretaire Générale," November 3, 1942, VNNA 1, GGI 89.

45. Raffin, *Youth Mobilization in Vichy Indochina,* 161.

46. Today, the site of the former École des Enfants de Troupe Eurasien is the University of Dalat.

47. Graffeuil to Lambert, October 19, 1940, VNNA 1, GGI 76.

48. "Circulaire," undated, presumably 1914–1916, VNNA 2, RSA 867.

49. "Rapport sur le Fonctionnement de la Société d'Assistance aux Enfants Franco-Indochinois du Cambodge," June 29, 1944, VNNA 1, GGI 90.

50. Note to GGI, November 3, 1942, VNNA 1, GGI 89.

51. "La question des eurasiens," undated, presumably 1940–1942, VNNA 2, Goucoch VIA.8/282(13).

52. "Notes au sujet du problème des Eurasiens," 1942, VNNA I, GGI 89.

53. Reference to a September 17, 1942, directive by Decoux asking for a census of fatherless *métis* children by 1943. Decoux à RST, April 16, 1943, VNNA 1, GGI 88.

54. Decoux to RSA, April 16, 1943, VNNA 1, Fonds GGI 88.

55. Decoux to President of JBF, August 12, 1941, VNNA 1, RST 71816.

56. "Notes au Sujet du Problèm des Eurasiens," undated, presumably 1942, VNNA 1, GGI 89.

57. Letter to President of JBF, December 8, 1942, VNNA 1, GGI 89; "Rapport sur l'Activité de la FBJ pendant l'Année 1943," VNNA 1, GGI 482; Letter from president of JBF, November 10, 1942, VNNA 1, GGI 89.

58. Letter from Lt. Col, Belloc, November 12, 1942, VNNA 1, GGI 89.

59. "Décret 2986 du 24 Novembre 1943 Portant Institution des Pupilles Eurasiens d'Indochine," VNNA 1, GGI 479.

60. Note from GGI, November 17, 1942, VNNA 1, GGI 89.

61. Letter from RS Rival, November 19, 1940, VNNA 1, MHN 5917.

62. RF Lang Son to RST, April 12, 1943, VNNA, GGI 494; "Rapport annuel sur la situation et le fonctionnement de la Sociéte de protection des métis d'Annam," November 3, 1940, VNNA 1, GGI 78.

63. Letter from Belloc, November 12, 1942, VNNA 1, GGI 89.

64. RF Lang Son to RST, April 12, 1943, VNNA, GGI 494.

65. Original text is underlined. "Notes au Sujet du Problèm des Eurasiens," undated, presumably 1942, VNNA 1, GGI 89.

66. "La question des eurasiens," undated, presumably 1940–1942, VNNA 2, Goucoch VIA.8/282(13); "Rapport annuel sur la situation et le fonctionnement de la Sociéte de protection des métis d'Annam," November 3, 1940, VNNA 1, GGI 78.

67. "Rapport Annuel sur la Situation et le Fonctionnement de la Société de Protection des Métis d'Annam," November 3, 1940, VNNA 1, GGI 78.

68. RST to Inspector of Political Affairs, January 5, 1945, VNNA 1, GGI 471.

69. Letter form Belloc, November 14, 1942, VNNA 1, GGI 89.

70. "Notes au Sujet du Problèm des Eurasiens," undated, presumably 1942, VNNA 1, GGI 89.

71. Letter from Belloc, November 12, 1942, VNNA 1, GGI 89.
72. Aumont to RST, November 7, 1944, VNNA 1, GGI 495.
73. "Maison de Nam Dinh 1944," VNNA 1, GGI 88.
74. "En Execution des Prescriptions de la Transmision n 19 /sd du Colonel, cdt la Subdivision de Phu Tho, Garnison de Tuyen Quang," undated, VNNA 1, GGI 10339.
75. The archival record does not indicate the children's fate. Belloc to President JBF, May 14, 1940, VNNA 1, GGI 10338.
76. Gazin to RST, February 29, 1940, CAOM, RSTNF 3923; "Institute de Notre Dame des Missions, Liste des Enfants pour l'Année 1944," VNNA 1, GGI 88.
77. Aumont to Mayor of Hai Phong, October 28, 1942, VNNA 1, GGI 495.
78. Letter from President of Society for the Protection of Métis of Annam, January 29, 1943, VNNA, GGI 75.
79. Letter to RST, September 1942, CAOM, RSTNF 3942.
80. Police Commissioner to Central Commissioner, 5 April 1941, VNNA 1, MHN 5817.
81. Letter to President of the Society, January 22, 1943, VNNA 1, Fonds GGI 75.
82. Letter from President of the Society for the Protection of Métis of Annam, January 29, 1943, VNNA, GGI 75.
83. Letter to Commissioner, July 9, 1940, VNNA 1, MHN 5917; "Liste des Enfants Eurasiens Abandonnés et dont les Mères Conseitent à se Dessaisir," 1939, VNNA 1, MHN 5917.
84. "Rapport annuel sur la situation et le fonctionnement de la Sociéte de protection des métis d'Annam," November 3, 1940, VNNA 1, Fonds GGI 78.
85. Aumont to Rivière, May 19, 1944, VNNA 1, GGI 495.
86. See letters from mothers in VNNA 1, GGI 495.
87. RST to President of the Society for Assistance to Franco-Indochinese Children of Tonkin, September 21, 1944, VNNA 1, GGI 479; "Fédération des Oeuvres de l'Enfance Francais d'Indochine, Exercice 1954, Assemblée Générale Ordinaire des 5,6,7 Mai 1955."
88. "Rapport sur l'Activité de la FJB pendant l'Année 1944," VNNA 1, GGI 131.
89. Letter to Mayor of Hanoi, January 13, 1940, VNNA 1, MHN 5917.
90. Aumont to Rivière, October 28, 1942, VNNA 1, GGI 495.
91. Rivière to Aumont, October 10, 1944, VNNA 1, GGI 495.
92. Tissot to Mayor of Hanoi, January 28, 1939, VNNA 1, MHN 5916.
93. "Problème des eurasiens," November 17, 1942, VNNA 1, GGI 89.
94. Letter from GGI, January 27, 1943, VNNA 1, GGI 89.
95. "FJB, Réunion Annuelle de 1944 du Conseil d'Administration de Procès Verbal de la Séance du 15 décembre 1944," VNNA 1, GGI 131.
96. "Notes a/s du Problème des Eurasiens," undated, most likely 1942, VNNA 1, GGI 89.
97. Letter from Guiriec, January 5, 1945, VNNA 1, GGI 471.

98. President JBF to RST, January 12, 1940, CAOM, RSTNF 3922.
99. Letter to Mayor of Hanoi, September 1, 1941, VNNA 1, MHN 5900; Rivière to Aumont, November 13, 1944, VNNA 1, GGI 495.
100. Letter from Chauvet, December 24, 1942, VNNA 1, GGI 89.
101. "Problème des eurasiens," November 17, 1942, VNNA 1, GGI 89.
102. Letter from Aumont, September 30, 1942, VNNA 1, GGI 495; Aumont to Mayor of HaiPhong, October 28, 1942, VNNA 1, GGI 495; Letter to Aumont, October 31, 1942, VNNA 1, GGI 495.
103. Aumont to Rivière, June 27, 1944, VNNA 1, GGI 495.
104. Aumont to Rivière, May 19, 1944, VNNA 1, GGI 495.
105. Rivière to Aumont, November 18, 1944, VNNA 1, GGI 495. While the paper trail for the girls went silent, the child was listed among protection society records in 1964, suggesting that the girls may have taken the soldier's name and entered into the *métis* protection society system. "Fédération des Oeuvres de l'Enfance Française d'indochine [hereafter FOEFI], Exercice 1963, Assemblée Générale Ordinaire Du 11 Aout 1964."
106. Aumont to Rivière, September 28, 1944, VNNA 1, GGI 495; Aumont to Rivière, October 7, 1944, VNNA 1, GGI 495; Aumont to Rivère, November 7, 1944, VNNA 1, GGI 495; Rivière to Aumont, November 18, 1944, VNNA 1, GGI 495.
107. "L'enfant de troupe eurasien," by JN, 1951, SHAT 10H108.
108. Ibid.

CHAPTER 5: THE LAST FRENCH ISLAND IN INDOCHINA

1. "Xin Bỏ Pháp Tịch" (request to relinquish citizenship), signed "NTG, JR," 28 January 1946, CAOM, GF 9; Signed Trân Huy Cá, January 30, 1946, CAOM, GF 9; "Extrait des Minutes du Greffe du Tribunal de Première Instance de Hanoi (Tonkin) du 17 Juin 1933, Jugement Suppletif d'Acte de Naissance de JR," CAOM, GF 9.
2. Though the protection society continued to cover all the territory of Indochina, because these leaders had Vietnamese mothers and were located in Cochinchina, they focused most of their efforts on *métis* children in Vietnam.
3. David G. Marr, *Vietnam 1945: The Quest for Power;* Ngu Chieu Vu, "Political and Social Change in Vietnam, 1940–1946."
4. This statistic includes 9,190 women. Association Nationale des Anciens et Amis de l'Indochine et du Souvenir Indochinois, www.anai-asso.org/NET /document/le_temps_de_la_guerre/la_guerre_dindochine/forces_Françaises _en_extreme_orient/index.htm, accessed July 27, 2014.
5. Isabelle Tracol-Huynh, "Entre Ordre Colonial et Sante Publique, La Prostitution au Tonkin de 1885 a 1954," 298.

6. The DRV allowed soldiers and their families to stay in Vietnam through the 1970s. During this time, the DRV rejected soldiers' requests to leave the country. "Con lại 30 năm nhặt rác mua vé máy bay tìm về quê cha," August 1, 2014, zing.vn, last accessed June 17, 2015; "Chuyện những người con lính lê dương tại Việt Nam," *Thanh Niên,* May 8, 2014 Nelcya Delanoe, *Poussières d'empires,* 19.

7. General Ely to Minister of Defense, undated, presumably January–May 1954, SHAT, 10H327; "Lời khẩn cầu của vợ con lính lê dương từng tham chiến tại Việt Nam," *Lao Động,* November 1, 2014.

8. Nadine Bari and Laby Camara, *L'enfant de seno,* 63–64; "Chuyện những người con lính lê dương tại Việt Nam—Kỳ 2: Những dòng họ cô đơn," *Thanh Niên Online,* May 8, 2014, www.thanhnien.com.vn/doi-song/chuyen-nhung -nguoi-con-linh-le-duong-tai-viet-nam-ky-2-nhung-dong-ho-co-don-393882 .html, accessed January 27, 2015.

9. Shawn McHale, "Ethnicity, Violence, and Khmer-Vietnamese Relations: The Significance of the Lower Mekong Delta, 1757–1954," 367–390.

10. Letter, undated, early 1946, CAOM, GF 9.

11. Kim Lefevre, *Métisse Blanche,* 44–49.

12. CAOM, XIV Slotfom 14–2.

13. Note from President of FOEFI, December 3, 1979, Personal Archives of FOEFI [heretofore FOEFI].

14. In 1945, Binh Xuyên leader Ba Nhỏ reportedly confessed to the crime in a Việt Minh courtroom and subsequently committed suicide in repentance. Văn Lê, "Khu trưởng khu 7 Nguyễn Bình và vụ án Ba Nhỏ cuối năm 1945," December 12, 2006, http://vnca.cand.com.vn/Truyen-thong/Khu-truong -khu-7-Nguyen-Binh-va-vu-an-Ba-Nho-cuoi-nam-1945-324522/, accessed September 27, 2014. For a similar account, see Christopher Goscha, *Historical Dictionary of the Indochina War (1945–1954): An International and Interdisciplinary Approach,* 201–202; Văn Giàu Trần, "Lược sử thành phố Sài Gòn từ khi Pháp xâm chiếm (1859) đến tháng 4 năm 1975," in *Địa Chí Văn Hóa Thành Phố Hồ Chí Minh,* ed. Trần Văn Giàu.

15. Pierre Journoud, *De Gaulle et le Vietnam (1945–1969),* 42.

16. "Truyện ký: 'Ông Tây Việt Minh'-Phương Đình," May 7, 2014, http://vanvn .net/news/7/4675-truyen-ky–ong-tay-viet-minh—phuong-dinh.html.

17. Dương Bá Lộc is a well-known actor who often portrays westerners in Vietnamese films. Nguyễn Thế Thanh, "Giăng Mô rô—người Pháp lạ lùng," *Báo Phụ Nữ,* October 6, 2009.

18. Interviews with PNL, San Luis Obispo, California, October 2011.

19. "Thông thư uy san nhan dan bac bo gui uy ban nhan dan cac tinh va cac thanh pho," [sic] September 25, 1945, CAOM, GF 9.

20. Untitled letter, September 24, 1945, CAOM, GF 9.

21. Administrative Committee of the North (DRV) to Minister from France, August 7, 1946, CAOM, GF 9; Letter to the Main Committee of Tonkin, July 26, 1946, CAOM, GF 9.

22. William Bazé, "L'Indispensable Solidarité," *L'Eurafricain*, 1952.

23. Letter, September 23, 1945, CAOM, GF 9; Decree of November 1, 1945, by the President of the Northern People's Committee, CAOM, GF 9.

24. "Revue de la presse," 2–9 October 1948, CAOM, Fonds HCC 1–2.

25. Virginia Thompson and Richard Adolff, *Minority Problems in Southeast Asia*, 140–143, 146–148.

26. In 1963, the Dutch government rescinded its claim to West New Guinea and the Eurasian settlers evacuated to the Netherlands; Christian Lambert and Maria Penders, *The West New Guinea Debacle: Dutch Decolonization and Indonesia*, 85–86; Robert C. Bone, *The Dynamics of the Western New Guinea Problem*, 89.

27. "Mutuelle des Français d'Indochine," *L'Eurafricain*, undated, 1950.

28. "Retour Vers Le Passé," *L'Eurafricain*, undated, 1951.

29. Mutiny, "Discours de M. Mutiny d'un Groupe des Jeunes Eurasiens," *L'Eurafricain*, 1949.

30. La Mutuelle des Français d'Indochine had ties to La Mutuelle des Français de l'Inde, La Mutuelle des Eurafricans, and La Mutuelle des Guyanais et Antillais. "Au Cimetière de Massiges à Saigon Inauguration d'une Stèle a la Mémoire de Henri Chavigny de la Chevrotière," *L'Eurafricain*, 1952.

31. For more on the Eurafrican community, see Owen White, *Children of the French Empire: Miscegenation and Colonial Society in French West Africa 1895–1960*; Bazé, "L'Indispensable Solidarité"; "Retour Vers Le Passé"; "Position Juridique des Métis," *L'Eurafricain*, 1949.

32. Philippe Devilliers, *Histoire du Viêtnam de 1940 à 1952*, 319.

33. Oscar Chapuis witnessed the outburst. Oscar Chapuis, *The Last Emperor of Vietnam: From Tu Duc to Bao Dai*, 148.

34. "Revue de Presse," undated, from December 1948 or January 1949, CAOM, Fonds HCC 1–2; President of the FOEFI to Mr. Head of Central Services of the Social Action, October 11, 1951, SHAT, 10h327.

35. "Extraits 'l'Union Française,' Discours de M William Bazé," *L'Eurafricain*, 1949.

36. "Assemblée de l'Union Française, Procès Verbal du 6 November 1952," *L'Eurafricain*, 1952.

37. Letter from Bazé, October 11, 1951, SHAT, 10H327.

38. William Bazé, "La Conference de Pau: La Conference Doit Régler dans l'Équité les Interests Français et Eurasiens," *L'Eurafricain*, 1950; Letter from Bazé, October 11, 1951, SHAT, 10H327.

39. Robert DuPont, "Le Dernier Ilot Français en Indochine," *L'Eurafricain*, undated, 1951.

40. Ibid.

41. "Proposition Tenant à Demander au Haut Conseil de l'Union Francias l'Etude d'un Statute Juridique en Faveur des Eurasiens," *L'Eurafricain*, c. 1953.

42. Letter from Bazé, October 11, 1951, SHAT, 10H327.

43. Bazé, "La Conference de Pau: La Conference Doit Régler dans l'Équité les Interests Français et Eurasiens."

44. Bazé, "L'Indispensable Solidarité."

45. Shawn Frederick McHale, "Understanding the Fanatic Mind? The Viet Minh and Race Hatred in the First Indochina War (1945–1954)," *Journal of Vietnamese Studies* 4, no. 3 (2009): 98–138.

46. "Another Editor Shot in Saigon," *Mercury*, July 19, 1950.

47. "M Henri de Lachevrotiere, Avocat Honoraire Président d'Honneur de la Mutuelle des Français de l'Indochine, Journaliste Assassiné à Saigon à Coup de Grenade," *L'Eurafricain*, 1951.

48. "Nuôi nắng trẻ con," *Việt Nữ*, December 10, 1945.

49. Decree 8 and Decree 9 of January 18, 1946, *Việt nam dân quốc công báo*, January 26, 1946, 44–45.

50. "Trẻ em Việt Nam trước và sau cách mạng tháng 8," *Thiếu Nhi*, October 1, 1946; *Thiếu Sinh*, October 29, 1945; *Thiếu Sinh*, November 29, 1945; "Đời sống của dân quân du kích," *Thiếu Sinh*, November 13, 1945; "Nam bắc một nhà," *Thiếu Sinh*, October 15, 1945.

51. "Khoa học," *Thiếu Sinh*, October 15, 1945; "Khoa học," *Thiếu Sinh*, October 29, 1945; "Khoa học," *Thiếu Sinh*, November 22, 1945; "Khoa học," *Thiếu Sinh*, November 29, 1945; "Thiếu sinh tập trận," *Thiếu Sinh*, October 1, 1945; "Một không chiến thiếu sinh," *Thiếu Sinh*, November 22, 1945.

52. Norodom Sihanouk and Ngô Đình Diệm can also attribute much of their success to militarized youth groups. Anne Raffin, *Youth Mobilization in Vichy Indochina and Its legacies, 1940 to 1970*, 194.

53. Trần Đình Tú, "Nữ vệ út và báu vật 60 năm," *Việt Báo*, February 13, 2006.

54. "'Vệ út' thủ đô và những bức ảnh xúc động," *Việt Báo*, February 8, 2006; Goscha, *Historical Dictionary of the Indochina War (1945–1954): An International and Interdisciplinary Approach*, 99–101, 353, 501; Thompson and Adolff, *Minority Problems in Southeast Asia*, 140–148.

55. "Rapport du conseil d'administration, FOEFI General Assembly of 8 November 1983."

56. In June 1946, the Fondation Jules Brévié became the Fondation Fédérale Eurasien. In May 1949, the name changed to the Fondation de l'Enfance Franco-Indochinois. In December 1950, the name changed again to FOEFI; "Une Oeuvre Humaine," *Le Populaire*, July 24, 1947.

57. "FOEFI: Exercice 1952, Assemblée Général Ordinaire des 10, 11, 12 Septembre 1953," (Saigon: Imprimerie Française d'Outre Mer, 1953).

58. "Status du FOEFI 1951," SHAT, Indo 10H327.

59. In 1947, there were 888 known Eurasian births and 974 European births. "Tableau III movement de certaines caté gories de la population 1937 à 1948," in Direction de la Statistique Générale, *Annuaire Statistique Abrégé, 1943–1949*, 321.
60. "FOEFI: Exercice 1952, Assemblée Général Ordinaire des 10, 11, 12 Septembre 1953."
61. Ibid.
62. "FOEFI, Exercice 1950: Assemblée Générale Ordinaire des 27, 28, 29 Juillet 1951," (Saigon: Imprimerie Française d'Outre Mer, 1951).
63. "FOEFI: Exercice 1952, Assemblée Général Ordinaire des 10, 11, 12 Septembre 1953," 21.
64. Philippe Rostan, "Inconnu, Présume Français," (France 2011).
65. Kim Lefèvre, *Métisse Blanche*, 44–51.
66. Letter from Sayabory, April 14, 1949, CAOM, RS Laos S-12.
67. "FOEFI: Exercice 1952, Assemblée Général Ordinaire des 10, 11, 12 Septembre 1953."
68. Conversation with PNL, San Luis Obispo, October 2011.
69. "FOEFI: Exercice 1952, Assemblée Général Ordinaire des 10, 11, 12 Septembre 1953."
70. Report of March 1948, CAOM, RS Laos S-11.
71. Report of October and November 1948, CAOM, RS Laos S-11.
72. Letter from Police Commissioner of Vientiane, April 1948, CAOM, RS Laos S-12.
73. Dufourcq to Laoec, March 4, 1949, CAOM, RS Laos S-11.
74. While some orphanages of the Jules Brévié Foundation and its predecessors did take in Afro-Asian children, this decision was rare and often made by low-ranking administrators.
75. As is policy for this book, these names are pseudonyms. For the original names, the mother also gave her child a French translation of her Vietnamese name. "Maison de Bac Ninh," 1944, VNNA 1, GGI 88; Ha Xuan Te to General Prosecutor of Saigon, April 16, 1954, SHAT, Indo 10 H-1113; General Prosecutor of Saigon to Prosecutor of Nha Trang, April 21, 1954, SHAT, Indo 10H1113.
76. There are no statistics on Afro-Asian or Indian-Asian birthrates. "Fiche á l'Attention de Général de Brigade Directeur du Cabinet Militaire," September 11, 1951, SHAT, Indo 10H327.
77. "Lời Khẩn câu của vợ con lính lê dương từng tham chiến tại Việt Nam," *Lao Động*, November 1, 2014; Delanoe, *Poussières d'empires*.
78. Letter from Bazé, October 11, 1951, SHAT, 10H327.
79. After the evacuation, FOEFI sent a few Afro-Asian children to the North African colonies, but the majority went to the *métropole*. "FOEFI, Exercice 1953, Assemblée Générale Ordinaire des 13, 14, 15 Septembre 1954."

80. During this time, the students moved to Phnom Penh, Pakse, Pakson, and Kampong Chhnang. "École des Enfants de Troupe de Dalat: Histoire," undated, after 1952, SHAT, 10H1108.

81. Letter to the Director of Cabinet of the High Commissioner of France in Indochina, October 25 1951, SHAT, 10H327; "Note de Service " June 8, 1948, SHAT, Indo 10H327.

82. Letter from Bazé, October 11, 1951, SHAT, 10H327.

83. As late as May 1947, the school was only accepting children born of Asian mothers and French fathers, or unknown fathers who were presumably French. By July 1947, the school had extended its enrollment to include children with French mothers and Asian fathers. "Note de Service, May 28, 1947, SHAT, Indo 10H1108; "Decision," July 11, 1947, SHAT, 10H327; "Note de Service," August 12, 1948, SHAT, 10H1108.

84. Leclerc to D'Escadre, April 12, 1946, SHAT, 10H1108.

85. "Anexe à la Note de Service n 1.687/3.1, Date du 23.8.48, Liste des Enfants Admis en 1948 à l'École d'Enfants de Troupe Eurasiens de Dalat," SHAT 10h327.

86. "L'Enfant de Troupe Eurasien," undated, SHAT, Indo 10H1108.

87. "Anexe à la Note de Service n 1.687/3.1, Date du 23.8.48, Liste des Enfants Admis en 1948 à l'École d'Enfants de Troupe Eurasiens de Dalat," SHAT 10h327.

88. Letter to Director of Cabinet of the High Commissioner of France in Indochina, October 25, 1951, SHAT, Indo 10H327.

89. "FOEFI: Exercice 1952, Assemblée Général Ordinaire des 10, 11, 12 Septembre 1953."

90. Ibid.

91. "L'Enfant de Troupe Eurasien," SHAT 10H1108.

92. Letter from Cheval, October 1949, SHAT, 10h1110.

93. Bazé to Alessandri, 21 April 1949, SHAT, Indo 10H1110; Letter from Morgand, 9 January 1955, SHAT, Indo 10H1113.

94. Ely to Mr. Minister of the National Defense Cabinet, undated, presumably January–May 1954, SHAT, 10H327.

95. "Nés de Pères Français et de Mères Asiatiques, 350 Jeunes Eurasiens ont Retrouvé, en France, une Famille," L'Eurafricain, 1952.

96. "La Question des Enfants Eurasiens Abandonées," undated, CAOM, RS Laos S-11; "L'Action Sociale," undated, presumably 1948 or 1949, CAOM, RS Laos S-11.

97. Lefèvre, Métisse Blanche, 73–74.

98. CAOM, FOEFI album 48.

99. "FOEFI: Exercice 1952, Assemblée Général Ordinaire des 10, 11, 12 Septembre 1953."

100. Juliette Varenne, Juliette du Tonkin.

101. The *sûreté* rejected the idea on the grounds that Vietnamese *métis* children could not speak Lao. Letter to Lao Provincial Counselors, May 21, 1948, CAOM, RS Lao S-12; *Sûreté* to Provincial Council in Vientiane, June 4, 1948, CAOM, RS Lao S-12.

102. Conversation with Leca, Paris, France, 2004.

103. "FOEFI, Exercice 1954, Assemblée Générale Ordinaire des 5,6,7 Mai 1955," (Saigon: Imprimerie Français d'Outre Mer, 1955).

104. It is not clear if her mother had consented to sending her to France. "Nés de pères français et de mères asiatiques, 350 jeunes eurasiens ont retrouvé, en France, une famille."

105. "FOEFI, Exercice 1953, Assemblée Générale Ordinaire des 13, 14, 15 Septembre 1954."

106. Ibid.

107. "FOEFI: Exercice 1952, Assemblée Général Ordinaire des 10, 11, 12 Septembre 1953."

108. In 1954, preliminary reports to FOEFI list one known death, one disappearance, and two prisoners of war; however, these numbers would likely be higher when counting wards from l'École d'Enfants de Troupe Eurasiens de Dalat. "FOEFI, Exercice 1953, Assemblée Générale Ordinaire des 13, 14, 15 Septembre 1954."

109. Jean Chesneaux, *Contribution a l'Histoire de la Nation Vietnamienne,* 306–310.

110. Minister of the Armed Forces to the Commanding Generals of the Military Regions and Territories, February 15, 1955, SHAT, 10H327; Secretary of State to the Armed Forces to the Military Governor Generals, December 16, 1954, SHAT, 10H327; Minister of National Defense and of the Armed Forces to General Distribution, July 7, 1955, SHAT, 10H327; "Note de Service," from the Commander in Chief of the Land, Naval and Air in Indochina, February 25, 1955, SHAT, 10H327.

111. "FOEFI: Exercice 1952, Assemblée Général Ordinaire des 10, 11, 12 Septembre 1953."

112. "FOEFI, Exercice 1953, Assemblée Générale Ordinaire des 13, 14, 15 Septembre 1954."

113. Ibid.

114. Ibid.

115. Ibid.; "FOEFI, Exercice 1954, Assemblée Générale Ordinaire des 5, 6, 7 Mai 1955."

116. Commander of the Ground, Naval, and Air Forces in Indochina to General of the Army Corps, January 10, 1956, SHAT, 10H1113.

117. Prothin to General of the Army Corps, December 9, 1955, SHAT, 10H1113; December 9, 1955, SHAT, 10H1113.

118. Commander in Chief of the Land, Naval and Air Forces in Indochina to the General of the Army Corps, January 10, 1956, SHAT, 10H1113.

119. Morgand to the General of the Army Corps, January 10, 1956, SHAT, 10H1113.

120. Widow H. to the General of the Army Corps, November 2, 1955, SHAT, 10H1113; "Fiche à l'Attention du Général, Commandant Chef," October 10, 1955, SHAT, 10H1113.

121. The fate of her child is unclear from the archives. Widow V. to Morgand, December 10, 1955, SHAT, 10H1113.

122. Letter to Morgand, 10 December 10, 1955, SHAT, 10H1113; Letter from Morgand, January 3, 1956, SHAT, 10H1113; Letter, December 8, 1956, SHAT, 10H1113.

123. Letter from Cheval, March 30, 1950, CAOM 90APC62.

124. Untitled document, September 1, 1955, SHAT, 10H1113.

125. Letter from Morgand, January 9, 1956, SHAT, 10H1113.

126. Letter from Morgand, January 9, 1956, SHAT, 10H1113; Commander to Chiefs of Forces, January 10, 1956. SHAT, 10H1111.

127. Ely to "General Diffusion," March 15, 1955, SHAT, 10H327.

128. "FOEFI, Assemblée Générale Ordinaire des 3, 4, 5 Juin 1957."

129. Rostan, "Inconnu, Présume Français."

130. Ibid.

131. Ibid.

132. "Bulletin de l'École d'Enfants de Troupe de Dalat, December 1954, nouvelle series n1," SHAT, 10H1113.

133. "Confidential objet: Repliement en Métropole de l' EETED," July 28, 1955, SHAT, 10H327.

134. See files on departure in SHAT, 10h1113.

135. "FOEFI, Exercice 1954, Assemblée Générale Ordinaire des 5, 6, 7 Mai 1955."

CHAPTER 6: VICTIMS OF DECOLONIZATION

1. "Les difficultés des *métis* Franco-Vietnamiens à emigrer en France et l'attitude de Paris" (reprint of an unlabeled source, most likely *Le Monde*, 18 September 1980), FOEFI private archives.

2. Ivan Jablonka, *Enfants en exil: Transfert de pupilles réunionnais en métropole (1963–1982)*.

3. Todd Shepard, *The Invention of Decolonization: The Algerian War and the Remaking of France*.

4. This estimate does not include returning military. Maura Kathryn Edwards, "*Le Mal Jaune:* The Memory of the Indochina War in France, 1954–2006," 133–173.

5. Roughly twelve thousand *rapatriés* passed through the camps. The camps integrated children through school curriculum and by encouraging them to

socialize with French children. *Rapatriés* organized together to teach their fellow migrants both Vietnamese and French languages and to build religious centers. Edwards, *"La Mal Jaune,"* chapter 4; Hoàng Thi Thư, "Người Việt trên đất Pháp," *Miền Nam,* May 14, 1968; Hoàng Thị Thư, "Người Việt trên đất Pháp," *Miền Nam,* May 16, 1968.

6. Edwards, *"La Mal Jaune"*; Hoàng Thi Thư, "Người Việt trên đất Pháp," *Miền Nam,* May 14, 1968.

7. "FOEFI, Exercice 1966, Assemblée Générale Ordinaire du 9 Octobre 1967."

8. Bazé's family may have migrated from another colony. "De son côté, M. William Bazé nous écrit," *Le Monde,* undated; "Le Dévouement de nos fondateurs," by Sister Francois Régis, FOEFI archives.

9. "FOEFI, Exercice 1966, Assemblée Générale Ordinaire du 9 Octobre 1967."

10. "FOEFI, Exercice 1961, Assemblée Générale Ordinaire du 31 Aout 1962"; "FOEFI, Exercice 1970, Assemblée Générale Ordinaire du 14 Octobre 1971."

11. "FOEFI, Exercice 1964, Assemblée Générale Ordinaire du 7 Octobre 1965."

12. "FOEFI, Exercice 1969, Assemblée Générale Ordinaire du 20 Octobre 1970."

13. "FOEFI, Exercice 1967, Assemblée Générale Ordinaire du 15 Octobre 1968."

14. "Convention sur la Nationalité," reprinted in "FOEFI, Exercice 1955, Assemblée Générale Ordinaire des 19, 20, 21 Mars 1956."

15. Michel Wintrebert to Nguyen Van Si, August 16, 1955, "Convention franco-viêtnamienne du 16 août 1955 sur la nationalite."

16. "Tây lai ăn khoai cả vỏ, ăn chó cả lông, ăn hồng cả hột," Conversation with PNL, October 2011, San Luis Obispo, California.

17. Xuân Triêm, "Nhận xét khái quát qua ca kịch phẩm xã hội trên sân khấu TMTN Những đứa con lai," *Miền Nam,* December 22, 1967.

18. Nadine Bari and Laby Camara, *L'enfant de seno,* 12.

19. "Hạnh phúc truân chuyên của người đàn ông lấy vợ 'lai Tây,'" July 17, 2014, *Báo Mới,* www.baomoi.com/Hanh-phuc-truan-chuyen-cua-nguoi-dan-ong-lay-vo-lai-Tay/139/14330569.epi accessed January 27, 2014.

20. Conversation with PNL, October 2011, San Luis Obispo, California.

21. Hoàng Thi Thư, "Người Việt trên đất Pháp," *Miền Nam,* May 14, 1968; Hoàng Thị Thư, "Người Việt trên đất Pháp," *Miền Nam,* May 16, 1968; Conversation with PNL October 2011, San Luis Obispo, California.

22. Juliette Varenne, *Juliette du Tonkin.*

23. For example, see the story of fifteen-year-old MTL, also known as AD. Mai Anh and Thanh Xuân, "Quanh vụ La-thoại-Tân bị thưa dụ dỗ gái vị thành niên, cô MTL đã trở về gia đình vào tối 16–2," *Saigon Mới,* February 18, 1963.

24. Rostan, *Inconnu, Présume Français.*

25. "FOEFI, Exercice 1961, Assemblée Générale Ordinaire du 31 Aout 1962."

26. "FOEFI, Exercice 1961, Assemblée Générale Ordinaire du 31 Aout 1962"; "FOEFI, Exercice 1962, Assemblée Générale Ordinaire du 24 Septembre 1963" (Saigon: Kim Lai An-Quan, 1963).

27. "FOEFI, Exercice 1961, Assemblée Générale Ordinaire du 31 Aout 1962."
28. "FOEFI, Exercice 1962, Assemblée Générale Ordinaire du 24 Septembre 1963."
29. "FOEFI, Assemblée Générale Ordinaire des 3, 4, 5 Juin 1957."
30. "FOEFI, Exercice 1954, Assemblée Générale Ordinaire des 5, 6, 7 Mai 1955."
31. "FOEFI, Assemblée Générale Ordinaire des 3, 4, 5 Juin 1957"; "FOEFI, Exercice 1959, Assemblée Générale Ordinaire des 5 et 6 Aout 1960."
32. Rostan, *Inconnu, Présume Français.*
33. "FOEFI, Assemblée Générale Ordinaire des 3, 4, 5 Juin 1957."
34. "FOEFI, Délégation Métropolitaine, Exercice 1957, Assemblée Générale Ordinaire des 28 et 29 Juillet 1958."
35. "FOEFI, Exercice 1964, Assemblée Générale Ordinaire du 7 Octobre 1965"; "FOEFI, Exercice 1963, Assemblée Générale Ordinaire du 11 Aout 1964."
36. "FOEFI, Exercice 1960, Assemblée Générale Ordinaire des 11 et 12 Aout 1961."
37. "Rapport sur les activites de la FOEFI," September 10, 1965, French National Archives [hereafter FNA], Centre des Archives Contemporaines at Fontainebleau [hereafter CAC], 0019960015 Art 22.
38. "FOEFI, Exercice 1954, Assemblée Générale Ordinaire des 5, 6, 7 Mai 1955."
39. "FOEFI, Délégation Métropolitaine, Exercice 1957, Assemblée Générale Ordinaire des 28 et 29 Juillet 1958"; "FOEFI, Exercice 1965, Assemblée Générale Ordinaire du 18 Octobre 1966."
40. "FOEFI, Exercice 1964, Assemblée Générale Ordinaire du 7 Octobre 1965."
41. "FOEFI, Exercice 1962, Assemblée Générale Ordinaire du 24 Septembre 1963."
42. "FOEFI, Exercice 1960, Assemblée Générale Ordinaire des 11 et 12 Aout 1961."
43. "FOEFI, Exercice 1961, Assemblée Générale Ordinaire du 31 Aout 1962."
44. "FOEFI, Délégation Métropolitaine, Exercice 1957, Assemblée Générale Ordinaire des 28 et 29 Juillet 1958."
45. "FOEFI, Exercice 1966, Assemblée Générale Ordinaire du 9 Octobre 1967."
46. "FOEFI, Certificat de Decharge," November 30, 1974, CAC 0019960015, ART 22.
47. "FOEFI, Exercice 1960, Assemblée Générale Ordinaire des 11 et 12 Aout 1961."
48. "FOEFI, Assemblée Générale Ordinaire des 3, 4, 5 Juin 1957."
49. "FOEFI, Exercice 1961, Assemblée Générale Ordinaire du 31 Aout 1962."
50. "FOEFI, Assemblée Générale Ordinaire des 3, 4, 5 Juin 1957."
51. "FOEFI, Exercice 1963, Assemblée Générale Ordinaire du 11 Aout 1964."
52. "Rapport sur les Activites de la FOEFI," September 10, 1965, French National Archives, CAC 0019960015, ART 22.
53. Rostan, *Inconnu, Présume Français.*
54. "FOEFI, Exercice 1955, Assemblée Générale Ordinaire des 19, 20, 21 Mars 1956."
55. "FOEFI, Délégation Métropolitaine, Exercice 1957, Assemblée Générale Ordinaire des 28 et 29 Juillet 1958."
56. "FOEFI, Exercice 1963, Assemblée Générale Ordinaire du 11 Aout 1964."

57. Rostan, *Inconnu, Présume Français.*
58. Tara Zahara, *The Lost Children: Reconstructing Europe's Families after World War II.*
59. Rostan, *Inconnu, Présume Français.*
60. Conversations with RR, Paris, France, February–April 2004; "FOEFI, Exercice 1961, Assemblée Générale Ordinaire du 31 Aout 1962."
61. It is not clear if his mother was living in France or if she traveled to France for a vacation. "FOEFI, Délégation Métropolitaine, Exercice 1957, Assemblée Générale Ordinaire des 28 et 29 Juillet 1958."
62. Mora-Kpai, *Indochina: Traces of a Mother.*
63. Rostan, *Inconnu, Présume Français.*
64. Ibid.
65. "FOEFI, Exercice 1967, Assemblée Générale Ordinaire du 15 Octobre 1968."
66. "FOEFI, Exercice 1966, Assemblée Générale Ordinaire du 9 Octobre 1967."
67. "FOEFI, Exercice 1961, Assemblée Générale Ordinaire du 31 Aout 1962."
68. "Introduction," by Luis Péré-Lahaille-Dab, Inspecteur Général, undated, after 1975, CAC 0019960015ART22.
69. "FOEFI, Exercice 1960, Assemblée Générale Ordinaire des 11 et 12 Aout 1961."
70. Conversation with Thu Uyên, producer of *Như chưa hề có cuộc chia ly,* a television show that attempted to aid this man in finding his family, December 3, 2012, Ho Chi Minh City, Vietnam.
71. "FOEFI, Exercice 1954, Assemblée Générale Ordinaire des 5, 6, 7 Mai 1955."
72. Rostan, *Inconnu, Présume Français.*
73. Conversations with RR, Paris, France, January–April 2004; email correspondence with JMJCA, November–December 2012.
74. In 1945, this child was listed at Asile St. Albert à Drapeau, VNNA 1, GGI 498; "FOEFI, Délégation Métropolitaine, Exercice 1957, Assemblée Générale Ordinaire des 28 et 29 Juillet 1958."
75. "FOEFI, Exercice 1967, Assemblée Générale Ordinaire du 15 Octobre 1968."
76. Rostan, *Inconnu, Présume Français.*
77. "FOEFI, Exercice 1960, Assemblée Générale Ordinaire des 11 et 12 Aout 1961"; Rostan, *Inconnu, Présume Français*; Conversations with RR, Paris, France, January–April 2004.
78. Rostan, *Inconnu, Présume Français.*
79. "Rapport sur les Activites de la FOEFI," September 10, 1965, French National Archives, CAC 0019960015, ART 22; Erica J. Peters, "Culinary Crossings and Disruptive Identities: Contesting Colonial Categories in Everyday Life."
80. "FOEFI, Exercice 1962, Assemblée Générale Ordinaire du 24 Septembre 1963."
81. "FOEFI, Exercice 1954, Assemblée Générale Ordinaire des 5, 6, 7 Mai 1955."

82. "FOEFI, Exercice 1960, Assemblée Générale Ordinaire des 11 et 12 Aout 1961."
83. My interview subjects were, however, a self-selecting group who came to my attention through their membership in the FOEFI social club. Former wards who had negative experiences are unlikely to be involved with such a group.
84. Rostan, *Inconnu, Présume Français*.
85. "FOEFI, Délégation Métropolitaine, Exercice 1957, Assemblée Générale Ordinaire des 28 et 29 Juillet 1958."
86. Rostan, *Inconnu, Présume Français*.
87. "FOEFI, Exercice 1975–1976"; "FOEFI, Exercice 1959, Assemblée Générale Ordinaire des 5 et 6 Aout 1960"; "FOEFI, Exercice 1972, Assemblée Générale Ordinaire du 23 Octobre 1973."
88. Elisa Camiscioli, *Reproducing the French Race: Immigration, Intimacy, and Embodiment in the Early Twentieth Century*.
89. Luis Péré-Lahaille-Dab, "Introduction," undated, after 1975, CAC 0019960015 ART 22.
90. Bazé to Lenoir, December 4, 1975, printed in "FOEFI, Exercice 1974–1975, Assemblée Générale Ordinaire du 28 Janvier 1976."
91. "FOEFI, Exercice 1960, Assemblée Générale Ordinaire des 11 et 12 Aout 1961."
92. "FOEFI, Exercice 1961, Assemblée Générale Ordinaire du 31 Aout 1962."
93. "FOEFI, Exercice 1954, Assemblée Générale Ordinaire des 5, 6, 7 Mai 1955."
94. "Marriages de 1975," December 4, 1975, CAC 0019960015.
95. "FOEFI, Exercice 1974–1975, Assemblée Générale Ordinaire du 28 Janvier 1976."
96. Rostan, *Inconnu, Présume Français*.
97. "FOEFI, Exercice 1961, Assemblée Générale Ordinaire du 31 Aout 1962"; "FOEFI, Exercice 1968, Assemblée Générale Ordinaire du 14 Octobre 1969."
98. "FOEFI, Exercice 1954, Assemblée Générale Ordinaire des 5, 6, 7 Mai 1955."
99. "FOEFI, Délégation Métropolitaine, Exercice 1957, Assemblée Générale Ordinaire des 28 et 29 Juillet 1958."
100. "FOEFI, Exercice 1972, Assemblée Générale Ordinaire du 23 Octobre 1973."
101. Ibid.
102. "FOEFI, Exercice 1959, Assemblée Générale Ordinaire des 5 et 6 Aout 1960."
103. "FOEFI, Exercice 1978, Rapport du Conseil d'Administration, Assemblée Générale Ordinaire du 5 Décembre 1979."
104. "FOEFI, Exercice 1982, Rapport du Conseil d'Administration, Assemblée Générale Ordinaire du Mardi 22 Mars 1983."
105. "FOEFI, Exercice 1972, Assemblée Générale Ordinaire du 23 Octobre 1973"; "Questions posées par l'État Civil et la Nationalité des Eurasiens, Octobre 1979," FOEFI Archives.
106. "FOEFI, Exercice 1982, Rapport du Conseil d'Administration, Assemblée Générale Ordinaire du Mardi 22 Mars 1983"; FOEFI, Exercice 1982, Rapport

du Conseil d'Administration, Assemblée Générale Ordinaire du Mardi 22 Mars 1983"; "FOEFI, Exercice 1972, Assemblée Générale Ordinaire du 23 Octobre 1973."

107. Files in FOEFI private archives. The FOEFI website (www.foefi.net) includes a page of detailed instructions for correcting citizenship problems, including form letters to send to the necessary ministries of the French government (www.foefi.net, accessed June 4, 2013).

108. Letter to Bazé, September 26, 1962, printed in "FOEFI, Exercice 1962, Assemblée Générale Ordinaire du 24 Septembre 1963"; Yves Denéchère, "Les 'rapatriements' d'enfants eurasiens en France à la fin de la guerre d'Indochine," 123–139.

109. Ed Miller suggests that the brothers saw negotiating with the DRV as a way to defeat the NLF. Edward Miller, *Misalliance: Ngo Dinh Diem, the United States, and the Fate of South Vietnam*, 303.

110. Thank you to Ed Miller for clarifying this point.

111. Miller, *Misalliance*, 305.

112. Ibid., 306.

113. Fredrik Logevall, *Choosing War: The Lost Chance for Peace and the Escalation of War in Vietnam*, 1–42.

114. "FOEFI, Exercice 1964, Assemblée Général Ordinaire du 7 Octobre 1965"; "FOEFI, Exercice 1966, Assemblée Générale Ordinaire du 9 Octobre 1967."

115. Some reports say there were 194 children; others indicate 198 children. "FOEFI, Exercice 1962, Assemblée Générale Ordinaire du 24 Septembre 1963"; "FOEFI, Exercice 1967, Assemblée Générale Ordinaire du 15 Octobre 1968."

116. Ibid.

117. Miller, *Misalliance*, 290–291.

118. "Lần đầu tiên, nhà viết sử Pháp tiết lộ: Pháp-Mỹ 'cãi nhau' như thế nào về chiến tranh VN," *Miền Nam*, January 31, 1967.

119. Pierre Journoud, *De Gaulle et le Vietnam: 1945–1969, La reconciliation*, 157–162, 188–196.

120. "FOEFI, Exercice 1963, Assemblée Générale Ordinaire du 11 Aout 1964."

121. "'Không thể nhìn nhận VC Đại diện cho dân chúng Miền nam' Hồ Chí Minh gửi thông điệp cho De Gualle," *Miền Nam*, February 2, 1966.

122. "Nhân cuộc viếng thăm Mạc T. Khoa, Pháp-Nga thỏa Thuận vận động cho hoà bình Việt Nam, Kế hoạch này sẽ thực hiện trong tháng tới," *Miền Nam*, January 15, 1966; "De Gaulle gửi thông điệp mới cho TT Johnson về chiến tranh VN," *Miền nam* 1966; Journoud, *De Gaulle et le Vietnam (1945–1969)*, 193–194.

123. "Rapport sur les Activites de la Fédération des Oeuvres de l'Enfance Française d'Indochine (FOEFI)," September 10, 1965, CAC 0019960015, ART 22.

124. Ibid.

125. Ibid.

126. Ibid.

127. Ibid.

128. "FOEFI, Exercice 1959, Assemblée Générale Ordinaire des 5 et 6 Aout 1960"; "FOEFI, Exercice 1963, Assemblée Générale Ordinaire du 11 Aout 1964"; "Rapport sur les Activites de la FOEFI," September 10, 1965, CAC 0019960015, ART 22.

129. "FOEFI, Délégation Métropolitaine, Exercice 1957, Assemblée Générale Ordinaire des 28 et 29 Juillet 1958"; "FOEFI, Exercice 1961, Assemblée Générale Ordinaire du 31 Aout 1962."

130. "FOEFI, Exercice 1959, Assemblée Générale Ordinaire des 5 et 6 Aout 1960." When the lease on the grave expired, the tomb was destroyed, and his body, along with those of the other wards, was disinterred and placed in the pauper grave at Père Lachaise Cemetery.

131. "Rapport sur les Activites de la Fédération des Oeuvres de l'Enfance Française d'Indochine (FOEFI)," September 10, 1965, CAC 0019960015, ART 22.

132. Ibid.

133. "FOEFI, Exercice 1968, Assemblée Générale Ordinaire du 14 Octobre 1969."

134. "FOEFI, Exercice 1967, Assemblée Générale Ordinaire du 15 Octobre 1968."

135. "FOEFI, Exercice 1966, Assemblée Générale Ordinaire du 9 Octobre 1967."

136. "FOEFI, Exercice 1965, Assemblée Générale Ordinaire du 18 Octobre 1966."

137. "FOEFI, Exercice 1966, Assemblée Générale Ordinaire du 9 Octobre 1967."

138. Letter to Bazé, March 14, 1967, and "Extrait du Droit de Vivre n334 de Janvier/février 1967, documents pour les antiracistes (propos revueillis par Geneviève Réach)," printed in "FOEFI, Exercice 1966, Assemblée Générale Ordinaire du 9 Octobre 1967"; "FOEFI, Exercice 1970, Assemblée Générale Ordinaire du 14 Octobre 1971."

139. "FOEFI, Exercice 1968, Assemblée Générale Ordinaire du 14 Octobre 1969."

140. "FOEFI, Exercice 1974–1975, Assemblée Générale Ordinaire du 28 Janvier 1976."

141. "FOEFI, Exercice 1966, Assemblée Générale Ordinaire du 9 Octobre 1967."

142. "FOEFI, Exercice 1964, Assemblée Générale Ordinaire du 7 Octobre 1965"; "FOEFI, Exercice 1974–1975, Assemblée Générale Ordinaire du 28 Janvier 1976."

143. "FOEFI, Exercice 1966, Assemblée Générale Ordinaire du 9 Octobre 1967."

144. Ibid.

145. "FOEFI, Exercice 1968, Assemblée Générale Ordinaire du 14 Octobre 1969."

146. "FOEFI, Exercice 1965, Assemblée Générale Ordinaire du 18 Octobre 1966."

147. "FOEFI, Exercice 1970, Assemblée Générale Ordinaire du 14 Octobre 1971."

148. "FOEFI, Exercice 1967, Assemblée Générale Ordinaire du 15 Octobre 1968."

149. "FOEFI, Exercice 1969, Assemblée Générale Ordinaire du 20 Octobre 1970."

150. "FOEFI, Exercice 1970, Assemblée Générale Ordinaire du 14 Octobre 1971."

151. In 1971, Vice Counsul at the U.S. embassy in Paris consulted with the FOEFI Paris office. "FOEFI, Exercice 1971, Assemblée Générale Ordinaire du 11 Octobre 1972"; "FOEFI, Exercice 1970, Assemblée Générale Ordinaire du 14 Octobre 1971."

152. "FOEFI, Exercice 1966, Assemblée Générale Ordinaire du 9 Octobre 1967."

153. "FOEFI, Exercice 1967, Assemblée Générale Ordinaire du 15 Octobre 1968."

154. "FOEFI, Exercice 1970, Assemblée Générale Ordinaire Du 14 Octobre 1971."

155. In 1976, after Bokassa announced the Kingdom of Central Africa and declared himself king, his Afro-Asian daughters became princesses. "Cô bé lọ lem VN trở thành công chúa Vương Quốc Kim Cương ở Châu Phi," *Việt Bao*, July 16, 2014; "Chuyện 2 cô gái Sài Gòn trở thành công chúa ở Châu Phi," zing.vn, May 4, 2013; Nguyễn Hoàng, "Muôn mặt báo chí Sài Gòn trước năm 1975," *Lao Động*, June 7, 2015.

156. "Nha kế hoạch, pháp chế và nghiên huấn," undated, 1970, VNNA 2, Fonds Phủ thủ thường Việt Nam Công Hoà [hereafter PTTVNCH], 30544. For example, in 1969 and 1970, the Hoà Bình orphanage in Kiên Giang was investigated, and in 1971, the Long Thành orphanage in Biên Hoà was found guilty of child abuse and starvation. See files of the Hoà Bình Orphanage in VNNA 2, PTTVNCH 30545. See files of the Long Thành Orphanage in VNNA 2, PTTVNCH 30768.

157. "Phiên họp ngày 29–1–1970 của ủy ban liên bộ cứu xét vấn đề cô nhi Việt Nam tại ngoại quốc tại văn phòng bộ xã hội," VNNA 2, PTTVNCH 30544.

158. "Nha kế hoạch, pháp chế và nghiên huấn," undated, 1970, VNNA 2, PTTVNCH 30544.

159. "Phiên họp ngày 29–1–1970 của ủy ban liên bộ cứu xét vấn đề cô nhi Việt Nam tại ngoại quốc tại văn phòng bộ xã hội," VNNA 2, PTTVNCH 30544.

160. "Nha kế hoạch, pháp chế và nghiên huấn," undated, 1970, VNNA 2, PTTVNCH 30544.

161. "Phiên họp ngày 29–1–1970 của ủy ban liên bộ cứu xét vấn đề cô nhi Việt Nam tại ngoài quốc tại văn phòng bộ xã hội," VNNA 2, PTTVNCH 30544.

162. "Tài liệu này do Tiểu ban của Ủy-ban Phụ-trách trẻ em của Hội Đồng các cơ quan Từ Thiện ngoại quốc chỉ định soạn thảo," October 1, 1969, VNNA 2, PTTVNCH 30544.

163. "Nha kế hoạch, pháp chế và nghiên huấn," undated, 1970, VNNA 2, PTTVNCH 30544.

164. Letter to Ô. Đồng Lý Văn phòng Bộ Tư-pháp Saigon, September 2, 1968, VNNA 2, PTTVNCH 19849.

165. French Consulate General in Saigon to Ministry of Foreign Affaires, November 16, 1972, CAC 0019960015 ART 22.

166. The family was accused of having ties to communists, and their case was dismissed. Letter, January 9, 1967, VNNA 2, PTTVNCH 19849.

167. Varet to Director, CAC 0019960015, ART 22.

168. "FOEFI, Exercice 1974–1975, Assemblée Générale Ordinaire du 28 Janvier 1976."

169. "FOEFI, Exercice 1973, Assemblée Générale Ordinaire du [illegible] Octobre 1974."

170. Patrick Amiot to Maurice Schumann, August 14, 1972, CAC 0019960015 ART 22.

171. French Consulate General to Ministry of Foreign Affairs, CAC 0019960015 ART 22.

172. Deschamps to Ministry of Foreign Affairs, undated, CAC 0019960015 ART 22.

173. "FOEFI, Exercice 1973, Assemblée Générale Ordinaire du [illegible] Octobre 1974."

174. Dana Sachs, *The Life We Were Given: Operation Babylift, International Adoption, and the Children of War in Vietnam,* 54, 65, 98–99.

175. Letter, April 1975, PTTVNCH 31652.

176. Letter, June 18, 1975, CAC 0019960015 ART 22.

177. Letter from Beauvais, June 23, 1975, CAC 0019960015 ART 22.

178. "Enfants eurasiens du Vietnam," November 1975, CAC 0019960015 ART 22.

179. FOEFI met October 2, 1977, at 7 Rue de Washington in Paris.

180. Conversations with PNL, October 2011.

181. Duiker, *Vietnam Since the Fall of Saigon,* 67, 85–86.

182. Georges Condominas and Richard Pottier, *Les Réfugiés originaires de l'Asie du Sud-Est: rapport présenté au Président de la République par un équipe du Centre de documentation et de recherche sur l'Asie du Sud-Est e t le monde insulindien,* 7.

183. George Bazé helped PNL. Conversations with PNL, October 2011, San Luis Obispo, CA.

184. "Fédération des Oeuvres de l'Enfance Français d'Indochine, Exercice 1975–1976."

185. Conversations with PNL, October 2011, San Luis Obispo, CA.

186. Conversations with PNL, November 2011, San Luis Obispo, CA.

187. "FOEFI, Exercice 1980, Rapport du Conseil d'Administration, Assemblée Générale Ordinaire du samedi 6 Décembre 1980."

188. "L'émigration des *métis* franco-vietnamiens," *Le Monde,* September 20, 1980.

189. "FOEFI, Exercice 1980, Rapport du Conseil d'Administration, Assemblée Générale Ordinaire du samedi 6 Décembre 1980."

190. Conversations with PNL, October 2011, San Luis Obispo, CA.

191. "FOEFI, Exercice 1980, Rapport du Conseil d'Administration, Assemblée Générale Ordinaire du samedi 6 Décembre 1980."

192. At the time of this observation, the Vietnamese government had just finished up its two-decade project to classify Vietnam into fifty-four ethnic groups, as well as encourage Vietnam's ethnic Chinese and Khmer populations to emigrate. Patricia Pelley argues that the classification process homogenized Vietnamese society and created a new national culture. Patricia Pelley, "'Barbarians' and 'Younger Brothers': The Remaking of Race in Post Colonial Vietnam," *Journal of Southeast Asian Studies* 29, no. 2 (1998); Van Tinh Nguyen, Hoang Van Nguyen, and Van Than Thai, "Les difficulties des *métis* Franco-Vietnamiens à émigrer en France et l'attitude de Paris," *Le Monde*, September 18, 1980; Conversations with PNL, October 2011, San Luis Obispo, CA.

193. Nguyen et al., "Les difficulties des *métis* Franco-Vietnamiens à émigrer en France et l'attitude de Paris."

194. "FOEFI, Exercice 1975–1976."

195. "Les difficulties des *métis* franco-Vietnamiens à émigrer en France et l'attitude de Paris."

196. "FOEFI, Exercice 1980, Rapport du Conseil d'Administration, Assemblée Générale Ordinaire Du samedi 6 Décembre 1980."

197. Trin Yarborough, *Surviving Twice: Amerasian Children of the Vietnam War*, 64; Steven DeBonis, *Children of the Enemy: Oral Histories of Vietnamese Amerasians and Their Mothers*, 2, 13, 115–116.

198. "FOEFI," 1977.

199. Luis Péré-Lahaille-Dab, "Introduction," undated, after April 30, 1975, CAC 0019960015 Art 22.

200. Rostan, *Inconnu, Présume Français*.

201. "FOEFI, Exercice 1982, Rapport du Conseil d'Administration, Assemblée Générale Ordinaire du Mardi 22 Mars 1983."

EPILOGUE

1. *Như chưa hề có cuộc chia ly*, episode 52, aired September 30, 2012.

2. "Ông muốn nói là Việt Nam trọng người của ông," *Như chưa hề có cuộc chia ly*, episode 52, aired September 30, 2012.

3. *Như chưa hề có cuộc chia ly*, episode 52, aired September 30, 2012.

4. Ibid.

5. Margaret Jacobs, *White Mother to a Dark Race: Settler Colonialism, Maternalism, and the Removal of Indigenous Children in the American West and Australia, 1880–1940*; Margaret D. Jacobs, *A Generation Removed: The*

Fostering and Adoption of Indigenous Children in the Postwar World (Lincoln: University of Nebraska Press, 2014).

6. Ivan Jablonka, *Enfants en exil: Transfert de pupilles réunionnais en métropole (1963–1982)* (Paris: Editions du Seuil, 2007).

7. Oficina del Alto Comisionado para los Derechos Humanos, "Observaciones preliminares del Grupo de Trabajo sobre las Desapariciones Forzadas o Involuntarias de la ONU al concluir su visita a España," www.ohchr.org/SP/NewsEvents/Pages/DisplayNews.aspx?NewsID=13800&LangID=S, accessed January 24, 2014.

8. Van Klinken, *Making Them Indonesians: Child Transfers out of East Timor.*

9. "Những người con lai Pháp ở Điện Biên," *Tài nguyên và Môi Trường,* April 11, 2014. http://baotainguyenmoitruong.com.vn/suc-khoe-doi-song/201404/nhung-nguoi-con-lai-phap-o-dien-bien-518330,.html accessed January 27, 2015; "Người con lai Pháp 20 năm viết đơn tìm cha," *Báo Mới,* July 17, 2014, www.baomoi.com/Nguoi-con-lai-Phap-20-nam-viet-don-tim-cha/139/14330861.epi, accessed January 27, 2014.

10. Conversation with MPB, June 2009, Paris, France; Conversation with PNL, October 2011, San Luis Obispo, CA; "Mihagui: Trong máu tôi . . . có nước mắm?"; "Robert Vaeza 'coi như là Pháp'"; "Tìm di ảnh," *Tuổi Trẻ,* March 3, 2012; "Chuyện những người con lính lê dương tại Việt Nam—Kỳ 2: Những dòng họ cô đơn," *Thanh Niên Online,* May 8, 2014. www.thanhnien.com.vn/doi-song/chuyen-nhung-nguoi-con-linh-le-duong-tai-viet-nam-ky-2-nhung-dong-ho-co-don-393882.html, accessed January 27, 2015.

11. Letter to Bazé, October 27, 1983, FOEFI Archives.

12. "Andre Epouse Constant Marie Claire tìm mẹ Phạm Thị Phong," *Hội Từ Thiện Quảng Nam,* January 5, 2015, http://hoituthienquangnam.com/tin-tuc/ms5631-andre-epouse-constant-marie-claire-tim-me-pham-thi-phong-t6ifc.html, accessed January 27, 2015.

13. CAOM, FOEFI album 48.

14. Philippe Rostan, *Inconnu, Présume Francais* (France, 2011).

15. Email correspondence with JMJCA, December 2012.

16. Francois Beroult, http://www.foefi.net/messages.htm, accessed June 17, 2015.

17. Rostan, *Inconnu, Présume Francais.*

18. "Mihagui: Trong máu tôi . . . có nước mắm?," *Việt Báo,* October 7, 2006.

19. Rostan, *Inconnu, Présume Francais.*

20. Ibid.

21. Conversations with RR. February–April 2004, Paris, France.

22. Rostan, *Inconnu, Présume Francais.*

23. Ibid.

24. "Mẹ là con gà ấp trứng vịt. Con vịt bơi qua sông, mẹ gà đứng bên này nhìn theo mà không thể làm gì được"; "Mihagui: Trong máu tôi . . . có nước mắm?"

25. Rostan, *Inconnu, Présume Francais.*

26. Correspondence with E.T., December 2014.
27. CAOM, FOEFI Album 48.
28. "Robert Vaeza 'coi như là Pháp,'" *Tuổi Trẻ Cuối Tuần,* July 26, 2009.
29. Rostan, *Inconnu, Présume Francais.*

APPENDIX

1. All mistakes in Vietnamese are from the original document. "FOEFI, Exercice 1966, Assemblée Générale Ordinaire Du 9 Octobre 1967"; "FOEFI, CERTIFICAT DE DECHARGE," CAC 0019960015, ART 22.

BIBLIOGRAPHY

Accampo, Elinor A. "Gender, Social Policy and the Third Republic." In *Gender and the Politics of Social Reform in France, 1870–1914,* edited by Elinor A. Accampo, Rachel G. Fuchs, and Mary Lynn Stewart. Baltimore: The John Hopkins University Press, 1995.

———. "The Gendered Nature of Contraception in France: Neo-Malthusianism, 1900–1920." *Journal of Interdisciplinary History* 34, no. 2 (2003): 235–262.

AJP. "Colonisation Familiale." *Indochine Hebdomadaire Illustré,* February 10, 1944, 29–30.

Albertini, Pierre. *L'école en France xixe–xx siècle: De la maternelle à l'université.* Paris: Hachette, 1998.

Allen, Theodore. *The Invention of the White Race.* London, New York: Verso, 1994.

"Allocution prononcée par m. Rignaux Nicolas, Président de l'union des eurafricains de L'aof, Togo, Aef." *L'Eurafricain,* 1951.

Althusser, Louis. *Lenin and Philosophy and Other Essays.* New York: Monthly Review Press, 1971.

Andersen, Margaret Cook. "A Colonial Fountain of Youth: Imperialism and France's Crisis of Depopulation, 1870–1940." PhD diss., University of Iowa, 2009.

———. "Creating French Settlements Overseas: Pronatalism and Colonial Medicine in Madagascar." *French Historical Studies* 33, no. 3 (2010): 417–444.

"Andre Epouse Constant Marie Claire tìm mẹ Phạm Thị Phong." *Hội Từ Thiện Quảng Nam.* January 5, 2015. http://hoituthienquangnam.com/tin-tuc /ms5631-andre-epouse-constant-marie-claire-tim-me-pham-thi-phong-t6ifc .html. Accessed January 27, 2015.

Andrew, Dudley, and Steven Ungar. *Popular Front Paris and the Poetics of Culture.* Cambridge: Harvard University Press, 2005.

"Ấn-Gia-Nả-Đại Thảo-Luận Sơ Bộ Về Vn Tại Tân-Đề-Ly. Theo Nguôn Tin Thong-Tấn-Xã Mỹ Ap: De Gualle Sẽ Đứng Trung—Gian Hòa-Giải Vấn Đề Vn." *Miền Nam Nhật Báo Thong Tinh Nghị Luận,* February 13–14, 1966.

Angleviel, Frédéric, ed. *La Nouvelle Calédonie, Terre De Métissages.* Paris: Les Indes Savantes, 2004.

Anh, Mai, and Thanh Xuân. "Quanh Vụ La-Thoại-Tân Bị Thừa Dụ Dỗ Gái Vị Thành Niên, Cô Mai Thị Liễu Đã Trở Về Gia Đình Vào Tối 16–2." *Saigon Mới,* February 18, 1963, 1–4.

"Another Editor Shot in Saigon." *Mercury*, July 19, 1950.

"Au Cimetière de Massiges à Saigon Inauguration d'une Stèle a la Mémoire de Henri Chavigny de la Chevrotière." *L'Eurafricain*, 1952.

Bác Hồ với thiếu niên nhi đồng. Hà Nội: NXB Chính Trị Quốc Gia, 2004.

Bari, Nadine, and Laby Camara. *L'enfant de Seno.* Paris: L'Harmattan, 2011.

Barry, Jonathan and Colin Jones, eds. *Medicine and Charity Before the Welfare State.* New York: Routledge, 1991.

Baudrit, André. "Bétail Humain: Rapt, vente, infanticide dans l'Indochine Française et dans la Chine du sud." In *Bétail Humaine: La traite des femmes et des enfants en Indochine et en Chine du sud, suivi de onze documentssur l'esclavage (1860–1940),* edited by Pierre Le Roux and Nicolas Lainez, 97–130. Paris: Connaissances et Savoirs, 2008.

———. "La naissance de dalat." *Indochine Hebdomadaire Illustré*, February 10, 1944, 23–24.

Bazé, William. "La conference de pau: La conference doit régler dans l'équité les interests Francais et eurasiens." *L'Eurafricain*, 1950.

———. "L'indispensable Solidarité." *L'Eurafricain*, 1952.

Bell, Susan G., and Karen M. Offen. *Women, the Family, and Freedom: The Debate in Documents.* Stanford: Stanford University Press, 1983.

Bernoville, Gaëtan. *Anne-Marie Javouhey, Fodatrice des Soeurs de St Joseph de Cluny.* Paris: Éditions Barnard Grasset, 1943.

Bilange, François, Charles Fourniau, and Alain Ruscio, eds. *Rapport de Mission en Indochine 1 January—14 Mars 1937.* Paris: L'Harmattan, 1994.

Blanchard, Pascal, and Sandrine Lemaire, eds. *Culture Impériale 1931–1961: les colonies au coeur de la République.* Paris: Éditions Autrement, 2004.

Blot, Docteur. "L'oeuvre scientifique du colonel A. Bonifacy." *Bulletins et Mémoires de la Société d'Anthropologie de Paris,* Tome II (1931): 9–10.

Bone, Robert C. *The Dynamics of the Western New Guinea Problem.* Singapore: Equinox Publishing, 2009.

Bonvicini, Henri. *Enfants de la Colonie.* Saigon: Orient-Occident, 1938.

Bowd, Gavin, and Daniel Clayton. "Tropicality, Orientalism, and French Colonialism in Indochina: The Work of Pierre Gourou, 1927–1982." *French Historical Studies* 28, no. 2 (2005): 297–327.

Britto, Karl Ashoka. *Disorientation: France, Vietnam, and the Ambivalence of Interculturality.* Hong Kong: Hong Kong University Press, 2004.

Brocheux, Pierre. "Elite, bourgeoisie, où la difficulté d'être." In *Saigon 1924–1945: De la "Belle Colonie" à l'eclosion révolutionnaire ou la fin des dieux blancs,* edited by Philippe Franchini. Paris: Éditions Autrement, 1992.

———. "Le métis dans la littérature indochinoise." In *Rêver l'Asie, Exotisme et Litérature coloniale aux Indes, Indochine et en Insulinde,* edited by Denis Lombard, 335–339. Paris: Éditions de l'École des Hautes Études en Sciences Sociales, 1993.

———. "The State and the 1930s Depression in French Indochina." In *Weathering the Storm: The Economies of Southeast Asia in the 1930s Depression*, edited by Peter Boomgaard and Ian Brown. Leiden: KITLV Press, 2000.

"Bulletin de la Société de Protection de l'Enfance en Annam." Hà Nội: Imprimerie Mac Dinh Tu, 1919.

Cách Mạng Tháng Tám (1945). Hà Nội: NXB Bản Sự Thật, 1970.

Camiscioli, Elisa. "Producing Citizens, Reproducing the 'French Race': Immigration, Demography, and Pronatalism in Early Twentieth-Century France." *Gender & History* 13, no. 3 (2001): 593–621.

———. *Reproducing the French Race: Immigration, Intimacy, and Embodiment in the Early Twentieth Century*. Durham: Duke University Press, 2009.

Canning, K., and S. O. Rose. "Gender, Citizenship and Subjectivity: Some Historical and Theoretical Considerations." *Gender & History* 13, no. 3 (2001): 427–443.

Cao Thi Nhu Quynh and John Schaefer. "Ho Bieu Chanh and the Early Development of the Vietnamese Novel." *Vietnam Forum* 12 (1988): 100–111.

Cauderlier, G. "Les Causes de la Dépopulation de France." *Bulletin de la Société d'Anthropology de Paris* (1901): 520.

Chafer, Tony, and Amanda Sackur. *French Colonial Empire and the Popular Front: Hope and Disillusion*. New York: St. Martin's Press, 1999.

Chaigneau, Michel Đức. *Souvenirs de Hué*. Paris: L'Imprimerie Impériale, 1857.

Chapman, Jessica. *Cauldron of Resistance: Ngo Dinh Diem, the United States, and 1950s Southern Vietnam*. Ithaca: Cornell University Press, 2013.

Chapuis, Oscar. *The Last Emperor of Vietnam: From Tu Duc to Bao Dai*. Westport: Greenwood Press, 2000.

Charle, Christophe. *La crise des sociétés Impériales: Allemagne, France, Grande-Bretagne 1900–1940*. Paris: Éditions du Seuil, 2001.

Chervin, Authour. "Étude de Resultants Generaux du Dénombrement de la Population." *Bulletin de la Societe Anthropologie de Paris* (1881): 428.

Chesneaux, Jean. *Contribution a l'Histoire de la Nation Vietnamienne*. Paris: Éditions Sociales, 1955.

Childers, Kristen Stromberg. *Fathers, Families, and the State in France, 1914–1945*. Ithaca: Cornell University Press, 2003.

Christiansen, Flemming, and Ulf Hedetoft. *The Politics of Multiple Belonging: Ethnicity and Nationalism in Europe and East Asia*. Research in Migration and Ethnic Relations Series. Aldershot, Hants, England, and Burlington, VT: Ashgate, 2004.

"Cho được sống lâu, vô bịnh, loài vật cũng cần tập thể thao như người." *Thanh Niên Đông Pháp*, 1944.

"Chuyện 2 cô gái Sài Gòn trở thành công chúa ở Châu Phi." May 4, 2013 zing.vn, accessed June 17, 2015.

"Chuyện những người con lính lê dương tại Việt Nam—Kỳ 2: Những dòng họ cô đơn." *Thanh Niên Online*. May 8, 2014. www.thanhnien.com.vn/doi-song

/chuyen-nhung-nguoi-con-linh-le-duong-tai-viet-nam-ky-2-nhung-dong-ho
-co-don-393882.html. Accessed January 27, 2015.

Clancy-Smith, Julia Ann, and Frances Gouda. *Domesticating the Empire: Race, Gender, and Family Life in French and Dutch Colonialism*. Charlottesville, VA: University Press of Virginia, 1998.

"Cô bé lọ lem VN trở thành công chúa Vương Quốc Kim Cương ở Châu Phi." *Việt Bao*. July 16, 2014.

Code Annamite: Lois Et Règlements du Royaume D'annam. Translated by G. Aubaret. Paris: Imprimerie Impériale, 1865.

Cole, Joshua. *The Power of Large Numbers: Population, Politics, and Gender in Nineteenth-Century France*. Ithaca: Cornell University Press, 2000.

———. "'There Are Only Good Mothers': The Ideological Work of Women's Fertility in France before World War I." *French Historical Studies* 19, no. 3 (1996): 639–672.

Comte D'Haussonville and Joseph Chailley-Bert. *L'émigration des femmes aux colonies*. Paris: Armand Colin & Cie., 1897.

"Con lai 30 năm nhặt rác mua vé máy bay tìm về quê cha." August 1, 2014. zing.vn, last accessed June 17, 2015.

Condominas, Georges, and Richard Pottier. *Les réfugiés originaires de l'asie du sud-est: Rapport Présenté au Président de la République par un Équipe du Centre de documentation et de recherche sur l'asie du sud-est e t le monde insulindien*. Paris: La Documentation Française, Collection des rapports officiels, 1982.

Congrès International pour la Protection de l'Enfance, Section IX: Comité Colonial National de l'Enfance. Paris: Imprimerie Beurq, 1933.

Constantin, L. "Le sanatorium du Langbian." *Revue Indochinois* (March-April 1916): 305–328.

Cooper, Frederick, and Ann Laura Stoler, eds. *Tensions of Empire: Colonial Cultures in a Bourgeois World*. Berkeley: University of California Press, 1997.

Coté, Joost. "'The Sins of Their Fathers': Culturally at Risk Children and the Colonial State in Asia." *Paedagogica Historica: International Journal of the History of Education* 45, no. 1 (2009): 129–142.

Crossley, Ceri. "Using and Transforming the French Countryside: The 'Colonies Agricole' (1820–1850)." *French Studies* 45, no. 1 (1991): 36–54.

Đặng, Thị Vân Chi. "Phan Bội Châu với vấn đề phụ nữ đầu thế kỉ xx." In *Phan Bội Châu: Con Người Và Sự Nghiệp*. Hà Nội: Đại Học Quốc Gia Hà Nội, 1998.

———. *Vấn Đề Phụ Nữ Trên Báo Chí Tiếng Việt Trước Năm 1945*. Hà Nội: Nhà xuất bản khoa học xã hội, 2008.

Đào Duy Anh. *Việt Nam văn hoá sử cương*. Hà Nội: NXB Văn hóa–Thông tin, 2000.

Dareste, Pierre. *Traité de droit coloniale*, Paris: Impr. Du Recueil de législation; de doctrine et de jurisprudence colonials, 1931.

Daughton, J. P. *An Empire Divided: Religion, Republicanism, and the Making of French Colonialism, 1880–1914.* Oxford: Oxford University Press, 2008.

Davin, Anna. "Imperialism and Motherhood." *History Workshop* 5 (1978): 9–65.

DeBonis, Steven. *Children of the Enemy: Oral Histories of Vietnamese Amerasians and Their Mothers.* London: McFarland, 1995.

de Gantès, Gilles. "Les métis franco-indochinois à l'époque coloniale. A l'interface des dominants et des dominés ou à leur marge?" In *Actes Du Colloque L'esprit Économique Impérial,* edited by Hubert Bonin, 735–752. Paris: Publications de la SFHOM, 2008.

"De Gualle gửi thong điệp mới cho TT Johnson về chiến tranh VN." *Miền nam,* 1966.

de la Chevrotière, Jacques. *Les chavigny de la Chevrotière: En nouvelle-France à la Martinique.* Québec: Septentrion, 1997.

Delanoe, Nelcya. *Poussières D'empires.* Paris: Presses Universitaires de France, 2002.

Del Testa, David W. "Workers, Culture, and the Railroads in French Colonial Indochina, 1905–1936." *French Colonial History* 2 (2002): 181–198.

Denéchère, Yves. "Les 'rapatriements' en France des enfants eurasiens de l'ex-Indochine: Pratiques, débats, mémoires." *Revue d'histoire de l'enfance "irrégulière"* 14 (2012): 123–139.

"De Son Côté, M. William Bazé Nous Écrit." *Le Monde,* undated.

Devilliers, Philippe. *Histoire du Viêtnam de 1940 à 1952.* Paris: Édition du Seuil, 1952.

Đinh, Xuân Lâm, ed. *Đại cương lịch sử Việt Nam.* Vol. 2. Hà Nội: Nhà xuất bản Giáo Dục, 2000.

Direction de la Statistique Générale. *Annuaire Statistique Abrégé, 1943–1949.* Paris: Imprimerie Nationale, 1949.

Donzelot, Jacques. *The Policing of Families.* New York: Pantheon Books, 1979.

Downs, Laura Lee. *Childhood in the Promised Land: Working-Class Movements and the Colonies de Vacances in France, 1880–1960.* Durham: Duke University Press, 2002.

Duong Duc Nhu. "Education in Vietnam under the French Domination 1862–1945." Ph.D. diss., Southern Illinois University at Carbondale, 1978.

Dreifort, John E. "Japan's Advance into Indochina, 1940: The French Response." *Journal of Southeast Asian Studies* 13, no. 2 (1982): 279–295.

du Basty, M. "Société d'aide et d'assistance aux oeuvres de bienfaisance en Annam." Paper presented at the Congrès International pour la Protection de l'Enfance, 1933.

Duiker, William J. *Vietnam since the Fall of Saigon.* Athens: Ohio University, 1989.

DuPont, Robert. "Le Dernier Ilot Français En Indochine." *L'Eurafricain,* undated, 1951.

Edington, Claire Ellen. "Beyond the Asylum: Colonial Psychiatry in French Indochina, 1880–1940." PhD diss., Columbia University, 2013.

Edwards, Coral, and Peter Read, eds. *The Lost Children: Thirteen Australians Taken from Their Families Tell of the Struggle to Find Their Natural Parents.* New York: Doubleday, 1989.

Edwards, Maura Kathryn. "*Le Mal Jaune:* The Memory of the Indochina War in France, 1954–2006." PhD diss., University of Toronto, 2010.

"Em Muốn Biết." *Thiếu Sinh,* November 22, 1945.

"Extraits de l'union Française, 'Discours de M William Bazé.'" *L'Eurafricain,* 1949.

Ezra, Elizabeth. "Colonialism Exposed: Miss France D'outre-Mer, 1937." In *Identity Papers: Contested Nationhood in Twentieth Century France,* edited by Steven Ungar and Tom Conley. Minneapolis: University of Minnesota Press, 1996.

Fall, Bernard B. "The Political-Religious Sects of Viet-Nam." *Pacific Affairs* 28, no. 3 (1955): 235–253.

Faron, Olivier. *Les Enfants du Deuil: Orphelins et Pupilles de la Nation de la Première Guerre Mondiale (1914–1941).* Paris: Éditions la Découverte, 2001.

"Fédération des oeuvres de l'enfance Française de l'Indochine, exercice 1950, Assemblée Générale Ordinaire des 27, 28, 29 juillet 1951." Saigon: Imprimerie Française d'Outre Mer, 1951.

"Fédération des oeuvres de l'enfance Française de l'Indochine, exercice 1953, Assemblée Générale Ordinaire des 13, 14, 15 septembre 1954." Saigon: Imprimerie Française d'Outre Mer, 1954.

"Fédération des oeuvres de l'enfance Française d'Indochine, exercice 1954, Assemblée Générale Ordinaire des 5, 6, 7 mai 1955." Saigon: Imprimerie Française d'Outre Mer, 1955.

"Fédération des oeuvres de l'enfance Française d'Indochine, exercice 1955, Assemblée Générale Ordinaire des 19, 20, 21 mars 1956." Saigon: Imprimerie Français d'Outre Mer, 1956.

"Fédération des oeuvres de l'enfance Française d'Indochine, Assemblée Générale Ordinaire des 3, 4, 5 juin 1957." Saigon: Saigon Án Quán, 1957.

"Fédération des oeuvres de l'enfance Française d'Indochine, délégation métropolitaine, exercice 1957, Assemblée Générale Ordinaire des 28 et 29 juillet 1958." Saigon: Kim Lai An-Quan, 1958.

"Fédération des oeuvres de l'enfance Française d'Indochine, exercice 1959, Assemblée Générale Ordinaire des 5 et 6 aout 1960." Saigon: Kim Lai An Quan, 1960.

"Fédération des oeuvres de l'enfance Française d'Indochine, exercice 1960, Assemblée Générale Ordinaire des 11 et 12 aout 1961." Saigon: Kim Lai An-Quan, 1961.

"Fédération des oeuvres de l'enfance Française d'Indochine, exercice 1961, Assemblée Générale Ordinaire du 31 aout 1962." Saigon: Kim Lai An-Quan, 1962.

"Fédération des oeuvres de l'enfance Française d'Indochine, exercice 1962, Assemblée Générale Ordinaire du 24 septembre 1963." Saigon: Kim Lai An-Quan, 1963.

"Fédération des oeuvres de l'enfance Française d'Indochine, exercice 1963, Assemblée Générale Ordinaire du 11 aout 1964." Saigon: Kim Lai An-Quan, 1964.

"Fédération des oeuvres de l'enfance Française d'Indochine, exercice 1964, Assemblée Général Ordinaire du 7 octobre 1965." Paris: Imprimerie René Belleville, 1965.

"Fédération des oeuvres de l'enfance Française d'Indochine, exercice 1965, Assemblée Générale Ordinaire du 18 octobre 1966." Paris: Imprimerie René Belleville, 1966.

"Fédération des oeuvres de l'enfance Française d'Indochine, exercice 1966, Assemblée Générale Ordinaire du 9 octobre 1967." Paris: Imprimerie René Belleville, 1967.

"Fédération des oeuvres de l'enfance Française d'Indochine, exercice 1967, Assemblée Générale Ordinaire du 15 octobre 1968." Paris: Imprimerie René Belleville, 1968.

"Fédération des oeuvres de l'enfance Française d'Indochine, exercice 1968, Assemblée Générale Ordinaire du 14 octobre 1969." Paris: Imprimerie René Belleville, 1969.

"Fédération des oeuvres de l'enfance Française d'Indochine, exercice 1969, Assemblée Générale Ordinaire du 20 octobre 1970." Paris: Imprimerie René Belleville, 1970.

"Fédération des oeuvres de l'enfance Française d'Indochine, exercice 1970, Assemblée Générale Ordinaire du 14 octobre 1971." Paris: Imprimerie René Belleville, 1971.

"Fédération des oeuvres de l'enfance Française d'Indochine, exercice 1971, Assemblée Générale Ordinaire du 11 octobre 1972." Paris: Imprimerie René Belleville, 1972.

"Fédération des oeuvres de l'enfance Française d'Indochine, exercice 1972, Assemblée Générale Ordinaire du 23 octobre 1973." Paris: Imprimerie René Belleville, 1973.

"Fédération des oeuvres de l'enfance Française d'Indochine, exercice 1973, Assemblée Générale Ordinaire du octobre 1974." Paris: Imprimerie René Belleville, 1974.

"Fédération des oeuvres de l'enfance Française d'Indochine, exercice 1974–1975, Assemblée Générale Ordinaire du 28 janvier 1976." 1976.

"Fédération des oeuvres de l'enfance Française d'Indochine, exercice 1975–1976."

"Fédération des oeuvres de l'enfance Française d'Indochine, exercice 1978, Rapport du Conseil D'administration, Assemblée Générale Ordinaire du 5 décembre 1979."

"Fédération des oeuvres de l'enfance Française d'Indochine, exercice 1980, Rapport du Conseil D'administration, Assemblée Générale Ordinaire du samedi 6 décembre 1980." 1980.

"Fédération des oeuvres de l'enfance Française d'Indochine, exercice 1981, Rapport du Conseil D'administration, Assemblée Générale Ordinaire du samedi 24 mars 1982." 1982.

"Fédération des oeuvres de l'enfance Française d'Indochine, exercice 1982, Rapport du Conseil D'administration, Assemblée Générale Ordinaire du mardi 22 mars 1983." 1983.

Firpo, Christina. "Lost Boys: 'Abandoned' Eurasian Children and the Management of the Racial Topography in Colonial Indochina, 1938–1945." *French Colonial History* 8 (2007): 203–224.

———. "Shades of Whiteness: Petits-Blancs and the Politics of Military Allocations Distribution in World War I Colonial Cochinchina." *French Historical Studies* 34, no. 2 (2011).

Foucault, Michel. *Discipline and Punish: The Birth of the Prison.* New York: Pantheon Books, 1977.

Fourniau, Charles. "Les Années 1930 et l'impasse coloniale en Indochine." In *Rapport de Mission en Indochine 1 Janvier–14 Mars 1937,* edited by François Bilange, Charles Fourniau, and Alain Ruscio. Paris: Éditions L'Harmattan, 1994.

Franchini, Philippe. *Continental Saigon.* Paris: Métailié, 1985.

———, ed. *Tonkin 1873–1954. Colonie et Nation: la delta des mythes.* Paris: Éditions Autrement, 1994.

Fuchs, Rachel G. *Abandoned Children: Foundlings and Child Welfare in Nineteenth Century France.* Albany: State University New York Press, 1998.

———. "Charity and Welfare." In *The History of the European Family: Volume 2, Family Life in the Long Nineteenth Century 1789–1913,* edited by David I. Kertzer and Marzio Barbagli, 155–195. New Haven: Yale University Press, 2002.

———. *Contested Paternity: Constructing Families in Modern France.* Baltimore: Johns Hopkins University Press, 2008.

———. *Gender and Poverty in Nineteenth-Century Europe.* Cambridge: Cambridge University Press, 2005.

Furuta, Motoo, and Takashi Shiraishi, eds. *Indochina in the 1940s and 1950s.* Ithaca: Cornell Southeast Asia Program, 1992.

Galuski, M. "Enquête sur la Situation des Métis, IV. Au Tonkin." *Revue Indochinoise* 16, no. 4 (1913): 402–408.

"Giăng Mô rô—người Pháp lạ lùng." *Báo Phụ Nữ,* October 6, 2009.

Girault, Arthur. "La condition juridique des métis dans les colonies français." *Revue Politique et Parlementaire* (1928): 124–131.

Gordon, Linda. "Family Violence, Feminism, and Social Control." In *Women, the State, and Welfare,* edited by Linda Gordon, 178–198. Madison: University of Wisconsin Press, 1990.

———, ed. *Women, the State, and Welfare.* Madison: University of Wisconsin Press, 1990.

———. *The Great Arizona Orphan Abduction.* Cambridge: Harvard University Press, 1999.

Goscha, Christopher. *Historical Dictionary of the Indochina War (1945–1954): An International and Interdisciplinary Approach.* Honolulu: University of Hawai'i Press, 2012.

———. *Vietnam or Indochina? Contesting Concepts of Space in Vietnamese Nationalism, 1887–1954.* Copenhagen: Nordic Institute of Asian Studies Publishing, 1995.

Gosh, Durba. *Sex in the Family in Colonial India: The Making of Empire.* Cambridge: Cambridge University Press, 2006.

Gouda, Frances. *Poverty and Political Culture: The Rhetoric of Social Welfare in the Netherlands and France, 1815–1854.* Amsterdam: Amsterdam University Press, 1995.

Gourou, Pierre. *Les Paysans du Delta Tonkinois.* Paris: École Française d'Extrême-Orient, 1936.

Gravelle, Charles. "Enquête sur la Question des Métis." *Revue Indochinois* 10 (January 1913): x–xii.

———. "Les métis et l'oeuvre de la protection de l'enfance au Cambodge." *Revue Indochinois* 16, no. 1 (January 1913).

Guillaume, Pierre. "Les métis en Indochine." *Annales de Demographie Historique* (1995): 185–195.

Ha, Marie-Paule. *French Women and the Empire: The Case of Indochina.* Oxford: Oxford University Press, 2014.

Habermas, Jürgen. "The European Nation-State: On the Past and Future of Sovereignty and Citizenship." *Public Culture* 10, no. 2 (1998): 397–416.

Hardy, Andrew. *Red Hills: Migrants and the State in the Highlands of Vietnam.* Honolulu University of Hawai'i Press, 2003.

Hartkopf Schloss, Rebecca. *Sweet Liberty: The Final Days of Slavery in Martinique.* Philadelphia: University of Pennsylvania Press, 2009.

"Henri De Lachevrotier." *L'Eurafricain,* 1951.

Heynssens, Sarah. "Practices of Displacement: Forced Migration of Mixed-Race Children from Colonial Ruanda-Urundi to Belgium." Presented at the Berkshire Conference, Toronto, Canada, May 22, 2014.

Hoàng, Khôi, and Hoàng Đình Thi. *Giai Thoại về Phụ Nữ Việt Nam.* Hà Nội: NXB Phụ Nữ, 1978.

Hoàng, Thi Thư. "Người Việt Trên Đất Pháp." *Miền Nam,* May 14, 1968.

———. "Người Việt Trên Đất Pháp." *Miền Nam,* May 16, 1968.

Hoang, Trong Phu Tong Do SE. "Les oeuvres de protection de la maternité et de l'enfance de la province de Hadong." Paper presented at the Congrès International pour la Protection de l'Enfance, 1933.

Huard, P., and Do Xuan Hop. "Recherches sur l'importance numérique des européens et des eurasiens." *Bulletin de l'Institut Indochinois pour l'Etude de l'Homme,* 1942, Part V, section 1 (1943).

Huỳnh, Kim Khánh. *Vietnamese Communism, 1925–1945.* Ithaca: Cornell University Press, 1982.

Hy Van Luong. *Revolution in the Village: Tradition and Transformation in North Vietnam, 1925–1988.* Honolulu: University of Hawai'i Press, 1992.

Jablonka, Ivan. *Enfants en exil: Transfert de pupilles réunionnais en métropole (1963–1982).* Paris: Seuil, 2007.

Jacobs, Margaret D. *A Generation Removed: The Fostering and Adoption of Indigenous Children in the Postwar World.* Lincoln: University of Nebraska Press, 2014.

———. *White Mother to a Dark Race: Settler Colonialism, Maternalism, and the Removal of Indigenous Children in the American West and Australia, 1880–1940.* Lincoln: University of Nebraska Press, 2009.

Jamieson, Neil L. *Understanding Vietnam.* Berkeley: University of California Press, 1995.

Jennings, Eric Thomas. *Curing the Colonizers: Hydrotherapy, Climatology, and French Colonial Spas.* Durham: Duke University Press, 2006.

———. "Đà Lạt, Capital of Indochina: Remolding Frameworks and Spaces in the Late Colonial Era." *Journal of Vietnamese Studies* 4, no. 2 (2009): 1–33.

———. *Imperial Heights: Dalat and the Making and Undoing of French Indochina.* Berkeley: University of California Press, 2011.

———. *Vichy in the Tropics: Pétain's National Revolution in Madagascar, Guadeloupe, and Indochina, 1940–1944.* Stanford, CA: Stanford University Press, 2001.

Jenson, Jane. "Representations of Gender: Policies to 'Protect' Women Workers and Infants in France and the United States before 1914." In *Women, the State and Welfare,* edited by Linda Gordon, 152–177. Madison: University of Wisconsin Press, 1990.

Jones, Hilary. *The Métis of Senegal: Urban Life and Politics in French West Africa.* Bloomington: Indiana University Press, 2013.

Journoud, Pierre. *De Gaulle et le Vietnam (1945–1969).* Paris: Éditions Tallandier, 2011.

Kahin, Audrey R., and George McT. Kahin. *Subversion as Foreign Policy: The Secret Eisenhower and Dulles Debacle in Indonesia.* Seattle: University of Washington Press, 1997.

Keith, Charles. *Catholic Vietnam: A Church from Empire to Nation.* Berkeley: University of California Press, 2012.

———. "Catholicisme, Bouddhisme et lois laïques au tonkin, 1899–1914." *Vingtième Siècle, Revue d'Histoire* 87 (2005): 113–128.

Kelly, Gail Paradise and David H. Kelly. *French Colonial Education: Essays on Vietnam and West Africa.* New York: AMS Press, 1998.

———. *Franco-Vietnamese Schools, 1918–1938: regional development and implications for national integration.* No. 6. Center for Southeast Asian Studies, University of Wisconsin-Madison, 1982.

Kenneison, Rebecca. *Playing for Malaya: A Eurasian Family in the Pacific War.* Singapore: NUS Press, 2012.

Kertzer, David I., and Marzio Barbagli, eds. *The History of the European Family: Volume 2. Family Life in the Long Nineteenth Century 1789–1913.* New Haven: Yale University Press, 2002.

———. *The History of the European Family: Volume 3. Family Life in the Twentieth Century.* New Haven: Yale University Press, 2003.

Khérian, Gregoire. "Le problème démographique en Indochine, extrait de la *Revue Indochinoise Juridique et Economique.*" Hanoi: Imprimerie d'Extrême-Orient, 1937.

"Khoa Học." *Thiếu Sinh,* October 15, 1945.

"'Không thể nhìn nhận vc đại diện cho dân chúng miền nam' Hồ Chí Minh gởi thông điệp cho De Gualle." *Miền Nam,* February 2, 1966.

Kranakis, Eda. *Constructing a Bridge: An Exploration of Engineering Culture, Design, and Nineteenth-Century France and America.* Cambridge: MIT Press, 1996.

Kroef, Justus M. van der. "The Eurasian Minority in Indonesia." *American Sociological Review* 18, no. 5 (1953): 484–493.

Lâm, Truong Buu. *Colonialism Experienced: Vietnamese Writings on Colonialism, 1900–1931.* Ann Arbor, MI: University of Michigan, 2000.

Lambert, Christian, and Maria Penders. *The West New Guinea Debacle: Dutch Decolonization and Indonesia.* Honolulu: University of Hawai'i Press, 2002.

"Lần đầu tiên, nhà việt sử pháp tiết lộ: Pháp-Mỹ 'cãi nhau' như thế nào về chiến tranh Vn." *Miền Nam,* January 31, 1967.

Langlois, Walter. *André Malraux: The Indochina Adventure.* New York: Frederick A. Praeger, 1967.

Lapouge, G. Vacher. "La Dépopulation de la France," *Revue Anthropologie* 16 (1887): 69–80.

Le, Manh Hung. *The Impact of World War II on the Economy of Vietnam 1939–1945.* New York: Eastern University Press, 2004.

Lê, Văn. "Khu trưởng khu 7 Nguyễn Bình và vụ án Ba Nhỏ cuối năm 1945." December 12, 2006. http://vnca.cand.com.vn/Truyen-thong/Khu-truong-khu-7 -Nguyen-Binh-va-vu-an-Ba-Nho-cuoi-nam-1945-324522. Accessed September 27, 2014.

Lefèvre, Kim. *Métisse blanche.* Paris: Éditions Bernard Barrault, 1989, 2003.

"L'émigration des *métis* Franco-Vietnamiens." *Le Monde,* September 20, 1980.

Les grands commis de l'empire colonial français: Actes du colloque de clermont-ferrand du 14 octobre 2005 organisé par les Indes Savantes avec le soutien de la Fondation Varenne. Paris: Indes savantes, 2010.

Lessard, Micheline. "Tradition for Rebellion: Vietnamese Students and Teachers and Anticolonial Resistance, 1888–1931." PhD diss., Cornell University, 1995.

Lịch Sử Phong Trào Phụ Nữ Hà Bắc. Hà Bắc: Hội Liên hiệp phụ nữ Hà Bắc, 1990.

Lịch Sử Phong Trào Phụ Nữ Nghệ An (1930–1975). Nghệ An: Hội Liên Hiệp Phụ Nữ Nghệ An, 1996.

Lịch Sử Phong Trào Phụ Nữ Tỉnh Bắc Ninh (1930–2000). Bắc Ninh: Hội Liên Hiệp Phụ Nữ Tỉnh Bắc Ninh, 2000.

Lịch Sử Phong Trào Phụ Nữ Tỉnh Vĩnh Phú (1930–1995). Vĩnh Phú: Hội Liên Hiệp Phụ Nữ Tỉnh Vĩnh Phú, 1996.

Lịch Sử Truyền Thống Cách Mạng Phụ Nữ Hà Tây. Hà Tây: Hội Liên Hiệp Phụ Nữ Hà Tây, 1997.

Lịch Sử Truyền Thống Phụ Nữ Nam Hà (1930–1995). Nam Hà: Hội Liên Hiệp Phụ Nữ Nam Hà, 1996.

Lionnet, Françoise. *Autobiographical Voices: Race, Gender, Self-Portraiture.* Ithaca: Cornell University Press, 1989.

Logevall, Fredrik. *Choosing War: The Lost Chance for Peace and Escalation of War in Vietnam.* Berkeley: University of California Press, 1999.

"Lời khẩn cầu của vợ con lính lê dương từng tham chiến tại Việt Nam." *Lao Động,* November 1, 2014.

Long, Ngô Vĩnh. *Before the Revolution: The Vietnamese Peasants Under the French.* New York: Columbia University Press, 1991 [1973].

Luc, Jean-Noël. *L'Invention du jeune enfant au XIXème siècle. De la sale d'asile à l'école maternelle.* Paris, Bernard Grasset, 1979.

Lusteguy, Pierre. *La Femme Annamite du Tonkin dans les Institutions des Biens Culturels (Huong Hoa).* Paris: Librarie Nizet et Bastard, 1935.

Lý, Nhân Phan Thứ Lang. *Sài Gòn Vang Bóng.* Hồ Chí Minh City: NXB Thành Phố Hồ Chí Minh, 2001.

Lydon, Ghislaine. "Women, Children and Popular Front's Missions of Inquiry in French West Africa." In *French Colonial Empire and the Popular Front: Hope and Disillusion,* edited by Tony Chafer and Amanda Sackur, 170–187. London: Macmillion Press LTD, 1999.

"M. Henri De Lachevrotiere, Avocat Honoraire Président D'honneur De La Mutuelle Des Français De L'indochine, Journaliste Assassiné À Saigon À Coup De Grenade." *L'Eurafricain,* 1951.

MacKinnon, Catherine A. *Toward a Feminist Theory of the State.* Cambridge: Harvard University Press, 1989.

Manceron, Gilles. *Marianne et les colonies: Une introduction à l'histoire coloniale de la France.* Paris: La Découverte, 2003.

Marquis, Edouard. *L'Oeuvre humaine de la France en Cochinchine.* Saigon: Imprimerie du Theatre, 1936.

Marr, David G. *Vietnam 1945: The Quest for Power.* Berkeley: University of California Press, 1995.

———. *Vietnamese Tradition on Trial, 1920–1945.* Berkeley: University of California Press, 1981.

Maxwell, Anne. *Colonial Photography and Exhibitions: Representations of the 'Native' and the Making of European Identities.* London: Leicester University Press, 1999.

Mayeur, Jean-Marie, and Madeleine Rebérioux. *The Third Republic from Its Origins to the Great War 1871–1914.* Cambridge: Cambridge University Press, 1987.

McClintock, Anne. *Imperial Leather: Race, Gender and Sexuality in the Colonial Conquest.* New York: Routledge, 1995.

McClintock, Anne, Aamir Mufti, and Ella Shohat, eds. *Dangerous Liasons: Gender, Nation, and Postcolonial Perspectives.* Minneapolis: University of Minnesota Press, 1997.

McHale, Shawn Frederick. "Ethnicity, Violence, and Khmer-Vietnamese Relations: The Significance of the Lower Mekong Delta, 1757–1954." *Journal of Asian Studies* 72, no. 2 (2013): 367–390.

———. "Printing and Power: Vietnamese Debates over Women's Place in Society, 1918–1934." In *Essays into Vietnamese Pasts,* edited by K.W. Taylor and John K. Whitmore, 173–194. Ithaca: Cornell University Press, 1995.

———. "Understanding the Fanatic Mind? The Viet Minh and Race Hatred in the First Indochina War (1945–1954)." *Journal of Vietnamese Studies* 4, no. 3 (2009): 98–138.

McMahon, Robert J. *Limits of Empire: The United States and Southeast Asia since World War II.* New York: Columbia University Press, 1999.

Meyer, Charles. *La Vie Quotidienne des Français en Indochine 1860–1910.* Paris: Hachette Littérature, 1985.

"Mihagui: Trong Máu Tôi . . . Có Nước Mắm?" *Việt Báo,* October 7, 2006.

Miller, Edward. *Misalliance: Ngo Dinh Diem, the United States, and the Fate of South Vietnam.* Cambridge: Harvard University Press, 2013.

Ministère des colonies office colonial. *Statistiques de la population dans les colonies françaises pour l'année 1906.* Melun: Imprimerie Administrative, 1909.

Mink, Gwendolyn. "The Lady and the Tramp: Gender, Race, and the Origins of the American Welfare State." In *Women, the State and Welfare,* edited by Linda Gordon, 92–122. Madison: University of Wisconsin Press, 1990.

———. *The Wages of Motherhood: Inequality in the Welfare State 1917–1942.* Ithaca: Cornell University Press, 1995.

Mizutani, Satoshi. *The Meaning of White: Race, Class, and the "Domiciled Community" in British India, 1858–1930.* London: Oxford University Press, 2011.

Monnais-Rousselot, Laurence. *Médecine et Colonisation: L'adventure Indochinoise, 1860–1939.* Paris: CNRS Éditions, 1999.

Montagnon, Pierre. *France-Indochine, un Siècle de Vie Commune 1858–1954.* Paris: Pygmalion, 2004.

Mora-Kpai, Idrissou. *Indochina: Traces of a Mother.* Noble Films, 2012.

Morlat, Patrice. *La Repression Coloniale au Vietnam 1908–1940*. Paris: L'Harmattan, 1990.

———. *Les affaires politiques de l'Indochine, 1895–1923: Les grands commis, du savior au pouvir*. Paris: Harmattan, 1995.

"Một khổng chiến thiếu sinh." *Thiếu Sinh*, November 22, 1945.

Muller, Gregor. *Colonial Cambodia's "Bad Frenchmen": The Rise of French Rule and the Life of Thomas Caraman, 1840–87*. New York: Routledge, 2006.

Murray, Martin. *The Development of Capitalism in Colonial Indochina (1870–1940)*. Berkeley: University of California Press, 1980.

Mutiny. "Discours De M. Mutiny D'un Groupe Des Jeunes Eurasiens." *L'Eurafricain* (1949): 24–25.

"Mutuelle des Françaises d'Indochine: compte rendu de l'Assemblée Générale Ordinaire du Dimanche 16 avril 1950." *L'Eurafricain*, undated, 1950.

"Nés de pères Français et de mères Asiatiques, 350 jeunes Eurasiens ont retrouvé, en France, une famille." *L'Eurafricain*, 1952.

Ngô, Van. *Viêt-Nam 1920–1945: Revolution et Contre-Revolution sous la Domination Coloniale*. Paris: L'Insomniaque, 1995.

Ngo, Van Chieu. *Journal d'un combattant Viet-Minh*. Translated by Jacques Despuech. Paris: Éditions du Seuil, 1955.

Ngô, Vinh Long. *Before the Revolution: The Vietnamese Peasants under the French*. New York: Columbia University Press, 1991.

"Người con lai Pháp 20 năm viết đơn tìm cha." *Báo Mới*. July 17, 2014. www.baomoi .com/Nguoi-con-lai-Phap-20-nam-viet-don-tim-cha/139/14330861.epi. Accessed January 27, 2014.

Nguyễn, Hoàng. "Muôn mặt báo chí Sài Gòn trước năm 1975." *Lao Động*, June 7, 2015.

Nguyễn, Khánh Toàn, Nguyễn Công Bình, Văn Tạo, Phạm Xuân Nam, and Bùi Đình Thanh, eds. *Lịch Sử Việt Nam Tập II 1858–1945*. Hà Nội: NXB Khoa Học Xã Hội, 2004.

Nguyen, Lien Hang. *Hanoi's War: An International History of the War for Peace in Vietnam*. Chapel Hill: University of North Carolina Press, 2012.

Nguyen, Martina Thucnhi. "The Self-Reliant Literary Group (Tự Lực Văn Đoàn): Colonial Modernism in Vietnam, 1932–1941." PhD diss., University of California, Berkeley, 2012.

Nguyen, Nathalie Huynh Chau. "Eurasian/Amerasian Perspectives: Kim Lefèvre's *Métisse blanche* (White Métisse) and Kien Nguyen's *The Unwanted*." *Asian Studies Review* 29 (June 2005): 107–122.

Nguyễn Phan Quang. *Việt Nam thế kỷ XIX (1802–1884)*. HCMC: NXB Thành Phố Hồ Chí Minh, 2002.

Nguyễn Q. Thắng and Nguyễn Bá Thế. *Từ Điển Nhân Vật Lịch Sử Việt Nam*. Hà Nội: NXB Văn Hóa, 1999.

Nguyễn, Thành. *Từ Điển Thư Tịch Báo Chí Việt Nam.* Hà Nội: NXB Văn Hóa-Thông Tin, 2001.

Nguyen, Van Tinh, Hoang Van Nguyen, and Van Than Thai. "Les difficulties des *métis* Franco-Vietnamiens à émigrer en France et l'attitude de Paris." *Le Monde,* September 18, 1980.

Nguyen-Marshall, Van. *In Search of Moral Authority: The Discourse on Poverty, Poor Relief, and Charity in French Colonial Indochina.* New York: Peter Lang, 2008.

"Nhân Cuộc Viếng Thăm Mạc T. Khoa, Pháp-Nga Thỏa Thuận Vận Động Cho Hoà Bình Việt Nam, Kế Hoạch Này Sẽ Thực Hiện Trong Tháng Tới." *Miền Nam,* January 15, 1966.

Nhất Linh. *Đoạn Tuyệt.* Saigon: Đời Nay, 1971.

"Nhiệm Vụ Thiêng Liêng Của Phụ Nữ: Chị Em Ta Phải Biệt Cách Nuôi Con." *Bạn Gái Mới,* November 27, 1945.

Như chưa hề có cuộc chia ly, episode 52, aired September 30, 2012.

Như Hiên Nguyễn, Ngọc Hiền. *Nữ Sĩ Việt Nam: Tiểu Sử & Giai Thoại Cổ-Cận Đại.* Hồ Chí Minh City: NXB Văn nghệ, 2000.

"Những Chiếc Áo Rét Gửi Cho Chiến Sĩ Ngoại Mặt Trận." *Thiếu Sinh,* October 15, 1945.

"Những người con lai Pháp ở Điện Biên." *Tài nguyên và Môi Trường.* April 11, 2014. http://baotainguyenmoitruong.vn/suc-khoe-doi-song/201404/nhung -nguoi-con-lai-phap-o-dien-bien-518330. Accessed January 27, 2015.

Nicholson, Barbara. "Stolen Generations." In *A Historical Companion to Postcolonial Thought in English,* edited by Prem Poḍar and David Johnson, 388–452. New York: Columbia University Press, 2005.

Norindr, Panivong. *Phantasmatic Indochina: French Colonial Ideology in Architecture, Film and Literature.* Durham: Duke University Press, 1996.

———. "The Popular Front's Colonial Policies in Indochina: Reassessing the Popular Front's 'Colonisation Altruiste.'" In *French Colonial Empire and the Popular Front: Hope and Disillusion,* edited by Tony Chafer and Amanda Sackur, 230–248. London: Macmillan Press, 1999.

Notice sur la Société d'Assistance aux Enfant Franco Indochinois du Tonkin. Hà Nội: Imprimerie G. Taupin, 1937.

"Nuôi Nắng Trẻ Con." *Việt Nữ,* December 10, 1945.

Oeuvre de la sainte enfance ou Association des enfants chrétiens pour le rachat des enfants infidèles en chine et dans les autres pays idolâtres. Paris: Bethune et Plon, 1844.

Paillard, Jean. *L'empire Français De Demain.* Paris: Institut d'etudes corporatives et sociales, 1943.

Papin, Philippe. *Histoire de Hanoi.* Paris, Fayard, 2001.

Paxton, Robert O. *Vichy France: Old Guard and New Order 1940–1945.* New York: Columbia University Press, 1972.

Pedersen, Jean Elisabeth. "'Special Customs': Paternity Suits and Citizenship in France and the Colonies, 1870–1912." In *Domesticating the Empire: Race, Gender, and Family Life in French and Dutch Colonialism,* edited by Julia Ann Clancy-Smith and Frances Gouda, 43–64. Charlottesville, VA: University Press of Virginia, 1998.

Pelaud, Isabelle Thuy. "Métisse blanche: Kim Lefèvre and Transnational Space." *Mixed Race Literature,* edited by Jonathan Brennan. Stanford, CA: Stanford University Press, 2002.

Pelley, Patricia. "'Barbarians' and 'Younger Brothers': The Remaking of Race in Post Colonial Vietnam." *Journal of Southeast Asian Studies* 29, no. 2 (1998): 374–391.

Perrens, Claude. "Lettre De Dalat." *Indochine Hebdomadaire Illustré* (1943): 14.

Peters, Erica J. *Appetites and Aspirations in Vietnam: Food and Drink in the Long Nineteenth Century.* New York: AltaMira, 2011.

———. "Culinary Crossings and Disruptive Identities: Contesting Colonial Categories in Everyday Life." In *Of Vietnam: Identities in Dialogue,* edited by Jane Winston. New York: Saint Martin's Press, 2001.

Petit Guide pour l'Application de Loi du 27 Juillet 1917 Instituant les Pupilles de la Nation. Paris: Chantenay Imprimerie, 1919.

Peycam, Philippe M. F. *The Birth of Vietnamese Political Journalism: Saigon, 1916–1930.* New York: Columbia University Press, 2012.

Phạm, Đình Tân. *Chủ Nghĩa Đế Quốc Pháp Và Tình Hình Công Nghiệp Ở Việt-Nam Dưới Thời Thuộc Pháp.* Hà Nội: NXB Bản Sự Thật, 1959.

Pham, Duy Khiem. "A propos de la famille annamite" *EST* no. 3 (March 1939): 275–279.

Phan, Boi Châu. *Overturned Chariot: The Autobiography of Phan-Bội-Châu.* Honolulu: University of Hawai'i Press, 1999.

Phinney, Harriet M. "Objets of Affection: Vietnamese Discourses on Love and Emancipation," *Positions: East Asia Cultures Critique* 16, no. 2 (2008): 329–358.

Phụ Nữ Hải Phòng Qua Các Chặng Đường Cách Mạng 1926–1955. Hải Phòng: NXB Hải Phòng, 1985.

Pigneau, L. G. "Dalat—Capital Administratif De L'indochine?" *La Revue Indochinoise Juridique et Economique* 2 (1937): 45–82.

Pierson, Ruth Roach, and Nupur Chaudhuri, eds. *Nation, Empire, Colony: Historicizing Gender and Race.* Bloomington: Indiana University Press, 1998.

Pomfret, David M. "Raising Eurasia: Race, Class, and Age in French and British Colonies." *Comparative Studies in Society and History* 51 (2009): 314–343.

"Position juridique des métis." *L'Eurafricain,* 1949.

Pouvourville, Albert (de), "l'Indochine et ses métis," *La Depeche Coloniale,* 16 September, 1911.

"Proposition tenant à demander au haut conseil de l'union Français l'etude d'un statute juridique en faveur des eurasiens." *L'Eurafricain,* 1953.

Prost, Antoine. *L'enseignement en France, 1800–1967.* Paris: Armand, 1968.

"Quan Báo Lược Lục." *Đông Dương Tạp Chí,* July 24, 1913.

"Quan Báo Trích Lục: Luật Nhận Cha Con." *Đông Dương Tạp Chí,* July 3, 1913, 5–6.

Quinn-Judge, Sophie. "Women in the Early Vietnamese Communist Movement: Sex, Lies, and Liberation." *South East Asia Research* 9, no. 3 (2001): 245–269.

Rabinow, Paul. *French Modern: Norms and Forms of the Social Environment.* Chicago: University of Chicago Press, 1989.

Raffin, Anne. "Easternization Meets Westernization: Patriotic Youth Organizations in French Indochina during World War II." *French Politics, Culture, and Society* 20, no. 2 (2002): 121–140.

———. *Youth Mobilization in Vichy Indochina and Its Legacies, 1940 to 1970.* Lanham: Lexington Books, 2005.

Ravi, Srilata. "Métis, Métisse and Métissage: Representations and Self-Representations." In *Asia in Europe, Europe in Asia,* edited by Srilata Ravi, Mario Rutten, and Beng-Lan Goh, 299–321. Singapore: Institute of Southeast Asian Studies, 2004.

———. "Métisse Stories and the Ambivalent Desire for Cultural Belonging." *Journal of Intercultural Studies* 28, no. 1 (2007): 15–26.

"Retour Vers Le Passé." *L'Eurafricain,* 1951.

Reynolds, Siân. *France Between the Wars: Gender and Politics.* New York: Routledge, 1996.

"Robert Vaeza 'Coi Như Là Pháp.'" *Tuổi Trẻ Cuối Tuần,* July 26, 2009.

Robin, René. "L'effort français en Indochine: Un problème bien posé qu'il reste à résoudre: Le problème démographique en Indochine." *Indochine Hebdomadaire Illustré* (1942): 4–7.

Rostan, Philippe. *Inconnu, présumé français.* France, 2011.

Saada, Emmanuelle. *Empire's Children: Race, Filiation, and Citizenship in the French Colonies.* Translated by Arthur Goldhammer. Chicago: University of Chicago Press, 2012.

———. *Les enfants de la colonie.* Paris: La Découverte, 2008.

Sachs, Dana. *The Life We Were Given: Operation Babylift, International Adoption, and the Children of War in Vietnam.* Boston: Beacon Press, 2010.

Said, Edward. *Orientalism.* New York, Pantheon, 1978.

Sambuc, Henri. "Notes et documents: Enquête sur la question des métis." *Revue Indochinoise* 19 (February 1913): 201–209.

———. "Les métis franco-annamites en Indochine." *La Revue du Pacifique* 10 (January 1931): 262–263.

———. "La Protection dans les Colonies Françaises des Enfants Métis Abandonnés." In *Congrès International pour la Protection de l'Enfance, Section IX: Comité Colonial National de l'Enfance.* Paris: Imprimerie Beurq, 1933.

Sarkissian, Margaret. "Cultural Chameleons: Portuguese Eurasian Strategies for Survival in Post-colonial Malaysia." *Journal of Southeast Asian Studies* 28, no. 2 (1997): 249–262.

Schafer, Sylvia. "Between Paternal Right and the Dangerous Mother: Reading Parental Responsibility in Nineteenth-Century French Civil Justice." *Journal of Family History* 23, no. 2 (1998): 173–189.

———. *Children in Moral Danger and the Problem of Government in Third Republic France.* Princeton, NJ: Princeton University Press, 1997.

Schneider, William H. *Quality and Quantity: The Quest for Biological Regeneration in Twentieth-Century France.* New York: Cambridge University Press, 1990.

Scott, James C. *Seeing Like a State: How Certain Schemes to Improve the Human Condition Have Failed.* New Haven: Yale University Press, 1998.

Shepard, Todd. *The Invention of Decolonization: The Algerian War and the Remaking of France.* Ithaca: Cornell University Press, 2008.

Simon, Pierre-Jean. *Rapatries d'Indochine: Un village franco-indochinois en Bourbonnais.* Paris: L'Harmattan, 1981.

Simon-Barouh, Ida. *Rapatries d'Indochine: deuxieme generation, Les enfants d'origine indochinoise à Noyant-d'Allier.* Paris: L'Harmattan, 1981.

Singaravélou, Pierre. *L'ecole française d'extrême-orient ou l'institution des marges (1898–1956): Essai d'histoire sociale et politique de la science coloniale.* Paris: L'Harmattan, 1999.

Smith, Ralph B. "The Japanese Period in Indochina and the Coup of 9 March 1945." *Journal of Southeast Asian Studies* 9, no. 2 (1978): 268–301.

Société d'Anthropologie de Paris. *Anthropologie des Métis Franco-Vietnamiens.* Paris: Masson et Cie, 1967.

Société d'Assistance aux Enfants Franco-Indochinois. *Assemblée Générale Annuelle Oridinaire du 23 Avril 1938.* Hanoi, 1938.

Société d'Assistance aux Enfants Franco-Indochinois du Cambodge. *Procèces-Verbal de l'Assemblée Générale du 28 Mars 1940, Exercice 1939.* Phnom-Penh: Imprimerie Albert Portail, 1940.

———. *Procèces-Verbal de l'Assemblée Générale du 21 Mars 1942, Exercice 1941.* Phnom-Penh: Imprimerie A. Portail, 1942.

Société de Protection aux Enfants Métis. *Assemblée Générale du 19 Janvrier 1918.* Hà Nội: Imprimerie d'Extreme Orient, 1918.

Société de Protection de l'Enfance au Cambodge. *Procèces-Verbal de l'Assemblée Générale du 31 Mars 1937, Exercice 1936.* Phnom-Penh: Imprimerie Société d'Editions Khmer, 1937.

———. *Procèces-Verbal de l'Assemblée Générale du 9 Mars 1938, Exercice 1937.* Phnom-Penh: Imprimerie Société d'Editions Khmer, 1938.

———. *Procèces-Verbal de l'Assemblée Générale du 30 Mars 1939, Exercice 1938.* Phnom-Penh: Imprimerie Albert Portail, 1939.

Springhall, John. "'Kicking Out the Vietminh': How Britain Allowed France to Reoccupy South Indochina, 1945–46." *Journal of Contemporary History* 40, no. 1 (2005): 115–130.

Statler, Kathryn C. *Replacing France: The Origins of American Intervention in Vietnam*. Lexington: University Press of Kentucky, 2007.

Stoler, Ann Laura. *Along the Archival Grain*. Princeton: Princeton University Press, 2009.

———. *Carnal Knowledge and Imperial Power: Race and the Intimate in Colonial Rule*. Berkeley: University of California Press, 2002.

———. "Making Empire Respectable: The Politics of Race and Sexual Morality in 20th-Century Colonial Cultures." *American Ethnologist* 16, no. 4 (1989): 634–660.

———. *Race and the Education of Desire: Foucault's "History of Sexuality" and the Colonial Order of Things*. Durham, NC: Duke University Press, 1995.

———. "Sexual Affronts and Racial Frontiers: European Identities and the Cultural Politics of Exclusions in Colonial Southeast Asia." In *Tensions of Empire: Colonial Cultures in a Bourgeois World*, edited by Frederick Cooper and Ann Laura Stoler, 198–237. Berkeley: University of California Press, 1997.

———. "Tense and Tender ties: The Politics of Comparison in North American History and (Post) Colonial Studies." *Journal of American History* 88 no.3, (2001): 829–865.

Stovall, Tyler. "Love, Labor, and Race: Colonial Men and White Women in France during the Great War." In *French Civilization and Its Discontents: Nationalism, Colonialism, Race*, edited by Tyler Edward Stovall and Georges Van den Abbeele, 297–322. Lanham, MD: Lexington Books, 2003.

Surkis, Judith. *Sexing the Citizen: Morality and Masculinity in France, 1870–1920*. Ithaca: Cornell University Press, 2006.

Tạ, Thị Thúy. *Việc Nhượng Đất, Khẩn Hoang ở Bắc Kỳ Từ 1919 Đến 1945*. Hà Nội: NXB Thế Giới, 2001.

Tableau de population, de culture, de commerce et de navigation, formant pour l'année 1872. Paris: Imprimerie Nationale, 1875.

"Tableau III, Movement de Certaines Catégories de la Population 1937 à 1948." In Direction de la Statistique Générale, *Annuaire Statistique Abrégé, 1943–1949*. Paris: Imprimerie Nationale, 1949.

Tai, Hue Tam Ho. *Radicalism and the Origins of the Vietnamese Revolution*. Cambridge: Harvard University Press, 1992.

Talbot, John E. *The Politics of Educational Reform in France, 1918–1940*. Princeton: Princeton University Press, 1969.

Tạo, Văn, and Moto Furuta. *Nạn Đói Năm 1945 ở Việt Nam: Những Chứng Tích Lịch Sử*. Hà Nội: Viện Sử Học Việt Nam xuất bản, 1995.

Taylor, Jean Gelman. *The Social World of Batavia: European and Eurasian in Dutch Asia*. Madison: University of Wisconsin Press, 1983.

Thiện, Mộc Lan. *Phụ-Nữ Tân-Văn: Phấn Son Tô Điểm Sơn Hà.* Ho Chi Minh City: NXB Văn Hóa Sài Gòn Công Ty Sách Thời Đại, 2010.

"Thiếu Sinh Tập Trận." *Thiếu Sinh,* October 1, 1945.

"Thời Sự Tổng Thuật." *Đông Dương Tạp Chí,* July 3, 1913.

Thompson, Virginia. *French Indo-China.* New York: Octagon Books, 1968.

Thompson, Virginia, and Richard Adolff. *Minority Problems in Southeast Asia.* Stanford: Stanford University Press, 1955.

"Tìm Di Ảnh." *Tuổi Trẻ,* March 3, 2012.

Tonnesson, Stein. *The Vietnamese Revolution: Roosevelt, Ho Chi Minh and De Gaulle in a World at War.* London: Sage, 1991.

———. *1946: Déclenchement de la guerre d'Indochine.* Paris: Editions l'Harmattan, 2000.

Tournebize, Cassilde. *Une enfance en Indochine: De la douceur à la tourmente.* Paris: L'Harmattan, 2003.

Touwen-Bouwsma, Elly. "Japanese Minority Policy: The Eurasians in Java and the Dilemma of Ethnic Loyalty." *Bijdragen tot de Taal-, Land- en Volkenkunde, Japan, Indonesia and the War Myths and Realities* 152, no. 4 (1996): 553–572.

Tracol-Huynh, Isabelle. "Entre Ordre Colonial et Sante Publique, La Prostitution au Tonkin de 1885 a 1954." PhD diss., Université Lumière Lyon 2, November 12, 2013.

"Traite des Fillettes Annamites," *Le Courrier Saigonnais,* September 7, 1908.

Trần, Đình Tú. "Nữ Vệ út và báu vật 60 năm." *Việt Báo,* February 13, 2006.

Trần, Huy Liệu, ed. *Cách Mạng Tháng Tám Tổng Khởi Nghĩa Ở Hà-Nội Và Các Địa Phương.* Vol. 1. Hà Nội: NXB Sử Học, 1960.

———. *Đảng Thanh Niên: Tài Liệu Và Hồi Ký.* Hà Nội: Nhà Xuất Bản Sử Học, 1961.

Trần, Huy Liệu, Lương Bích Nguyễn, Tạo Văn, and Tân Hường, eds. *Cách Mạng Cận Đại Việt-Nam.* Vol. 6. Hà Nội: Ban Nghiên Cứu Văn Sử Địa xuất bản, 1956.

Tran, Quang Anh Richard. "From Red Lights to Red Flags: A History of Gender in Colonial to Contemporary Vietnam." PhD diss., University of California, Berkeley, 2011.

Trần, Quy Nhơn. *Tưởng Hồ Chí Minh về trở thành niên trong cách mạng Việt Nam.* Hà Nội: NXB Thanh Niên, 2004.

Trần, Văn Giàu. *Chống Xâm Lăng: Lịch sử Việt Nam từ 1858 đến 1898.* Hồ Chí Minh City: NXB TPHCM, 2001.

Trần, Văn Giàu, Đinh Xuân Lâm, and Kiều Xuân Bá, eds. *Lịch Sử Cận Đại Việt Nam Tập IV 1919–1930,* Hà Nội: NXB Giáo Dục, 1963.

Trần, Văn Giàu, and Trần Bạch Đằng, eds. *Địa Chí Văn hóa Thành Phố Hồ Chí Minh tập 1: Lịch Sử.* Hồ Chí Minh City: NXB TPHCM, 1998.

"Trẻ Em Việt Nam Trước Và Sau Cách Mạng Tháng 8." *Thiếu Nhi,* October 1, 1946.

Triêm, Xuân. "Nhận Xét Khái Quát Qua Ca Kich Phẩm Xã Hội Trên Sân Khấu Tmtn Những Đứa Con Lai." *Miên Nam,* December 22, 1967.

Trinh, Dinh Khai. *Décolonisation du Viêt Nam, un Avocat Témoigne.* Paris: L'Harmattan, 1994.

Trinh, Van Thao, *L'Ecole français en Indochine.* Paris, Karthala, 1995.

"Trong Vườn Khoa Học, Sanh Tố K Là Gì?" *Thanh Niên Đông Pháp,* March 7, 1944.

Truong, Chinh, and Nguyen Giap Vo. *The Peasant Question (1937–1938).* Translated by Christine Pelzer White. Ithaca: Cornell University Press, 1974.

"Truyện ký: 'Ông Tây Việt Minh'-Phương Đình." May 7, 2014. http://vanvn.net /news/7/4675-truyen-ky—ong-tay-viet-minh—phuong-dinh.html.

Tú, Trần Đình. "Nữ Vệ Út Và Báu Vật 60 Năm." *Việt Báo,* February 13, 2006.

Tuck, Patrick J. N. *French Catholic Missionaries and the Politics of Imperialism in Vietnam, 1857–1914: A Documentary Survey.* Liverpool: Liverpool University Press, 1987.

"Une Oeuvre Humaine." *Le Populaire,* July 24, 1947.

Ungar, Steven, and Tom Conley. *Identity Papers: Contested Nationhood in Twentieth-Century France.* Minneapolis: University of Minnesota Press, 1996.

Van Der Kroef, Justus M. "The Indonesian Eurasian and His Culture." *Phylon* 16, no. 4 (1955): 448–462.

Van Klinken, Helene. *Making Them Indonesians: Child Transfers Out of East Timor.* Monash: Monash University Publishing, 2012.

Văn Tạo and Furuta Motoo. *Nạn Đói Năm 1945 ở Việt Nam: Những Chứng Tích Lịch Sử.* Hà Nội: Viện Sử Học Việt Nam xuất bản, 1995.

Vann, Michael G. "White Blood on Rue Hue: The Murder of 'Le Négrier' Bazin." *Proceedings for the Western Society of French History* 34 (2006): 247–262.

Varenne, Juliette. *Juliette du Tonkin.* Paris: Publibook, 2008.

Vaudon, Chanoine Jean. *Les filles de Saint-Paul en Indo-Chine.* Chartres: Procure des Soeurs de Saint-Paul, 1931.

"Vệ Sanh Thương Thực." *Thanh Niên Đông Pháp,* January 25, 1945.

"'Vệ Út' Thủ Đô Và Những Bức Ảnh Xúc Động." *Việt Báo,* February 8, 2006.

Vergès, Françoise. *Monsters and Revolutionaries: Colonial Family Romance and Métissage.* Durham: Duke University Press, 1999.

Võ, Văn Lộc, ed. *Bác Hồ với Thiếu Niên Nhi Đồng,* Hà Nội: NXB Chính Trị Quốc Gia, 2003.

Vu, Ngu Chieu. "Political and Social Change in Vietnam, 1940–1946." PhD diss., University of Wisconsin, 1984.

Vũ, Trọng Phụng. "Kỹ nghệ lấy tây." In *Kỹ nghệ lấy tây & cơm thấy cơm cô,* 9–101. Hà Nội: Nhà xuất bản văn học, 2004.

———. *Lục Sì.* Hà Nội: NXB Văn Hóa Thông Tin, 2002.

———. (translated by Thúy Tranviet) *The Industry of Marrying Europeans.* Ithaca: Cornell Southeast Asia Program, 2006.

Webber, Eugen. *France Fin de Siècle.* Cambridge: Harvard University Press, 1986.

———. *My France: Politics, Culture, Myth.* Cambridge: Harvard University Press, 1991.

———. *The Hollow Years: France in the 1930s.* New York: W.W. Norton Co., 1994.

Weil, Patrick. *La France et ses étrangers. L'adventure d'une politique d'immigration, 1938–1991.* Paris, Calmann-Lévy, 1991.

Weissbach, Lee Shai. *Child Labor Reform in Nineteenth-Century France: Assuring the Future Harvest.* Baton Rouge: Louisiana State University Press, 1989.

Werbner, Pnina, and Nira Yuval-Davis, "Women and the New Discourse of Citizenship." In *Women, Citizenship and Difference,* edited by Nira Yuval-Davis and Pnina Werbner, 1–38. New York: Zed Books, 1999.

White, Owen. *Children of the French Empire: Miscegenation and Colonial Society in French West Africa, 1895–1960.* Oxford: Oxford University Press, 1999.

Wolfe, Patrick. "Land, Labor, and Difference: Elementary Structures of Race." *American Historical Review* 106, no. 3 (2001): 866–905.

Xuan Tue, Nguyen. "Congai: Une race de femmes annamites, produit de la colonisation." In Bernard Hue, *Indochine: Reflets littéraires,* 69–77. Rennes: Presses de l'université Rennes, 1992.

Yap, Felicia. "Eurasians in British Asia during the Second World War." *Journal of the Royal Asiatic Society* 21, no. 4 (2011): 485–505.

Yarborough, Trin. *Surviving Twice: Amerasian Children of the Vietnam War.* Washington, DC: Potomac Books, 2005.

Yeager, Jack. "Kim Lefèvre's Retour à la saison des pluies: Rediscovering the Landscapes of Childhood." *Esprit Créateur* 23, no. 2 (2003).

Yuval-Davis, Nira, and Floya Anthias. Introduction to *Women, Nation, State,* edited by Floya Anthias and Nira Yuval-Davis, 1–15. Basingstoke: Macmillan Press, 1989.

Zahara, Tara. *The Lost Children: Reconstructing Europe's Families after World War II.* Cambridge: Harvard University Press, 2011.

INDEX

abandonment: agriculture schools and, 33; FOEFI and, 151, 154; JBF and, 95–96; paternal divestiture law (1889), 3, 26–29, 46, 50, 97; village traditions and, 21. *See also* maternal consent; mothers

Ách, Suzanne, 66, 70

L'Action Sociale, 120, 121, 127, 160

adolescence and modernity, 63–65

adoption: international, 156–157, 168; of *métis* orphans in France, 124; state ownership as, 46–54, 69–70; Vietnamese traditional practice of, 9, 21. *See also* guardianship

adults. See *métis* adults

Afro-Asian children: of Bokassa, 156, 219n.155; FOEFI on, 119, 160, 209n.79; JBF on, 209n.74; placement of, 103–104; postwar population of, 108, 119–120, 161; rejection of, 50, 53, 97, 102. See also *métis* children

Afro-European children. *See* Eurafrican children

agency: of children, 53–54, 70; of mothers, 9, 14, 27, 46, 68–73, 86

agreement, FOEFI legal, 140–142, 151, 175–177

agricultural schools and settlements, 55–60; in Annam district, 15, 55–56, 73, 79–80; financial management of, 34–36; in Netherlands Indies, 186n.78; penitentiary programs, 31–32, 80–81; protests at, 18, 35; purpose of, 15, 17, 31–34, 55, 56, 186n.75; in Tonkin district, 32, 56, 79–80, 92; during World War II, 89, 93. *See also* École des Enfants de Troupe; education system; penitentiary programs; *specific schools*

Aguinaldo, Emilio, 48

Aix-en-Provence FOEFI archives, 13, 86, 170, 173

Alain, Jacques Marie Jean Charles, 145, 170

Albertini, Pierre, 25

Algeria, 108, 109, 134, 135, 153

Amerasian Act (1982), 162

Amerasian children, 155–156, 158, 162. See also *métis* children

Amerasian Homecoming Act (1988), 162

Amicale des Français d'Indochine in Cambodia, 78

Ancian, Mademoiselle, 121–122

Andaman scheme, 5, 55

André, Henri, 110

André, Marie Claire, 170

André, Vincent, 43–44

Anglo-Indian (term), 190n.57

Annam protectorate, Vietnam: agricultural settlements in, 15, 55–56, 73, 79–80; French colonial division of, 179n.7; military population in, 19; political history of, 19, 20, 26, 125; resettlement programs of, 39, 92

anthropologists' studies on *métis* children, 145

anticlerical movement, 24–25

anticolonialism. *See* rebellion and social unrest

Argentina, 168

arranged marriage, 63–64, 125

Asile Saint Joseph, 123–124

assassinations, 114–115, 124, 150

assimilation program of FOEFI, 144–148

L'Assistance Publique, 153–155, 160

L'Assistance Sociale, 117, 168, 193n.6

Association for the Protection of and Assistance to Franco-Annamite Children, 28

ABOUT THE AUTHOR

Christina Firpo earned a BA at George Washington University and a PhD at the University of California, Los Angeles. She is the president-elect of the Vietnam Studies Group, an international organization for scholars of Vietnam. She publishes regularly on the history of race, gender, childhood, sexuality, and black markets in Vietnam and is presently an associate professor of Southeast Asian history and an affiliate in the Women's and Gender Studies Department at California Polytechnic State University in San Luis Obispo.

OTHER VOLUMES IN THE SERIES